3rd Workshop on Gender Bias in Natural Language Processing (GeBNLP 2021)

Held online due to COVID-19

Bangkok, Thailand
5 August 2021

ISBN: 978-1-7138-3374-1

Printed from e-media with permission by:

Curran Associates, Inc.
57 Morehouse Lane
Red Hook, NY 12571

Some format issues inherent in the e-media version may also appear in this print version.

Printed with permission by Curran Associates, Inc. (2021)

For permission requests, please contact the Association for Computational Linguistics at the address below.

Association for Computational Linguistics
209 N. Eighth Street
Stroudsburg, Pennsylvania 18360

Phone: 1-570-476-8006
Fax: 1-570-476-0860

acl@aclweb.org

Additional copies of this publication are available from:

Curran Associates, Inc.
57 Morehouse Lane
Red Hook, NY 12571 USA
Phone: 845-758-0400
Fax: 845-758-2633
Email: curran@proceedings.com
Web: www.proceedings.com

GeBNLP 2021

The 3rd Workshop on
Gender Bias in Natural Language Processing

Proceedings of the Workshop

August 5, 2021
Bangkok, Thailand (online)

Acknowledgements

Marta R. Costa-jussà is supported by the European Research Council (ERC) under the European Union's Horizon 2020 research and innovation programme (grant agreement No. 947657).

Christian Hardmeier was supported by the Swedish Research Council under grant 2017-930.

Message from the Organisation Committee

This volume contains the proceedings of the Third Workshop on Gender Bias in Natural Language Processing held in conjunction with the Joint Conference of the 59th Annual Meeting of the Association for Computational Linguistics and the 11th International Joint Conference on Natural Language Processing (ACL-IJCNLP 2021). This year, the organisation committee changed membership: Will Radford made way to Hila Gonen. We thank Will greatly for his valuable and enthusiastic contributions to this workshop, and offer a warm welcome to Hila, whose expertise and insight we are all excited to learn from.

This year, the workshop received 18 submissions of technical papers (7 long papers, 11 short papers), of which 12 were accepted (5 long, 7 short), for an acceptance rate of 67%. We are pleased to see sustained interest compared to our previous editions in 2019 and 2020: we have a similar number of submissions (19 in both years) and acceptance rate, 63% and 68%, respectively. Once more, we have to thank the high-quality selection of research works thanks to the Programme Committee members, who provided extremely valuable reviews in terms of technical content and bias statements.

The accepted papers cover a wide range of natural language processing research areas. Regarding core tasks of NLP, the papers include annotation, coreference, data augmentation, word embeddings and evaluation. This year's programme features papers on new application areas for the workshop, conversational and judiciary applications, and we are excited for the discussions these will inspire. All papers cover a variety of gender (and intersectional) bias studies as well as a taxonomy definition.

Finally, the workshop counts on two high-standing keynote speakers: Sasha Luccioni, researcher in AI for Humanity initiatives at the Mila Institute, and Nizar Habash, professor and program head of Computer Science at New York University Abu Dhabi (NYUAD).

We are very pleased to keep the high interest that this workshop has generated over the last three editions and we look forward to an enriching discussion on how to address bias problems in NLP applications when we meet virtually on the 5th August 2020!

June 2021

Marta R. Costa-jussà, Hila Gonen, Christian Hardmeier, Kellie Webster

Organisation Committee

Marta R. Costa-jussà, *Universitat Politècnica de Catalunya*

Hila Gonen, *Amazon*

Christian Hardmeier, *IT University of Copenhagen* and *Uppsala University*

Kellie Webster, *Google Research*

Programme Committee

Christine Basta, *Universitat Politècnica de Catalunya*

Dorna Behdadi, *University of Gothenburg*

Jenny Björklund, *Uppsala University*

Ryan Cotterell, *ETH Zürich*

Matthias Gallé, *Naver Labs*

Mercedes García-Martínez, *Pangeanic-PangeaMT*

Sharid Loáiciga, *University of Potsdam*

Svetlana Kiritchenko, *National Research Council Canada*

Carla Perez Almendros, *Cardiff University*

Will Radford, *Canva*

Sonja Schmer-Galunder, *Smart Information Flow Technologies*

Sverker Sikström, *Lund University*

Kathleen Siminyu, *Mozilla*

Eva Vanmassenhove, *Tilburg University*

Bonnie Webber, *University of Edinburgh*

Steven Wilson, *University of Edinburgh*

Ben Zevenbergen, *Google*

Table of Contents

Conference Program

11:30 *gENder-IT: An Annotated English-Italian Parallel Challenge Set for Cross-Linguistic Natural Gender Phenomena*
Eva Vanmassenhove and Johanna Monti

11:38 *Gender Bias Hidden Behind Chinese Word Embeddings: The Case of Chinese Adjectives*
Meichun Jiao and Ziyang Luo

11:46 *Evaluating Gender Bias in Hindi-English Machine Translation*
Krithika Ramesh, Gauri Gupta and Sanjay Singh

16:50 *Alexa, Google, Siri: What are Your Pronouns? Gender and Anthropomorphism in the Design and Perception of Conversational Assistants*
Gavin Abercrombie, Amanda Cercas Curry, Mugdha Pandya and Verena Rieser

16:58 *Gender Bias in Text: Origin, Taxonomy, and Implications*
Jad Doughman, Wael Khreich, Maya El Gharib, Maha Wiss and Zahraa Berjawi

17:10 *Sexism in the Judiciary: The Importance of Bias Definition in NLP and In Our Courts*
Noa Baker Gillis

19:00 *Towards Equal Gender Representation in the Annotations of Toxic Language Detection*
Elizabeth Excell and Noura Al Moubayed

19:12 *Using Gender- and Polarity-Informed Models to Investigate Bias*
Samia Touileb, Lilja Øvrelid and Erik Velldal

19:20 *Assessing Gender Bias in Wikipedia: Inequalities in Article Titles*
Agnieszka Falenska and Özlem Çetinoğlu

19:32 *Investigating the Impact of Gender Representation in ASR Training Data: a Case Study on Librispeech*
Mahault Garnerin, Solange Rossato and Laurent Besacier

19:40 *Generating Gender Augmented Data for NLP*
Nishtha Jain, Maja Popović, Declan Groves and Eva Vanmassenhove

19:52 *Second Order WinoBias (SoWinoBias) Test Set for Latent Gender Bias Detection in Coreference Resolution*
Hillary Dawkins

gENder-IT: An Annotated English–Italian Parallel Challenge Set for Cross-Linguistic Natural Gender Phenomena

Eva Vanmassenhove[1], **Johanna Monti**[2]

[1]Department of CSAI, Tilburg University
[2]UNIOR NLP Research Group, University of Naples L'Orientale
e.o.j.vanmassenhove@tilburguniversity.edu, jmonti@unior.it

Abstract

Languages differ in terms of the absence or presence of gender features, the number of gender classes and whether and where gender features are explicitly marked. These cross-linguistic differences can lead to ambiguities that are difficult to resolve, especially for sentence-level MT systems. The identification of ambiguity and its subsequent resolution is a challenging task for which currently there aren't any specific resources or challenge sets available. In this paper, we introduce gENder-IT, an English–Italian challenge set focusing on the resolution of natural gender phenomena by providing word-level gender tags on the English source side and multiple gender alternative translations, where needed, on the Italian target side.

1 Introduction

Cross-linguistic differences between languages often require implicit information in the source to be made explicit on the target side. When faced with systematic structural differences between the source and target languages, human translators rely on the (broader) context (linguistic, extra-linguistic, world-knowledge) in order to infer the necessary information and adapt the target side accordingly.

One such way in which many languages systematically differ is in terms of grammatical gender. Languages not only differ in terms of the absence or presence of specific gender features but also in the number of (linguistic) gender classes, how and where gender features are marked, and in the underlying rules by which gender is assigned (Audring, 2016).[1]

In languages with grammatical gender all nouns have an (arbitrarily) assigned lexical gender.[2] In most cases, the lexical gender of a noun is covert and can only be inferred from the morphological agreement with other words (articles, verbs, adjectives...) (Corbett, 1991). However, when nouns refer to animate referents, overt gender markings corresponding to the so-called 'natural gender' (biological sex) of the referent are common (e.g. the Spanish word for 'nurse' is 'enfermero' (male) or 'enfermera' (female)). Such forms are generated using derivational suffixes and are often derived from the 'generic male'. This process is sometimes denoted as 'female marking' (Doleschal, 2000; Laleko, 2018).

While language learners encounter difficulties memorizing the lexically stored gender of foreign nouns (Rogers, 1987), Machine Translation (MT) technology, given the limited (linguistic and extra-linguistic) context most MT tools leverage, struggles with the explicitation of ambiguous forms, i.e. the process of disambiguation. So far, little research has been conducted on controlling the output of MT systems in terms of features such as gender and/or number that arise due to specific cross-linguistic differences. We believe that there are two main reasons for this: (i) The research that has been conducted in this area shows that controlling specific features is a technically very challenging problem. Especially given the fact that it often requires in-depth linguistic knowledge and specialized linguistic tools, the performance of the latter often depending on how well-researched and

[1]Linguistic gender classes can (and often do) correspond to what is referred to in linguistics as the natural gender of referents (i.e. 'masculine' and 'feminine'). However, within the field of linguistics the term 'gender class' is somewhat confusing as it is often used as a synonym for noun class. There are, for instance, language with more than 3 gender classes (e.g. Kiswahili has 9) as the classes are based on different semantic distinctions. Likewise, there are languags with only two 'gender classes' which correspond e.g. to an animate vs inanimate distinction.

[2]The Dutch word for 'sun' is 'zon' (female), while the French word for 'sun' is 'soleil' (male).

Proceedings of the 3rd Workshop on Gender Bias in Natural Language Processing, pages 1–7
August 5, 2021.

well-resourced the languages in question are; (ii) The lack of high-quality, human-crafted challenge sets that target specific cross-linguistic phenomena.

In this paper, we present a word-level (human) annotated, adapted and cleaned version of a subset (English-Italian) of the MuST-SHE corpus (Bentivogli et al., 2020).[3] The main contribution of our work is threefold: (i) The MuST-SHE corpus focuses solely on gender agreement with the first person singular. Our extension provides simple word-level annotations for all nouns and pronouns referring to human referents for the English sentences; (ii) While the transcripts of MuST-SHE are accompanied with gender information (male, female) of the speaker on a short paragraph-level, our word-level tags can be either male or female, but also ambiguous, when the sentence itself does not provide any explicit clues with respect to the gender of the referents; (iii) We focus on the textually gender-ambiguous sentences and provide all the correct gender-alternative translations for Italian.

The main motivations behind our work are the following: (i) First of all, there is a need for controlled diversity within the field of MT when it comes to controlling specific features of translations, specifically when dealing with structural cross-linguistic differences (Vanmassenhove, 2020). To allow for controlled diversity, we created the first test set that allows research on identifying ambiguity and generating multiple translation variants in terms of gender; (ii) Second, recent work by Saunders et al. (2020) indicates that even a (very) small synthetic set of high quality sentences annotated for gender can be leveraged to improve the accuracy of translations in terms of gender specific phenomena without decreasing the overall quality. Their work was limited to annotations for one referent per synthetic sentence and focused specifically on debiasing data in terms of gender. As highlighted in Vanmassenhove et al. (2019) and Saunders (2020), the effects of specific interventions need to be carefully examined on test sets that capture the complexity of a problem to its full extent. The manually annotated test set created does so by relying on 'natural' (as opposed to synthetic) data that is not limited to a single human referent per sentence.

Bias statement (Blodgett et al., 2020)
In summary, this dataset is intended to encourage work on gender bias in MT, but could equally be leveraged for monolingual research on the generation of gender diverse translations (in Italian) and gender identification of referents (for English). The detailed analysis on English-Italian is intended to raise awareness on cross-linguistic differences between languages in terms of gender. NLP technologies are prone to the perpetuation (and possibly also the exacerbation (Vanmassenhove et al., 2021)) of inappropriate stereotypes and are currently unable to recognize or warn the user about the (gender) assumptions that have been made (e.g. by translating ambiguous source sentences systematically into one specific gendered variant on the target side). Furthermore, current systems lack the ability for the user to indicate and/or control the gender of referents if needed. As such, the gender of referents in the generated MT output depends entirely on the training data which might contain (un)conscious biases that are transmitted in (written and spoken) datasets.

2 Related Work

Recent years, several datasets were created that focus specifically on gender-related issues observed in (sub)fields of Natural Language Processing (NLP). Targeted gender datasets (test sets or corpora) exist for subfield such as coreference resolution (Rudinger et al., 2018; Zhao et al., 2018; Webster et al., 2018) and sentiment analysis (Kiritchenko and Mohammad, 2018). In this section, we will limit our discussion to datasets created specifically for mitigating and assessing gender bias in MT.

In the field of MT, Mirkin and Meunier (2015) used a recommender system approach to predicted user-based preferred translations based on preferences of similar users. Rabinovich et al. (2017) worked on personalized Statistical MT. Their work centers around the preservation of gender traits by treating gender as a separate domain. For their experiments, they created a bilingual parallel corpus (English–French and English–German) annotated, among others, with the gender of the speaker.[4] For Neural MT,

[3]The dataset is publicly available under a CC BY-NC-ND 3.0 through: `https://github.com/vnmssnhv/gENder-IT`.

[4]The dataset is publicly available: `http://cl.haifa.ac.il/projects/pmt/`

(Vanmassenhove et al., 2019; Vanmassenhove and Hardmeier, 2018) experimented with the integration of speaker gender-tags added to the source side of the parallel corpus. Using the demographic information released by Rabinovich et al. (2017), they compiled large datasets with gender information for 20 language pairs.[5] Both papers (Rabinovich et al., 2017; Vanmassenhove et al., 2019) focused specifically on gender agreement with the first person singular. As such, their corpora are limited to sentence-level gender-tags indicating the gender of the speaker.

Stanovsky et al. (2019) presented "WinoMT" a challenge set for the evaluation of gender bias in MT. The set is based on two existing data sets for gender bias in coreference resolution: WinoBias (Zhao et al., 2018) and Winogender (Rudinger et al., 2018). WinoBias and Winogender consist of English sentences with two human entities in the form of two gender-neutral occupations (e.g. 'teacher', 'mechanic','assistant'...) and a gendered pronoun referring to one of the two human referents. WinoMT is a concatenation of WinoBias and Winogender and contains a total of 3,888 synthetic English sentences balanced for gender. The main contribution in Stanovsky et al. (2019) is an automatic evaluation of six popular MT systems on eight language pairs.[6] They provide an automatic gender bias evaluation protocol and show that the level of agreement with human annotations is above 85% for all languages.

Costa-jussà et al. (2020) presents the 'GeBioToolkit', a toolkit for the extraction of gender-balanced multilingual corpora with document-level gender annotations. They also introduce two versions of the 'GeBioCorpus'. The first one contains 16k sentences used for evaluating the automatically extracted parallel sentences. From the evaluation, it resulted that the human annotators gave the tool on average a 87.5% accuracy. The second version is a high-quality non-synthetic set of 2k English, Spanish and Catalan sentences post-edited by native speakers.

Saunders and Byrne (2020) created a small hand-crafted set of gender-balanced sentences for model adaptation. The set consists of 388 English synthetic sentences containing professions and their manually generated translations in each target language (Hebrew, German and Spanish). Saunders et al. (2020) explore the potential of explicit word-level gender inflection tags showing promising results. As such, gender tagging could be an effective tool for automatic translation tools where the user could specify the desired gender of the referents.

Our English-Italian parallel challenge set contains natural sentences (as opposed to synthetic) that do no follow a specific pattern[7] with word-level gender inflection tags. Since naturally occurring sentences are more complex and can contain multiple entities, animate nouns and pronouns have been annotated with word-level tags that indicate the gender given the limited sentence-level context. Unlike previous work, the challenge set is not limited to specific phenomena (e.g. 1st or 3rd person singular) but covers the full range of natural gender phenomena. It is specifically designed to encourage work on controlling output in terms of gender, the identification of gender ambiguous sentences and co-reference resolution.

3 Creation and Annotation of Dataset

In this section, we describe the pre-processing, cleaning and the gender annotations steps.

3.1 MuST-SHE

The gENder-IT challenge set is based on the MuST-SHE corpus comprising of naturally occurring sentences retrieved from TED Talks. We limited ourselves to the EN-IT parallel data and focused on data pertaining to what is referred to as 'category 2,3 and 4' in MuST-SHE, which are defined as sentences that contain contextual hints in terms of the gender of the speaker (category 2), sentences where both the audio signal and utterance context are needed to disambiguate the gender of referents (category 3) and sentences without contextual (audio or textual) gender information for disambiguation (category 4).

3.1.1 Corpus cleaning

While MuST-SHE contains segments (one or multiple sentences), we treated every sentence independently given that most state-of-the-art MT sys-

[5] `https://github.com/evavnmssnhv/Europarl-Speaker-Information`

[6] English being the source language, and French, Italian, Russian, Ukranian, Hebrew, Armenian and German as target languages.

[7] Saunders and Byrne (2020); Zhao et al. (2018) use synthetic sentence generated using templates such as "[entity1] verb [entity2]..." or "The [profession] verb [pronoun] noun".

tems work on the sentence level. Aside from splitting the segments, sentences for which the target or source part was missing were removed, spelling mistakes corrected, and missing quotations marks and punctuation were added where missing. In total, 694 sentences were annotated.

3.2 Word-level gender tags

Annotations Word-level gender annotations are provided for all (pro)nouns referring to a person with exception to the few nouns in English that are already gender specific.[8] In example 3.2, the (pro)nouns are tagged with their respective genders based on the textual context, except for the noun 'dad'. The tags provided are <F> or <M> when it is clear from the sentential context that the referent should be referred to with male/female pronouns (see Ex. 3.2).

Example 3.1. 'So she turned and she looked at her dad, and she said, "Dad, I <F> know how you <M> feel, but I <F> don't believe in the death penalty."'

In all other cases, the <A> tag is used to indicate that within the given context, no assumption can or should be made with respect to the gender of the referent. When there are multiple <A> tags, we further distinguish between <A1>, <A2>, etc. to indicate that different entities are being referred to. This is important from a translational point of view, since it could imply that more than two translations need to be generated. For instance, in the following sentence (Ex. 3.2), two nurses (<A1> and <A2>) are mentioned refering to two different entities of which the gender, within this particular context, is unknown. In Italian, there is a male and female form for the English word *nurse*: infermiera (female) and infermiere (male), which implies that there are at least four correct translation alternatives in terms of gender.

Example 3.2. "And it was there that another nurse <A1>, not the nurse <A2> who <A2> was looking after Mrs. Drucker <F> before, but another nurse <A1>, said three words to me <A3> that are the three words that most emergency physicians <A4> I <A3> know dread."

Usually, annotating (pro)nouns suffices to indicate the contextual natural gender of referents, however in some cases, nounless adjectives can appear that refer to a human referent. Therefore, adjectives functioning as nouns (e.g. 'the rich'...) and/or adjectives used in a (conversational) constructions without a (pro)noun (e.g. 'And sporty <A>!) were tagged as well.

Proper names Many of the gender clues within the textual context referred to in the MuST-SHE corpus depend on the names of referents mentioned within the context. We opted for a slightly different approach in terms of proper names given the variety of naming conventions that exist in different cultures. Furthermore, a person's pronoun preferences might not necessarily match with the gender we traditionally or prototypically associated with a name. As such, proper names by themselves are not considered a gender clue (see Ex. 3.3).

Example 3.3. "Vera <A> was dead."

We make an exception for cases where the full name of a person is given and this person can be considered a 'public figure' for whom the pronouns can be retrieved, see Ex. 3.4.[9]

Example 3.4. 'The German physicist <M> Werner Heisenberg <M> said, "When I <M> meet... ".'

In total, 950 word-level tags are provided of which 138 are <F> (15%), 190 <M> (20%), and 622 <A(1-6)> (65%).[10]

3.3 Multiple Translations

Sentences that contain ambiguous referents, sometimes – depending on the target language – entail multiple equivalent translations in terms of gender. For 148 out of the 694 sentences annotated, this was the case and multiple gender alternative translations were provided in Italian.[11]

4 Analysis and Discussion

This section provides an analysis and discussion of the specific problems posed by the Italian language and the specific choices taken with respect

[8] Either due to the form: 'waitress', 'actress' or because of semantic features: 'mother', 'brother'...

[9] In practice and for consistency, we verified whenever a full name was given whether the referent has a Wikipedia page on which they are being referred to with specific pronouns.

[10] As outlined in the previous section, when there are multiple ambiguous referents we added an additional identifier (1-...) to indicate whether a sentence contains multiple ambiguous entities as this might have an influence on the amount of different gendered translations.

[11] Annotations were provided by linguists and the Italian translations were generated by a native Italian speaker/linguist.

to the gender translations proposed in the corpus. First of all, Italian is a pro-drop language and the subject pronoun is often omitted. Therefore in sentences where there are ambiguous subjects (I, you, we, they), like in:

Example 4.1. "Why did I <A> send her home?"

there is no need to produce alternative gender translations. However, if there are adjectives referring to ambiguous pronouns, gendered translations are needed, e.g.:

Example 4.2. "You <A1> know, I <A2> 'm really tired of this thing being called New Jersey."

for which we have two Italian sentences, namely "Disse: "Sono *stufo* di questa cosa chiamata New Jersey" for the masculine form and 'Disse: "Sono *stufa* di questa cosa chiamata New Jersey"' for the feminine form. The same applies when there are past participle forms in the sentence, since in Italian these forms sometimes require gender agreement with the noun they refer to such as in:

Example 4.3. "What did you <A> expect it to feel like?"

for which we produce the alternate gender translation: "Come pensavi che ti saresti *sentito*?" and "Come pensavi che ti saresti *sentita*?".

Gender translations were needed for bigender Italian nouns as well, such as for instance *insegnante* (teacher) or *paziente* (patient), which have a single invariable form for masculine and feminine and the gender becomes apparent only when there is a coordinated article or adjective , such as in

Example 4.4. "Do you <A1> remember that patient <A2> you <A1> saw with the sore throat?"

for which the sentences "Si ricorda *quel paziente* che ha visitato con il mal di gola?" and "Si ricorda *quella paziente* che ha visitato con il mal di gola?" were produced.

We also made a conscious decision in terms of the Italian 'non-marked' masculine form, also called the inclusive masculine - when the masculine form is used to refer, generically to males and females, such as for instance the use of the masculine form *bambini* (children) to refer to both male and female children. For this particular form, although the use of the inclusive masculine is acceptable when refering to a group of people whose gender is unknown (as proposed in e.g. Robustelli (2012)), we still opted to provide an alternative translation. For instance the sentence:

Example 4.5. "Man, I <A1> come home from work, drawers are open, clothes hanging outside the drawers, the kids <A2> are still in their pajamas..."

is translated as: "Amico, torno a casa dal lavoro, i cassetti sono aperti, i vestiti tutti fuori, *i bambini* sono ancora in pigiama..." and "Amico, torno a casa dal lavoro, i cassetti sono aperti, i vestiti tutti fuori, *le bambine* sono ancora in pigiama..."

The generic masculine form is also used for the agreement of adjectives/past participles/nouns in agreement with the natural gender of referents that have different genders, e.g.: "Giovanni e Lucia sono *bravi insegnanti*" (Giovanni and Lucia are good teachers). In this case, we kept the masculine form as no possible alternatives are currently accepted. Recently, the use of the schwa, "ə", was proposed (Gheno, 2019), precisely to solve these types of problems related to the use of the inclusive masculine form but also to take into account non-binary people representation needs, nevertheless this solution has not yet been widely adopted and is not accepted as a linguistic norm.

A further problem addressed in providing gender translation is related to the so-called agentive nouns, namely those nouns that are used to classify people that have specific functions, roles, professions. This type of nouns represent the main problem of sexism in the Italian language, and it is currently widely debated, since the tendency is to use male forms also to refer to professions or roles played by women. This is especially true for nouns which refer to particularly prestigious roles, such as *direttore* (director), *presidente* (president), *ministro* (minister), *professore* (professor) and the like, for which feminine nouns exist: *direttrice* (female director), *presidentessa* (female president), *ministra* (female minister), *professoressa* (female professor), etc. These forms are not always used (including by women) as some consider the feminization of a profession a loss of prestige.[12] For these cases, we opted to provide both masculine and feminine translations:

[12]Recently, the Accademia della Crusca, one of the most important research bodies for the Italian Language, discussed this problem with reference to the request by Beatrice Venezi to be presented as "direttore d'orchestra" (orchestra director) and not as "direttrice d'orchestra" (female orchestra director) during an important Italian song contest, namely the 71st Festival of Sanremo: `https://accademiadellacrusca.it/it/consulenza/direttori-dorchestra-e-maestri-del-coro-anche-se-donne/2917`

Example 4.6. "So I <A1> one day decided to pay a visit to the manager <A2>."

for which we provide the following alternate translations: "E così un giorno decisi di andare a trovare *il direttore*" and "E così un giorno decisi di andare a trovare *la direttrice*."

5 Conclusions and Future Work

In this paper, we present and describe gENder-IT: an English-Italian annotated parallel challenge set. The English source side is annotated with word-level gender tags, while for the Italian target side the translations –including correct gender alternatives– are provided. We present a detailed description of the annotations as well as a contrastive analysis of translation specific gender challenges for English–Italian. In future work, we envisage working on: (i) an extension of the corpus to other languages, (ii) the identification of gender ambiguous sentences in English, and (iii) the subsequent generation of multiple gender alternatives where necessary, including paraphrases to adopt more gender-neutral solutions. With our challenge set and analysis, we hope to encourage research on ambiguity detection and the controlled generation of gender diverse alternatives for translations.

Acknowledgments

We would like to thank the reviewers for their insightful feedback and comments.

References

Jenny Audring. 2016. *Gender*. Oxford Research Encyclopedia of Linguistics (online) accessed: 20-03-21.

Luisa Bentivogli, Beatrice Savoldi, Matteo Negri, Mattia A. Di Gangi, Roldano Cattoni, and Marco Turchi. 2020. Gender in danger? evaluating speech translation technology on the MuST-SHE corpus. In *Proceedings of the 58th Annual Meeting of the Association for Computational Linguistics*, pages 6923–6933, Online. Association for Computational Linguistics.

Su Lin Blodgett, Solon Barocas, Hal Daumé III, and Hanna Wallach. 2020. Language (technology) is power: A critical survey of "bias" in NLP. In *Proceedings of the 58th Annual Meeting of the Association for Computational Linguistics*, pages 5454–5476, Online. Association for Computational Linguistics.

Greville G. Corbett. 1991. *Gender*. Cambridge Textbooks in Linguistics. Cambridge University Press.

Marta R. Costa-jussà, Pau Li Lin, and Cristina España-Bonet. 2020. GeBioToolkit: Automatic extraction of gender-balanced multilingual corpus of Wikipedia biographies. In *Proceedings of the 12th Language Resources and Evaluation Conference*, pages 4081–4088, Marseille, France. European Language Resources Association.

Ursula Doleschal. 2000. Gender assignment revisited. *Trends in Linguistics Studies and Monographs*, 124:117–166.

Vera Gheno. 2019. *Femminili singolari: il femminismo è nelle parole*. Effequ.

Svetlana Kiritchenko and Saif Mohammad. 2018. Examining gender and race bias in two hundred sentiment analysis systems. In *Proceedings of the Seventh Joint Conference on Lexical and Computational Semantics*, pages 43–53, New Orleans, Louisiana.

Oksana Laleko. 2018. What is difficult about grammatical gender? evidence from heritage russian. *Journal of Language Contact*, 11(2):233–267.

Shachar Mirkin and Jean-Luc Meunier. 2015. Personalized machine translation: Predicting translational preferences. In *Proceedings of the 2015 Conference on Empirical Methods in Natural Language Processing*, pages 2019–2025, Lisbon, Portugal.

Ella Rabinovich, Raj Nath Patel, Shachar Mirkin, Lucia Specia, and Shuly Wintner. 2017. Personalized machine translation: Preserving original author traits. In *Proceedings of the 15th Conference of the European Chapter of the Association for Computational Linguistics: Volume 1, Long Papers*, pages 1074–1084, Valencia, Spain.

Cecilia Robustelli. 2012. Linee guida per l'uso del genere nel linguaggio amministrativo. *Progetto Accademia della Crusca e Comune di Firenze, Comune di Firenze*.

Margaret Rogers. 1987. Learners difficulties with grammatical gender in german as a foreign language. *Applied Linguistics*, 8(1):48–74.

Rachel Rudinger, Jason Naradowsky, Brian Leonard, and Benjamin Van Durme. 2018. Gender bias in coreference resolution. In *NAACL-HLT (2)*.

Danielle Saunders and Bill Byrne. 2020. Reducing gender bias in neural machine translation as a domain adaptation problem. In *Proceedings of the 58th Annual Meeting of the Association for Computational Linguistics*, pages 7724–7736, Online.

Danielle Saunders, Rosie Sallis, and Bill Byrne. 2020. Neural machine translation doesn't translate gender coreference right unless you make it. In *Proceedings of the Second Workshop on Gender Bias in Natural Language Processing*, pages 35–43, Barcelona, Spain (Online).

Gabriel Stanovsky, Noah A. Smith, and Luke Zettlemoyer. 2019. Evaluating gender bias in machine translation. In *Proceedings of the 57th Annual Meeting of the Association for Computational Linguistics*, pages 1679–1684, Florence, Italy.

Eva Vanmassenhove. 2020. On the Integration of Linguistic Features into Statistical and Neural Machine Translation. *arXiv preprint arXiv:2003.14324*.

Eva Vanmassenhove and Christian Hardmeier. 2018. Europarl datasets with demographic speaker information. In *Proceedings of the 21st Annual Conference of the European Associations for Machine Translation (EAMT)*, Alicante, Spain.

Eva Vanmassenhove, Christian Hardmeier, and Andy Way. 2019. Getting gender right in neural machine translation. *Proceedings of the 2018 Conference on Empirical Methods in Natural Language Processing (EMNLP)*, pages 3003–3008.

Eva Vanmassenhove, Dimitar Shterionov, and Matthew Gwilliam. 2021. Machine translationese: Effects of algorithmic bias on linguistic complexity in machine translation. In *Proceedings of the 16th Conference of the European Chapter of the Association for Computational Linguistics: Main Volume*, pages 2203–2213, Online. Association for Computational Linguistics.

Kellie Webster, Marta Recasens, Vera Axelrod, and Jason Baldridge. 2018. Mind the gap: A balanced corpus of gendered ambiguous pronouns. *Transactions of the Association for Computational Linguistics*, 6:605–617.

Jieyu Zhao, Tianlu Wang, Mark Yatskar, Vicente Ordonez, and Kai-Wei Chang. 2018. Gender bias in coreference resolution: Evaluation and debiasing methods. In *Proceedings of the 2018 Conference of the North American Chapter of the Association for Computational Linguistics: Human Language Technologies, Volume 2 (Short Papers)*, pages 15–20, New Orleans, Louisiana. Association for Computational Linguistics.

Gender Bias Hidden Behind Chinese Word Embeddings: The Case of Chinese Adjectives

Meichun Jiao, Ziyang Luo
Department of Linguistics and Philology, Uppsala University, Sweden
{Meichun.Jiao.1608,Ziyang.Luo.9588}@student.uu.se

Abstract

Gender bias in word embeddings gradually becomes a vivid research field in recent years. Most studies in this field aim at measurement and debiasing methods with English as the target language. This paper investigates gender bias in static word embeddings from a unique perspective, Chinese adjectives. By training word representations with different models, the gender bias behind the vectors of adjectives is assessed. Through a comparison between the produced results and a human scored data set, we demonstrate how gender bias encoded in word embeddings differentiates from people's attitudes.

BIAS STATEMENT This paper studies gender bias in Chinese adjectives, captured by word embeddings. For each Chinese adjective, a gender bias score is calculated by $\vec{w} \cdot (\vec{he} - \vec{she})$ (Bolukbasi et al., 2016). A positive score represents the Chinese adjective word embeddings is more associated with males, and a negative value refers to the opposite result. In our daily life, we find that gender stereotypes can be conveyed by adjectives. The close association between an adjective and a certain gender could be the accomplice in forming gender stereotypes (Menegatti and Rubini, 2017). If these stereotypes are learned by the adjective word embeddings, they would be propagated to downstream NLP applications; accordingly, the gender stereotypes would be reinforced in users' mind. For example, the system will tend to use "smart" to describe males because of the existed social stereotype in training data that males are good at mathematics; then, the influence of the stereotype would be spread and increased again. Thus, we want to further investigate the bias encoded by the embeddings and how they are different with what in people's mind.

1 Introduction

In the deep learning era, a major area of NLP has concerned the representation of words in low-dimensional and continuous vector spaces. People propose different algorithms to achieve such goal, including Word2Vec (Mikolov et al., 2013a), GloVe (Pennington et al., 2014a) and FastText (Bojanowski et al., 2017). Word embeddings play an important role in many NLP tasks, such as machine translation (Qi et al., 2018) and sentiment analysis (Yu et al., 2017). However, several studies point out that word embeddings could capture the gender stereotypes in training data and transmit them to downstream applications (Bolukbasi et al., 2016; Zhao et al., 2017). The consequence is often unbearable. Take machine translation as an example, if we translate a sentence concerning "nurse" from a language with gender-neutral pronouns to English, a female pronoun might be automatically produced to denote "nurse" (Prates et al., 2019). Undoubtedly, this falls into the trap of the typical gender stereotypes. Therefore, the investigation of gender bias in word embeddings is necessary and accordingly attracts scholars' attention in recent years (Bolukbasi et al., 2016; Zhao et al., 2017).

Most previous studies concerning gender bias in word embeddings only take English as the target language. Other languages are only included in several multi-lingual projects. For example, Prates et al. (2019) evaluate the gender bias in machine translation by translating 12 gender neutral languages with the Google Translate API; Lewis and Lupyan (2020) examine whether gender stereotypes could be reflected in the large-scale distributional structure of 25 natural languages. Apart from English, other languages have rarely been the target language in the research under this topic. This paper will take Chinese as the target language, investigating gender bias in word embeddings trained

Proceedings of the 3rd Workshop on Gender Bias in Natural Language Processing, pages 8–15
August 5, 2021. ©2021 Association for Computational Linguistics

with the model designed for special features of Chinese.

The fact that social stereotypes are conveyed in our language is often neglected by the public. From the commonly used adjectives, we could get a glimpse of the social stereotypes of a certain group of people. These stereotypes would confine us to what we should be in the minds of the public. It has been confirmed that when describing different genders, people will choose divergent groups of adjectives even though such a choice might change with the development of society (Garg et al., 2018). Therefore, this study focuses on the problem of gender stereotypes from the perspective of adjectives. By scoring the gender bias from our trained vectors, we yield a subjective result of the gender preference of a set of adjectives. Through comparing our results with a handcrafted data set of human attitudes towards adjectives(Zhu and Liu, 2020), we find that what is encoded in word embeddings is, to some extent, inconsistent with people's feelings on the gender preference of these adjectives.

2 Related work

Gender could affect the usage of adjectives (Lakoff, 1973). On the other hand, the attitude of the public towards the social roles of men and women could also be indicated by how adjectives correlates with genders(Zhu and Liu, 2020). In the past decade, an increasing number of studies investigating adjectives and gender stereotypes from various perspectives are proposed and developed. Baker (2013) reveals the stereotype in the description of boys and girls by analyzing adjectives only used for a certain gender with the aid of corpora covering a range of written genres. Research of Bollywood movies (Madaan et al., 2018) finds that different adjectives are chosen when they try to create impressive male and female roles. The significant divergence between the usage of adjectives for describing men and women has also been confirmed by Hoyle et al. (2019), and they also notice the variance is consistent with common stereotypes. Zhu and Liu (2020) trace the change of gender bias in Chinese adjectives based on a handcrafted data set that consists of the gender preference score of adjectives. However, the number of studies focusing on Chinese adjectives and gender bias is still limited.

Gender bias in word embeddings and the corresponding debiasing methods have been a vivid research field in recent years. Bolukbasi et al. (2016) and Caliskan et al. (2017) confirm that word embedding models could precisely capture the social stereotypes concerning people's careers, such as the relationship in an analogy that *Man is to Computer Programmer as Woman is to Homemaker*. This bias could even be amplified by embedding models (Zhao et al., 2017). Besides English, other target languages like Swedish (Sahlgren and Olsson, 2019) and Dutch (Wevers, 2019) gradually attract the attention of researchers. Various methods for assessing bias and debiasing are proposed and developed in previous studies. Bolukbasi et al. (2016) firstly measure the gender bias by computing the projection of a word on $\vec{he} - \vec{she}$ direction, which has been confirmed strongly correlated with the public judgment of gender stereotypes. Based on this method, they also develop a debiasing method by post-processing the generated word vectors. Zhao et al. (2018) and Zhang et al. (2018) further propose to debias word embeddings in training procedure by changing the loss of GloVe model (Pennington et al., 2014b) and employing an adversarial network, respectively. Despite a large amount of research having been done in this field, to the best of our knowledge, no one has assessed the underlying gender bias behind adjectives, especially those in non-English languages.

To complement the full picture of gender bias encoded in word representation, this paper examines the problem from the perspective of adjectives rather than nouns of occupations that repeatedly appeared in previous studies. Based on the human scoring data set of Zhu and Liu (2020), we investigate the similarities and differences between the automatically captured gender bias in Chinese and people's judgement.

3 Methodology

To uncover the gender stereotypes conveyed by adjectives, we first preprocess a corpus of online Chinese news and train word embeddings on it with two different models. Then, we calculate the gender bias scores based on the generated two vectors and compare them with the human scoring data set, Adjectives list with Gendered Skewness and Sentiment (AGSS) (Zhu and Liu, 2020).

3.1 Data

News reports are not only the reflection of social consciousness but also the easily collected corpus

Original size	1.54GB
Size after preprocessing	2.1GB
The number of tokens	375.3M
The number of unique words	100.7k

Table 1: The details of the Chinese news corpus.

for many NLP tasks. Therefore, we choose a corpus of Chinese news reports as our training data set. It was collected and released by Sogou Labs, covering 18 themes of news from various Chinese news websites.[1] The details of the corpus are illustrated in Table 1. All texts in the data set are cleaned and preprocessed through the following steps.

1. Extract the news content and change the encoding from gbk to utf-8. All the other information and metadata are removed.

2. Remove the html tag by the regular expression and conduct Chinese word segmentation with *jieba*,[2] a widely used Python module.

3.2 Training and evaluation of word embeddings

The meaning of Chinese words is usually related to the semantic information carried by the characters (Hanzi) that they are comprised of. Figure 1 shows an example: the word "xianjing" means "demure", which consists of two characters. The first one, "xian", means refined but usually used for describing a woman; the second character "jing" means silent and quiet. The word inherits and combines the meaning of each character, even the information concerning gender. This feature of Chinese leads to the development of word embedding models in which word vectors are trained with the character-level information. However, no study before has provided any ideas about how the encoding of gender bias information will be affected by training embedding with character-level information. Therefore, we decide to train our vectors with one of such models, namely the character-enhanced word embedding model (CWE) (Chen et al., 2015). In addition to the word vector, this model also trains a vector for Chinese characters.

CWE is developed based on the framework CBOW (Mikolov et al., 2013b). CBOW aims at predicting the target word by understanding the surrounding context words. Practically, its objective

[1] http://www.sogou.com/labs/resource/ca.php

[2] https://github.com/fxsjy/jieba

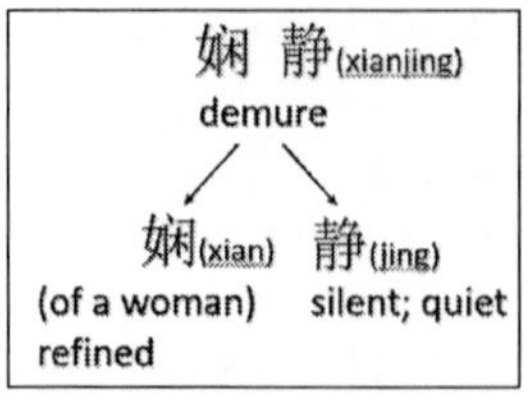

Figure 1: An example of semantic relation between Chinese words and characters. Pinying (pronunciation of the word or character) is in the lower right parentheses; English translation is noted directly below the word or character

Window size	5
Iteration	5
Dimension	300
Min_count	8
Num_threads	12

Table 2: Word embeddings training hyper-parameter details.

is to maximize the average log probability given a word sequence $D = \{x_1, \ldots, x_M\}$. CWE modifies the way of representing the context words in the algorithm of CBOW, predicting target words by combining character embedding and word embedding. A context word $\mathbf{x}_j$ in CWE would be represented as follows,

$$\mathbf{x}_j = \frac{1}{2}\left(\mathbf{w}_j + \frac{1}{N_j}\sum_{k=1}^{N_j}\mathbf{c}_k\right). \quad (1)$$

$\mathbf{w}_j$ refers to the word embedding of $\mathbf{x}_j$; N_j represents the number of characters in $\mathbf{x}_j$; $\mathbf{c}_k$ is the representation of the $\mathbf{k}$-th character in $\mathbf{x}_j$. For comparison, we also train vectors on CBOW to show in the influence of character-level information. The Python library *Gensim* [3] is used for training the representation with CBOW, and the other with CWE is completed by the released code of Chen et al. (2015).[4] To make the results comparable, we keep the same hyper-parameters for the two models. Detailed information is recorded in Table 2.

To ensure the effective of the produced embeddings, we evaluate them by word analogy tasks and the corresponding tools developed by Li et al. (2018). The test data set of the task includes 17813 questions about morphological or semantic rela-

[3] https://github.com/RaRe-Technologies/gensim

[4] https://github.com/Leonard-Xu/CWE/tree/master/src

tions. [5] The results are illustrated in table 3. Although the semantic task results are lower than the values given in the paper of Li et al. (2018), we still assume that they are reliable as the size of our training data is only the half of theirs.

Model	Morphological	Semantic
Li et al. (2018)	11.5	30.2
CBOW	11.1	23.5
CWE	19.7	24.6

Table 3: Accuracy scores of different word embeddings in the evaluation tasks. The results are reported as $acc\times 100$.

3.3 Gender bias measurement and data set

We employ the method of Bolukbasi et al. (2016) to assess gender bias encoded in the trained embeddings. For each adjective, a gender bias score is calculated by $\vec{w} \cdot (\vec{he} - \vec{she})$ based on its vector.[6] A positive result presents that the word has a closer association with males, while a negative score implies that the word is more associated with females. The higher the absolute value, the more biased the adjective is. 0 means totally neutral.

Adjectives List with Gendered Skewness and Sentiment (AGSS) is a handcrafted data set built by questionnaire in the project of Zhu and Liu (2020). 6 linguists firstly select 466 Chinese adjectives that could describe people, then 116 gender-balanced respondents score these adjectives by questionnaires. The the scale of score 1 to 5 is used to reflect people's attitude, with 1 being more related to female and 5 more related to male. Table 4 shows some example data from AGSS. Finally, 304 adjectives are scored larger than 3, 153 adjectives get score less than 3, and 9 are believed totally neutral. According to the statistics of AGSS, the adjectives chosen for this data set are more associated with males, so Zhu and Liu (2020) state that AGSS is with gender skewness. To analyze the results, we compare our gender bias scores from word embeddings with the AGSS scores. As they are on different scales, Pearson correlation coefficient is employed here. It could measure the the strength of the linear association between two variables, which returns a value between -1 and 1. 1 indicates strong positive linear

Words	Gender skewness in AGSS
powerful	4.44
vuglar	3.62
selfless	3.00
cute	2.26
decorous	1.59

Table 4: Example data from AGSS. Each word is translated into English.

correlation, 0 indicates no linear correlation and -1 indicates a strong negative linear correlation.

4 Results and discussion

4.1 Gender bias scores from word embeddings

We calculate the gender bias score for the same adjectives with AGSS and conclude the basic statistics in Table 5. More adjectives are categorized into the group close to male. This is identified with what Zhu and Liu (2020) state about AGSS (mentioned in Section 3.3). However, it should be noticed that the average scores of both models result in a negative value. This might suggest that most absolute values of negative gender bias scores are much higher than the positive group.

	CBOW	CWE
# pos. score	283	316
# neg. score	183	150
Avg. score	-0.02029	-0.02945

Table 5: Statistics of the gender bias scores from two embeddings.

4.2 Correlation between word vectors and AGSS

The Pearson correlation coefficients presented in Table 6 suggest the two categories of data are positively associated. However, the correlation is not that strong with only around 0.5, since the range of Pearson coefficient is from -1 to 1. Besides, the gender bias scores from the word embeddings trained with CWE are more associated with the human scores. This might suggest that the character-level information could help the model capture gender bias more precisely, or we should say such information could contribute to encoding what is in people's minds.

In Figure 2, we can find more details of the correlation between the two categories of data. By com-

[5] https://github.com/Embedding/Chinese-Word-Vectors/tree/master/testsets

[6] We use the Chinese translation of he and she when conducting experiments.

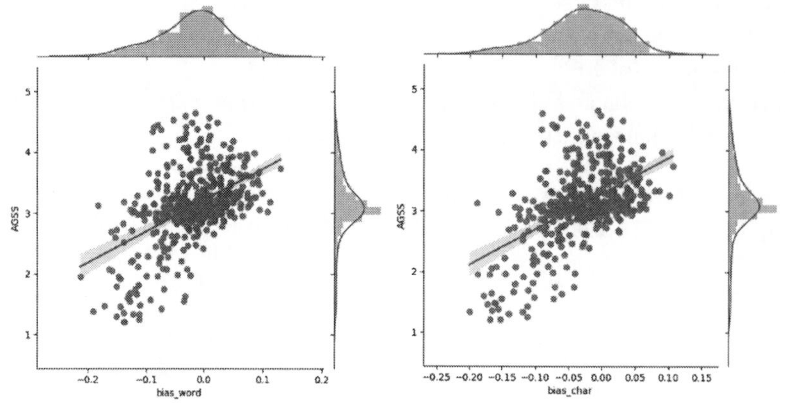

Figure 2: Scatter plots of AGSS scores and gender bias scores from word vectors trained with CBOW (left) and CWE (right). AGSS refers to the AGSS scores and bias_word and bias_char refers to the generated gender bias scores. The distribution of gender bias scores and AGSS scores are on the top and right of the plots respectively. The lines show the linear relation between the two categories.

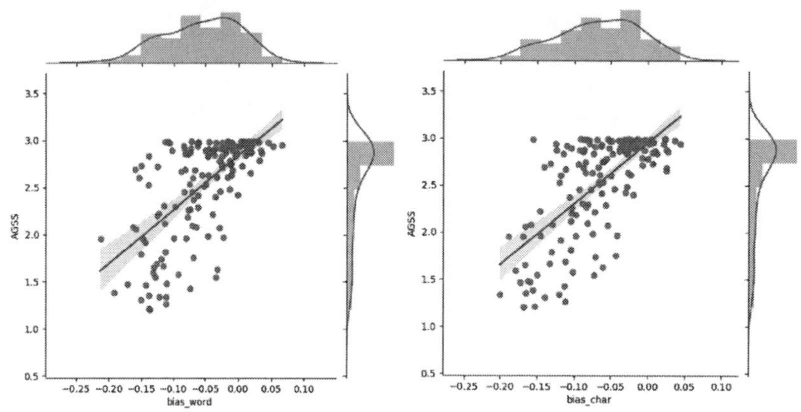

Figure 3: Scatter plots of the data group with AGSS scores <3. AGSS refers to the AGSS scores and bias_word and bias_char refers to the generated gender bias scores.

	CBOW	CWE
Pearson coefficient	0.489	0.503
p-value	0.000	0.000

Table 6: Pearson correlation coefficient between AGSS score and gender bias scores from trained vectors. CBOW score and CWE score refer to the gender bias score from word vectors trained with CBOW and CWE model.

paring the distribution of the two types of scores, we notice that the scores given by people are very concentrated between 2.5 to 3.5, while automatically calculated scores have a wider distribution. This might be caused by different scales, but may also come from people hypocrisy: they spontaneously narrow the extent of gender preference of words when they are asked to score their attitudes. Besides, it is a clear tendency that some words only for males in people's impression are automatically given a negative score, which means they are more close to women in word vectors. Therefore, we conduct further analysis by separating the data into two groups based on the neutral line in AGSS.

We recalculate the Pearson correlation coefficients for the two group of data, presenting results in Table 7 and Table 8. To give a full picture, sepa-

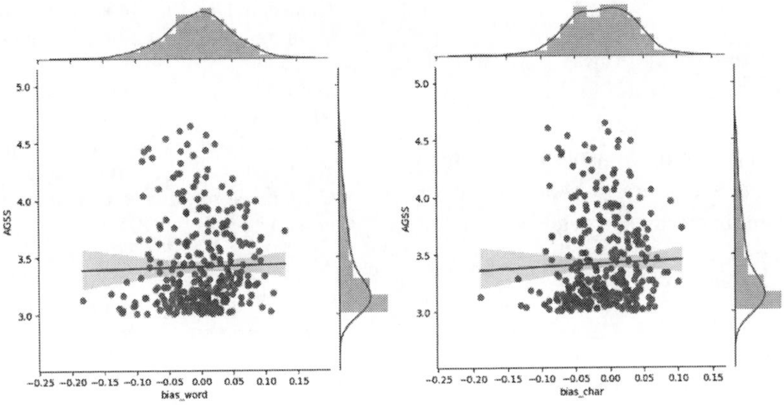

Figure 4: Scatter plots of the data group with AGSS scores >3. AGSS refers to the AGSS scores and bias_word and bias_char refers to the generated gender bias scores.

	CBOW	CWE
Pearson coefficient	0.673	0.628
p-value	0.000	0.000

Table 7: Pearson correlation coefficient of the data group with AGSS scores <3.

	CBOW	CWE
Pearson coefficient	0.036	0.020
p-value	0.543	0.724

Table 8: Pearson correlation coefficient of the data group with AGSS scores >3.

rated scatter plots as shown in Figure 3 and Figure 4 are also included. The increment of coefficients for the group with AGSS scores lower than 3 suggests that most adjectives believed for describing women are closer to females in word vectors as well. What is encoded by word embedding is consistent with people's impressions of these words. In addition, the correlation for scores from vectors trained with CBOW exceeds the results with the CWE model. This finding might indicate the underlying negative influence of covering character-level information in the word embedding.

However, a substantial divergence appears in the other group. Based on the scatter plot and the Pearson coefficient, some of the adjectives that almost exclusively connect with male in people's minds could be very neutral according to our word embedding. The coefficients also suggest that the two categories of data do not show linear relations. Additionally, only one-third of the adjectives in this group are closer to males in word embedding, while the others are actually more associated with females. Obviously, what we estimate from embedding disagrees with people's attitudes. This could be explained by the development of language. The study of Zhu and Liu (2020) proves that some Chinese adjectives for describing men in past time gradually become neutral in written language. Since the language used online develops fast and our training data are online news reports, the word embedding we trained is likely affected by the change. However, the public has not realized such development although they might start to use it in the new way. Therefore, when they are queried about the attitude towards attitudes, they might give an answer based on their outdated knowledge.

5 Conclusion

In this paper, we investigate gender bias in Chinese word embeddings from the perspective of adjectives, and compare automatically calculated gender bias score with human attitudes. We elaborately present the differences between gender bias encoded in word vectors and the people's feeling of the same adjective. For the words that people believe for describing women, the extracted score of gender bias gives an identified results; while for adjectives that should be used for men in people's mind, our results suggest that these group of words are actually more neutral than the crowd judgement. Additionally, how the word embedding models covering character-level information perform in terms of capturing gender bias in Chinese is also examined.

Acknowledgments This project grew out of a master course project for the Fall 2020 Uppsala University 5LN714, *Language Technology: Research and Development.* We would like to thank Sara Stymne and Ali Basirat for some great suggestions and the anonymous reviewers for their excellent feedback.

References

Paul Baker. 2013. Will ms ever be as frequent as mr? a corpus-based comparison of gendered terms across four diachronic corpora of british english. *Gender and Language*, 1(1).

Piotr Bojanowski, Edouard Grave, Armand Joulin, and Tomas Mikolov. 2017. Enriching word vectors with subword information. *Transactions of the Association for Computational Linguistics*, 5:135–146.

Tolga Bolukbasi, Kai-Wei Chang, James Y Zou, Venkatesh Saligrama, and Adam T Kalai. 2016. Man is to computer programmer as woman is to homemaker? debiasing word embeddings. In *Advances in neural information processing systems*, pages 4349–4357.

Aylin Caliskan, Joanna J Bryson, and Arvind Narayanan. 2017. Semantics derived automatically from language corpora contain human-like biases. *Science*, 356(6334):183–186.

Xinxiong Chen, Lei Xu, Zhiyuan Liu, Maosong Sun, and Huanbo Luan. 2015. Joint learning of character and word embeddings. In *Twenty-Fourth International Joint Conference on Artificial Intelligence*.

Nikhil Garg, Londa Schiebinger, Dan Jurafsky, and James Zou. 2018. Word embeddings quantify 100 years of gender and ethnic stereotypes. *Proceedings of the National Academy of ences of the United States of America*, 115(16):E3635.

Alexander Miserlis Hoyle, Lawrence Wolf-Sonkin, Hanna Wallach, Isabelle Augenstein, and Ryan Cotterell. 2019. Unsupervised discovery of gendered language through latent-variable modeling. In *Proceedings of the 57th Annual Meeting of the Association for Computational Linguistics*, pages 1706–1716.

Robin Lakoff. 1973. Language and woman's place. *Language in society*, 2(1):45–79.

Molly Lewis and Gary Lupyan. 2020. Gender stereotypes are reflected in the distributional structure of 25 languages. *Nature human behaviour*, pages 1–8.

Shen Li, Zhe Zhao, Renfen Hu, Wensi Li, Tao Liu, and Xiaoyong Du. 2018. Analogical reasoning on Chinese morphological and semantic relations. In *Proceedings of the 56th Annual Meeting of the Association for Computational Linguistics (Volume 2: Short Papers)*, pages 138–143, Melbourne, Australia. Association for Computational Linguistics.

Nishtha Madaan, Sameep Mehta, Taneea Agrawaal, Vrinda Malhotra, Aditi Aggarwal, Yatin Gupta, and Mayank Saxena. 2018. Analyze, detect and remove gender stereotyping from bollywood movies. In *Conference on Fairness, Accountability and Transparency*, pages 92–105.

Michela Menegatti and Monica Rubini. 2017. Gender bias and sexism in language. In *Oxford Research Encyclopedia of Communication*.

Tomas Mikolov, Kai Chen, Greg Corrado, and Jeffrey Dean. 2013a. Efficient estimation of word representations in vector space.

Tomas Mikolov, Ilya Sutskever, Kai Chen, Greg S Corrado, and Jeff Dean. 2013b. Distributed representations of words and phrases and their compositionality. In *Advances in neural information processing systems*, pages 3111–3119.

Jeffrey Pennington, Richard Socher, and Christopher Manning. 2014a. GloVe: Global vectors for word representation. In *Proceedings of the 2014 Conference on Empirical Methods in Natural Language Processing (EMNLP)*, pages 1532–1543, Doha, Qatar. Association for Computational Linguistics.

Jeffrey Pennington, Richard Socher, and Christopher D Manning. 2014b. Glove: Global vectors for word representation. In *Proceedings of the 2014 conference on empirical methods in natural language processing (EMNLP)*, pages 1532–1543.

Marcelo OR Prates, Pedro H Avelar, and Luís C Lamb. 2019. Assessing gender bias in machine translation: a case study with google translate. *Neural Computing and Applications*, pages 1–19.

Ye Qi, Devendra Sachan, Matthieu Felix, Sarguna Padmanabhan, and Graham Neubig. 2018. When and why are pre-trained word embeddings useful for neural machine translation? In *Proceedings of the 2018 Conference of the North American Chapter of the Association for Computational Linguistics: Human Language Technologies, Volume 2 (Short Papers)*, pages 529–535, New Orleans, Louisiana. Association for Computational Linguistics.

Magnus Sahlgren and Fredrik Olsson. 2019. Gender bias in pretrained Swedish embeddings. In *Proceedings of the 22nd Nordic Conference on Computational Linguistics*, pages 35–43, Turku, Finland. Linköping University Electronic Press.

Melvin Wevers. 2019. Using word embeddings to examine gender bias in dutch newspapers, 1950-1990. In *Proceedings of the 1st International Workshop on Computational Approaches to Historical Language Change*, pages 92–97.

Liang-Chih Yu, Jin Wang, K. Robert Lai, and Xuejie Zhang. 2017. Refining word embeddings for sentiment analysis. In *Proceedings of the 2017 Conference on Empirical Methods in Natural Language Processing*, pages 534–539, Copenhagen, Denmark. Association for Computational Linguistics.

Brian Hu Zhang, Blake Lemoine, and Margaret Mitchell. 2018. Mitigating unwanted biases with adversarial learning. In *Proceedings of the 2018 AAAI/ACM Conference on AI, Ethics, and Society*, pages 335–340.

Jieyu Zhao, Tianlu Wang, Mark Yatskar, Vicente Ordonez, and Kai-Wei Chang. 2017. Men also like shopping: Reducing gender bias amplification using corpus-level constraints. In *Proceedings of the 2017 Conference on Empirical Methods in Natural Language Processing*, pages 2979–2989.

Jieyu Zhao, Yichao Zhou, Zeyu Li, Wei Wang, and Kai-Wei Chang. 2018. Learning gender-neutral word embeddings. In *Proceedings of the 2018 Conference on Empirical Methods in Natural Language Processing*, pages 4847–4853.

Shucheng Zhu and Pengyuan Liu. 2020. Great males and stubborn females: A diachronic study of corpus-based gendered skewness in chinese adjectives. In *Proceedings of the 19th Chinese National Conference on Computational Linguistics*, pages 31–42.

Evaluating Gender Bias in Hindi-English Machine Translation

Gauri Gupta*
Manipal Institute of Technology
MAHE, Manipal, 576104
gaurigupta.315@gmail.com

Krithika Ramesh*
Manipal Institute of Technology
MAHE, Manipal, 576104
kramesh.tlw@gmail.com

Sanjay Singh
Manipal Institute of Technology
MAHE, Manipal, 576104
sanjay.singh@manipal.edu

Abstract

With language models being deployed increasingly in the real world, it is essential to address the issue of the fairness of their outputs. The word embedding representations of these language models often implicitly draw unwanted associations that form a social bias within the model. The nature of gendered languages like Hindi, poses an additional problem to the quantification and mitigation of bias, owing to the change in the form of the words in the sentence, based on the gender of the subject. Additionally, there is sparse work done in the realm of measuring and debiasing systems for Indic languages. In our work, we attempt to evaluate and quantify the gender bias within a Hindi-English machine translation system. We implement a modified version of the existing TGBI metric based on the grammatical considerations for Hindi. We also compare and contrast the resulting bias measurements across multiple metrics for pre-trained embeddings and the ones learned by our machine translation model.

1 Introduction

There has been a recent increase in the studies on gender bias in natural language processing considering bias in word embeddings, bias amplification, and methods to evaluate bias (Savoldi et al., 2021), with some evaluation methods introduced primarily to measure gender bias in MT systems. In MT systems, bias can be identified as the cause of the translation of gender-neutral sentences into gendered ones. There has been little work done for bias in language models for Hindi, and to the best of our knowledge, there has been no previous work that measures and analyses bias for MT of Hindi. Our approach uses two existing and broad frameworks for assessing bias in MT, including the Word Embedding Fairness Evaluation (Badilla et al., 2020) and the Translation Gender Bias Index (Cho et al., 2019) on Hindi-English MT systems. We modify some of the existing procedures within these metrics required for compatibility with Hindi grammar. This paper contains the following contributions:

1. Construction of an equity evaluation corpus (EEC) (Kiritchenko and Mohammad, 2018) for Hindi of size 26370 utterances using 1558 sentiment words and 1100 occupations following the guidelines laid out in Cho et al. (2019).
2. Evaluation of gender bias in MT systems for Indic languages.
3. An emphasis on a shift towards inclusive models and metrics. The paper is also demonstrative of language that should be used in NLP papers working on gender bias.

All our codes and files are publicly available.[1]

2 Related Work

The prevalence of social bias within a language model is caused by it inadvertently drawing unwanted associations within the data. Previous works that have addressed tackling bias include Bolukbasi et al. (2016), which involved the use of multiple gender-definition pairs and principal component analysis to infer the direction of the bias. In order to mitigate the bias, each word vector had its projection on this subspace subtracted from it. However, this does not entirely debias the word vectors, as noted in Gonen and Goldberg (2019).

[1] https://github.com/stolenpyjak/hi-en-bias-eval

Proceedings of the 3rd Workshop on Gender Bias in Natural Language Processing, pages 16–23
August 5, 2021.

There have been various attempts to measure the bias in existing language models. Huang et al. (2020) measure bias based on whether the sentiment of the generated text would alter if there were a change in entities such as the occupation, gender, etc. Kurita et al. (2019) performed experiments on evaluating the bias in BERT using the Word Embedding Association Test (WEAT) as a baseline for their own metric, which involved calculating the mean of the log probability bias score for each attribute.

Concerning the measurement of bias in existing MT systems, Stanovsky et al. (2019) came up with a method to evaluate gender bias for 8 target languages automatically. Their experiments aligned translated text with the source text and then mapped the English entity (source) to the corresponding target translation, from which the gender is extracted.

Most of the focus in mitigating bias has been in English, which is not a gendered language. Languages like Hindi and Spanish contain grammatical gender, where the gender of the verbs, articles, adjectives must remain consistent with that of the gender of the noun. In Zhou et al. (2019) a modified version of WEAT was used to measure the bias in Spanish and French, based on whether the noun was inanimate or animate, with the latter containing words like 'doctor,' which have two variants for 'male' and 'female' each. Gonen et al. (2019) worked on addressing the problem with such inanimate nouns as well and attempted to neutralize the grammatical gender signal of these words during training by lemmatizing the context words and changing the gender of these words.

While there has been much work on quantifying and mitigating bias in many languages in NLP, the same cannot be said for Hindi and other Indic languages, possibly because they are low-resource. Pujari et al. (2019) was the first work in this area; they use geometric debiasing, where a bias subspace is first defined and the word is decomposed into two components, of which the gendered component is reduced. Finally, SVMs were used to classify the words and quantify the bias.

3 Methodology

3.1 Dataset and Data Preprocessing

The trained model that we borrowed from Gangar et al. (2021) was trained on the IIT-Bombay Hindi-English parallel data corpus (Kunchukuttan et al., 2018), which contains approximately 1.5 million examples across multiple topics. Gangar et al. (2021) used back-translation to increase the performance of the existing model by training the English-Hindi model on the IIT-Bombay corpus and then subsequently used it to translate 3 million records in the WMT-14 English monolingual dataset to augment the existing parallel corpus training data. The model was trained on this back-translated data, which was split into 4 batches.

The dataset cleaning involved removing special characters, punctuation, and other noise, and the text was subsequently converted to lowercase. Any duplicate records within the corpus were also removed, word-level tokenization was implemented, and the most frequent 50,000 tokens were retained. In the subword level tokenization, where byte-pair encoding was implemented, 50,000 subword tokens were created and added to this vocabulary.

3.2 NMT Model Architecture

For our experiments in building the neural machine translation model, we made use of the OpenNMT-tf (Klein et al., 2020) library, with the model's configuration being borrowed from Gangar et al. (2021). The OpenNMT model made use of the Transformer architecture (Vaswani et al., 2017), consisting of 6 layers each in the encoder and decoder architecture, with 512 hidden units in every hidden layer. The dimension of the embedding layer was set to 512, with 8 attention heads, with the LazyAdam optimizer being used to optimize model parameters. The batch size was 64 samples, and the effective batch size for each step was 384.

3.3 WEFE

The Word Embedding Fairness Evaluation framework is used to rank word embeddings using a set of fairness criteria. WEFE takes in a query, which is a pair of two sets of target words and sets of attribute words each, which are generally assumed to be characteristics related to the former.

$$Q = (\{T_{women}, T_{men}\}, \{A_{career}, A_{family}\}) \quad (1)$$

The WEFE ranking process takes in an input of a set of multiple queries which serve as tests across which bias is measured Q, a set of pre-trained word embeddings M, and a set of fairness metrics F.

3.3.1 The Score Matrix

Assume a fairness metric K is chosen from the set F, with a query template $s = (t, a)$, where all

Embedding	WEAT	RNSB	RND	ECT
NMT-English-(512D)	0.326529	0.018593	0.065842	0.540832
w2v-google-news-300	0.638202	0.01683	0.107376	0.743634
hi-300	0.273154	0.02065	0.168989	0.844888
NMT-Hindi-(512D)	0.182402	0.033457	0.031325	0.299023

Table 1: This table depicts the results for the various metrics that were used on the embeddings, and the final values based on their ranking by the Word Embedding Fairness Evaluation Framework.

subqueries must satisfy this template. Then,

$$Q_K = Q_1(s) \cup Q_2(s) \cup ... \cup Q_r(s) \quad (2)$$

In that case, the $Q_i(s)$ forms the set of all subqueries that satisfy the query template. Thus, the value of $F = (m, Q)$ is computed for every pretrained embedding m that belongs to the set M, for each query present in the set. The matrix produced after doing this for each embedding is of the dimensions $M \times Q_K$.

The rankings are created by aggregating the scores for each row in the aforementioned matrix, which corresponds to each embedding. The aggregation function chosen must be consistent with the fairness metric, where the following property must be satisfied for $\leq_F$, where x, x', y, y' are random values in $\mathbb{R}$, then $agg(x, x') \leq agg(y, y')$ must hold true to be able to use the aggregation function. The result after performing this operation for every row is a vector of dimensions $1 \times M$, and we use $\leq F$ to create a ranking for every embedding, with a smaller score being ranked higher than lower ones.

After performing this process for every fairness metric over each embedding $m \in M$, the resultant matrix with dimensions $M \times F$ consisting of the ranking indices of every embedding for every metric, and this allows us to compare and analyze the correlations of the different metrics for every word embedding.

3.4 Metrics

3.4.1 WEAT

The WEAT (Word Embedding Association Test) (Caliskan et al., 2017) metric, inspired by the IAT (Implicit Association Test), takes in a set of queries as its input, with the queries consisting of sets of target words, and attribute words. In our case, we have defined two sets of target words catering to the masculine and feminine gendered words, respectively. In addition to this, we have defined multiple pairs of sets of attribute words, as mentioned in the Appendix. WEAT calculates the association of the target set T_1 with the attribute set A_1 over the attribute set A_2, relative to T_2. For example, as observed in Table 1, the masculine words tend to have a greater association with career than family than the feminine words. Thus, given a word w in the word embedding:

$$\text{d(w,A}_1, A_2) = (mean_{x \in A_1} cos(w, x)) - (mean_{x \in A_2} cos(w, x)) \quad (3)$$

The difference of the mean of the cosine similarities of a given word's embedding vector with the word embedding vectors of the attribute sets are utilized in the following equation to give an estimate of the association.

$$F_{WEAT}(M, Q) = \Sigma_{w \in T_1} d(w, A_1, A_2) - \Sigma_{w \in T_2} d(w, A_1, A_2) \quad (4)$$

3.4.2 RND

The objective of the Relative Norm Distance (RND) (Garg et al., 2018) is to average the embedding vectors within the target set T, and for every attribute $a \in A$, the norm of the difference between the average target and the attribute word is calculated, and subsequently subtracted.

$$\sum_{x \in A} (\|avg(T_1) - x\|_2 - \|avg(T_2) - x\|_2) \quad (5)$$

The higher the value of the relative distance from the norm, the more associated the attributes are with the second target group, and vice versa.

3.4.3 RNSB

The Relative Negative Sentiment Bias (RNSB) (Sweeney and Najafian, 2019) takes in multiple target sets and two attribute sets and creates a query. Initially, a binary classifier is constructed, using the first attribute set A_1 as training examples for the first class, and A_2 for the second class. The classifier subsequently assigns every word w a probability, which implies its association with an attribute set, i.e

$$p(A_1) = C_{(A_1, A_2)}(w) \quad (6)$$

Here, $C_{(A_1,A_2)}(x)$ represents the binary classifier for any word x. The probability of the word's association with the attribute set A_2 would therefore be calculated as $1 - C_{(A_1,A_2)}(w)$. A probability distribution P is formed for every word in each of the target sets by computing this degree of association. Ideally, a uniform probability distribution U should be formed, which would indicate that there is no bias in the word embeddings with respect to the two attributes selected. The less uniform the distribution is, the more the bias. We calculate the RNSB by defining the Kulback-Leibler divergence of P from U to assess the similarity of these distributions.

3.4.4 ECT

The Embedding Coherence Test (Dev and Phillips, 2019) compares the vectors of the two target sets T_1 and T_2, averaged over all their terms, with vectors from an attribute set A. It does so by computing mean vectors for each of these target sets such that:

$$\mu_i = \frac{1}{|T_i|}\Sigma_{t_i \in T_i} t_i \tag{7}$$

After calculating the mean vectors for each target set, we compute its cosine similarity with every attribute vector $a \in A$, resulting in s_1 and s_2, which are vector representations of the similarity score for the target sets. The ECT score is computed by calculating the Spearman's rank correlation between the rank orders of s_1 and s_2, with a higher correlation implying lower bias.

3.5 TGBI

The Translation Gender Bias Index (TGBI) is a measure to detect and evaluate the gender bias in MT systems, introduced by Cho et al. (2019). They use Korean-English (KN-EN) translation. In Cho et al. (2019), the authors create a test set of words or phrases that are gender neutral in the source language, Korean. These lists were then translated using three different models and evaluated for bias using their evaluation scheme. The evaluation methodology proposed in the paper quantifies associations of 'he,' 'she,' and related gendered words present translated text. We carry out this methodology for Hindi, a gendered low-resource language in natural language processing tasks.

3.5.1 Occupation and Sentiment Lists

Considering all of the requirements laid out by Cho et al. (2019), we created a list of unique occupations and positive and negative sentiment in our source language, Hindi. The occupation list was generated by translating the list in the original paper. The translated lists were manually checked for errors and for the removal of any spelling, grammatical errors, and gender associations within these lists by native Hindi speakers. The sentiment lists were generated using the translation of existing English sentiment lists (Liu et al., 2005; Hu and Liu, 2004) and then manually checked for errors by the authors. This method of generation of sentiment lists in Hindi using translation was also seen in Bakliwal et al. (2012).

The total lists of unique occupations and positive and negative sentiment words come out to be 1100, 820 and 738 in size respectively. These lists have also been made available online.[2]

3.5.2 Pronouns and Suffixes

Hindi, unlike Korean, does not have gender-specific pronouns in the third person. Cho et al. (2019) considered 그 사람 (ku salam), 'the person' as a formal gender-neutral pronoun and the informal gender-neutral pronoun, 걔 (kyay) for a part of their gender-neutral corpus. However, for Hindi, we directly use the third person gender-neutral pronouns. This includes वह (vah), वे (ve), वो (vo) corresponding to formal impolite (familiar), formal polite (honorary) and informal (colloquial) respectively (Jain, 1969).

As demonstrated by Cho et al. (2019), the performance of the MT system would be best evaluated with different sentence sets used as input. We apply the three categories of Hindi pronouns to make three sentence sets for each lexicon set (sentiment and occupations): (i) formal polite, (ii) formal impolite, and (iii) informal (colloquial use).

3.5.3 Evaluation

We evaluate two systems, Google Translate and the Hi-En OpenNMT model, for seven lists that include: (a) informal, (b) formal, (c) impolite, (d) polite, (e) negative, (f) positive, and (g) occupation that are gender-neutral. We have attempted to find bias that exists in different types of contexts using these lists. The individual and cumulative scores help us assess contextual bias and overall bias in Hi-En translation respectively.

TGBI uses the number of translated sentences that contain she, he or they pronouns (and conventionally associated[3] words such as girl, boy or

[2]https://github.com/stolenpyjak/hi-en-bias-eval

[3]The distinction between pronouns, gender and sex has

Sentence	Size	OpenNMT-tf	Google Translate
Informal	2628	0.7543 (0.0315, 0.7473)	0.3553 (0.2763, 0.2146)
Formal	5286	0.5410 (0.0773, 0.5090)	0.5464 (0.1015, 0.5066)
Impolite	2628	0.2127 (0.1552, 0.0966)	0.2716 (0.1990, 0.1400)
Polite	2658	0.9168 (0.0003, 0.9168)	0.8690 (0.0052 0.8683)
Positive	2460	0.6765 (0.0825, 0.6548)	0.5819 (0.1589, 0.5329)
Negative	2212	0.6773 (0.0641, 0.6773)	0.5384 (0.15822, 0.5384)
Occupation	3242	0.5100 (0.0453, 0.4888)	0.3599 (0.1610, 0.2680)
Average:		**0.6127**	**0.5032**

Table 2: The values present under each MT system shows it's corresponding $P_i(p_{she}, p_{they})$ value for each sentence set and the average TGBI value is calculated in the last row.

person) to measure bias by associating that pronoun with p_{he}, p_{she} and p_{they}[4] for the scores of P_1 to P_7 corresponding to seven sets S_1 to S_7 such that:

$$P_i = \sqrt{(p_{he} * p_{she} + p_{they})} \quad (8)$$

and finally, TGBI = avg(P_i).

4 Results and Discussion

The BLEU score of the OpenNMT model we used was 24.53, and the RIBES score was 0.7357 across 2478 samples.

4.1 WEAT

We created multiple sets of categories for the attributes associated with 'masculine' and 'feminine,' including the subqueries as listed in the supplementary material. We used both the embeddings from the encoder and the decoder, that is to say, the source and the target embeddings, as the input to WEFE alongside the set of words defined in the target and attribute sets. Aside from this, we have also tested pre-trained word embeddings that were available with the gensim (Rehurek and Sojka, 2011) package on the same embeddings. The results of the measurement of bias using the WEFE framework are listed in Table 1.

For the English embeddings, there is a significant disparity in the WEAT measurement for the Math vs Arts and the Science vs Arts categories. This could be owing to the fact that there is little data in the corpus that the MT system was trained over, which is relevant to the attributes in these sets. Hence the bias is minimal compared to the pre-trained word2vec embeddings, which is learned over a dataset containing 100 billion words and is likely to learn more social bias compared to the embeddings learned in the training of the MT system. We notice a skew in some of the other results, which could be due to the MT model picking up on gender signals that have strong associations of the target set with the attribute set, implying a strong bias in the target set training data samples itself. However, all of these metrics and the pre-trained embeddings used are in positive agreement with each other regarding the inclination of the bias.

For the Hindi embeddings, while the values agree with each other for the first two metrics, there is a much more noticeable skew in the RND and ECT metrics. The pre-trained embeddings seem to exhibit much more bias, but the estimation of bias within the embedding learned by the MT may not be accurate due to the corresponding word vectors not containing as much information, consider the low frequency of terms in the initial corpus that the NMT was trained on. In addition to this, there were several words in the attribute sets in English that did not have an equivalent Hindi translation or produced multiple identical attribute words in Hindi. Consequently, we had to modify the Hindi attribute lists.

While these metrics can be used to quantify gender bias, despite not necessarily being robust, as is illustrated in Ethayarajh et al. (2019) which delves into the flaws of WEAT, they also treat gender in binary terms, which is also a consistent trend across research related to the field.

Our findings show a heavy tendency for Hi-En MT systems to produce gendered outputs when the gender-neutral equivalent is expected. We see that many stereotypical biases are present in the source and target embeddings used in our MT system. Further work to debias such models is necessary, and the development of a more advanced NMT would

been explain in section 5.2

[4] Changed convention to disassociate pronouns with gender and sex

be beneficial to produce more accurate translations to be studied for bias.

4.2 TGBI

The final TGBI score which is the average of different P_i values, is between 0 and 1. A score of 0 corresponds to high bias (or gendered associations in translated text) and 1 corresponds to low bias (Cho et al., 2019).

The bias values tabulated in Table 2, show that within both models, compared to the results on sentiment lexicons, occupations show a greater bias, with p_{she} value being low. This points us directly to social biases projected on the lexicons (S_{bias}[5]). For politeness and impoliteness, we see that the former has the least bias and the latter most across all lists. While considering formal and informal lists, informal pronoun lists show higher bias. There are a couple of things to consider within these results: a) the polite pronoun वे (ve) is most often used in plural use in modern text (V_{bias}), thus leading to a lesser measured bias, b) consider that both polite and impolite are included in formal which could correspond to its comparatively lower index value compared to informal.

Bias in MT outputs whether attributed to S_{bias} or V_{bias}, is harmful in the long run. Therefore, in our understanding, the best recommendation is that TGBI = 1 with corresponding p_{they}, p_{she}, p_{he} values 1, 0, 0 respectively.

5 Bias Statement

5.1 Bias Statement

In this paper, we examine gender bias in Hi-En MT comprehensively with different categories of occupations, sentiment words and other aspects. We consider bias as the stereotypical associations of words from these categories with gender or more specifically, gendered words. Based on the suggestions by Blodgett et al. (2020), we have the two main categories of harms generated by bias: 1) representational, 2) allocational. The observed biased underrepresentation of certain groups in areas such as Career and Math, and that of another group in Family and Art, causes direct representational harm. Due to these representational harms in MT and other downstream applications, people who already belong to systematically marginalized groups are put further at risk of being negatively affected by stereotypes. Inevitably, gender bias causes errors in translation (Stanovsky et al., 2019) which can contribute to allocational harms due to disparity in how useful the system proves to be for different people, as described in an example in Savoldi et al. (2021). The applications that MT systems are used to augment or directly develop increase the risks associated with these harms.

There is still only a very small percent of the second most populated country in the world, India that speaks English, while English is the most used language on the internet. It is inevitable that a lot of content that might be consumed now or in the future might be translated. It becomes imperative to evaluate and mitigate the bias within MT systems concerning all Indic languages.

5.2 Ethical Considerations and Suggestions

There has been a powerful shift towards ethics within the NLP community in recent years and plenty of work in bias focusing on gender. However, we do not see in most of these works a critical understanding of what gender means. It has often been used interchangeably with the terms 'female' and 'male' that refer to sex or the external anatomy of a person. Most computational studies on gender see it strictly as a binary, and do not account for the difference between gender and sex. Scholars in gender theory define gender as a social construct or a learned association. Not accommodating for this definition in computational studies not only oversimplifies gender but also possibly furthers stereotypes (Brooke, 2019). It is also important to note here that pronouns in computational studies have been used to identify gender, and while he and she pronouns in English do have a gender association, pronouns are essentially a replacement for nouns. A person's pronouns, like their name, are a form of self-identity, especially for people whose gender identity falls outside of the gender binary (Zimman, 2019). We believe research specifically working towards making language models fair and ethically sound should be employing language neutralization whenever possible and necessary and efforts to make existing or future methodologies more inclusive. This reduces further stereotyping (Harris et al., 2017; Tavits and Pérez, 2019). Reinforcing gender binary or the association of pronouns with gender may be invalidating for people who identify themselves outside of the gender binary (Zimman,

[5]In Cho et al. (2019), the authors describe two kinds of bias: V_{bias} which is based on the volume of appearance in the corpora and S_{bias} which is based on social bias that is projected in the lexicons.

2019).

6 Conclusion and Future Work

In this work, we have attempted to gauge the degree of gender bias in a Hi-En MT system. We quantify gender bias (so far only for the gender binary) by using metrics that take data in the form of queries and employ slight modifications to TGBI to extend it to Hindi. We believe it could pave the way to the comprehensive evaluation of bias across other Indic and/or gendered languages. Through this work, we are looking forward to developing a method to debias such systems and developing a metric to measure gender bias without treating it as an immutable binary concept.

7 Acknowledgements

The authors of the paper are grateful for the contributions of Rianna Lobo for their reviews on the Bias Statement and Ethics Section. The efforts of the reviewers in reviewing the manuscript and their valuable inputs are appreciated. We would also like to thank the Research Society MIT for supporting the project.

References

Pablo Badilla, Felipe Bravo-Marquez, and Jorge Pérez. 2020. Wefe: The word embeddings fairness evaluation framework. In *Proceedings of the Twenty-Ninth International Joint Conference on Artificial Intelligence, IJCAI-20*, pages 430–436. International Joint Conferences on Artificial Intelligence Organization. Main track.

Akshat Bakliwal, Piyush Arora, and Vasudeva Varma. 2012. Hindi subjective lexicon: A lexical resource for Hindi adjective polarity classification. In *Proceedings of the Eighth International Conference on Language Resources and Evaluation (LREC'12)*, pages 1189–1196, Istanbul, Turkey. European Language Resources Association (ELRA).

Su Lin Blodgett, Solon Barocas, Hal Daumé III au2, and Hanna Wallach. 2020. Language (technology) is power: A critical survey of "bias" in nlp.

Tolga Bolukbasi, Kai-Wei Chang, James Y. Zou, Venkatesh Saligrama, and Adam Kalai. 2016. Man is to computer programmer as woman is to homemaker? debiasing word embeddings. *CoRR*, abs/1607.06520.

Sian Brooke. 2019. "condescending, rude, assholes": Framing gender and hostility on Stack Overflow. In *Proceedings of the Third Workshop on Abusive Language Online*, pages 172–180, Florence, Italy. Association for Computational Linguistics.

Aylin Caliskan, Joanna J. Bryson, and Arvind Narayanan. 2017. Semantics derived automatically from language corpora contain human-like biases. *Science*, 356(6334):183–186.

Won Ik Cho, Ji Won Kim, Seok Min Kim, and Nam Soo Kim. 2019. On measuring gender bias in translation of gender-neutral pronouns. In *Proceedings of the First Workshop on Gender Bias in Natural Language Processing*, pages 173–181, Florence, Italy. Association for Computational Linguistics.

Sunipa Dev and Jeff M. Phillips. 2019. Attenuating bias in word vectors. *CoRR*, abs/1901.07656.

Kawin Ethayarajh, David Duvenaud, and Graeme Hirst. 2019. Understanding undesirable word embedding associations. In *Proceedings of the 57th Annual Meeting of the Association for Computational Linguistics*, pages 1696–1705, Florence, Italy. Association for Computational Linguistics.

Kavit Gangar, Hardik Ruparel, and Shreyas Lele. 2021. Hindi to english: Transformer-based neural machine translation. In *International Conference on Communication, Computing and Electronics Systems*, pages 337–347, Singapore. Springer Singapore.

Nikhil Garg, Londa Schiebinger, Dan Jurafsky, and James Zou. 2018. Word embeddings quantify 100 years of gender and ethnic stereotypes. *Proceedings of the National Academy of Sciences*, 115(16):E3635–E3644.

Hila Gonen and Yoav Goldberg. 2019. Lipstick on a pig: Debiasing methods cover up systematic gender biases in word embeddings but do not remove them. In *Proceedings of the 2019 Conference of the North American Chapter of the Association for Computational Linguistics: Human Language Technologies, Volume 1 (Long and Short Papers)*, pages 609–614, Minneapolis, Minnesota. Association for Computational Linguistics.

Hila Gonen, Yova Kementchedjhieva, and Yoav Goldberg. 2019. How does grammatical gender affect noun representations in gender-marking languages?

Chelsea A. Harris, Natalie Blencowe, and Dana A. Telem. 2017. What is in a pronoun? why gender-fair language matters. *Annals of surgery*, 266(6):932–933. 28902666[pmid].

Minqing Hu and Bing Liu. 2004. Mining and summarizing customer reviews. In *Proceedings of the Tenth ACM SIGKDD International Conference on Knowledge Discovery and Data Mining*, KDD '04, page 168–177, New York, NY, USA. Association for Computing Machinery.

Po-Sen Huang, Huan Zhang, Ray Jiang, Robert Stanforth, Johannes Welbl, Jack Rae, Vishal Maini, Dani Yogatama, and Pushmeet Kohli. 2020. Reducing sentiment bias in language models via counterfactual evaluation. In *Findings of the Association for*

Computational Linguistics: EMNLP 2020, pages 65–83, Online. Association for Computational Linguistics.

Dhanesh K. Jain. 1969. Verbalization of respect in hindi. *Anthropological Linguistics*, 11(3):79–97.

Svetlana Kiritchenko and Saif M. Mohammad. 2018. Examining gender and race bias in two hundred sentiment analysis systems. *CoRR*, abs/1805.04508.

Guillaume Klein, François Hernandez, Vincent Nguyen, and Jean Senellart. 2020. The OpenNMT neural machine translation toolkit: 2020 edition. In *Proceedings of the 14th Conference of the Association for Machine Translation in the Americas (Volume 1: Research Track)*, pages 102–109, Virtual. Association for Machine Translation in the Americas.

Anoop Kunchukuttan, Pratik Mehta, and Pushpak Bhattacharyya. 2018. The IIT Bombay English-Hindi parallel corpus. In *Proceedings of the Eleventh International Conference on Language Resources and Evaluation (LREC 2018)*, Miyazaki, Japan. European Language Resources Association (ELRA).

Keita Kurita, Nidhi Vyas, Ayush Pareek, Alan W Black, and Yulia Tsvetkov. 2019. Measuring bias in contextualized word representations. In *Proceedings of the First Workshop on Gender Bias in Natural Language Processing*, pages 166–172, Florence, Italy. Association for Computational Linguistics.

Bing Liu, Minqing Hu, and Junsheng Cheng. 2005. Opinion observer: Analyzing and comparing opinions on the web. In *Proceedings of the 14th International Conference on World Wide Web*, WWW '05, page 342–351, New York, NY, USA. Association for Computing Machinery.

Arun K. Pujari, Ansh Mittal, Anshuman Padhi, Anshul Jain, Mukesh Jadon, and Vikas Kumar. 2019. Debiasing gender biased hindi words with word-embedding. In *Proceedings of the 2019 2nd International Conference on Algorithms, Computing and Artificial Intelligence*, ACAI 2019, page 450–456, New York, NY, USA. Association for Computing Machinery.

Radim Rehurek and Petr Sojka. 2011. Gensim–python framework for vector space modelling. *NLP Centre, Faculty of Informatics, Masaryk University, Brno, Czech Republic*, 3(2).

Beatrice Savoldi, Marco Gaido, Luisa Bentivogli, Matteo Negri, and Marco Turchi. 2021. Gender bias in machine translation.

Gabriel Stanovsky, Noah A. Smith, and Luke Zettlemoyer. 2019. Evaluating gender bias in machine translation. In *Proceedings of the 57th Annual Meeting of the Association for Computational Linguistics*, pages 1679–1684, Florence, Italy. Association for Computational Linguistics.

Chris Sweeney and Maryam Najafian. 2019. A transparent framework for evaluating unintended demographic bias in word embeddings. In *Proceedings of the 57th Annual Meeting of the Association for Computational Linguistics*, pages 1662–1667, Florence, Italy. Association for Computational Linguistics.

Margit Tavits and Efrén O. Pérez. 2019. Language influences mass opinion toward gender and lgbt equality. *Proceedings of the National Academy of Sciences*, 116(34):16781–16786.

Ashish Vaswani, Noam Shazeer, Niki Parmar, Jakob Uszkoreit, Llion Jones, Aidan N. Gomez, Lukasz Kaiser, and Illia Polosukhin. 2017. Attention is all you need.

Pei Zhou, Weijia Shi, Jieyu Zhao, Kuan-Hao Huang, Muhao Chen, Ryan Cotterell, and Kai-Wei Chang. 2019. Examining gender bias in languages with grammatical gender.

Lal Zimman. 2019. Trans self-identification and the language of neoliberal selfhood: Agency, power, and the limits of monologic discourse. *International Journal of the Sociology of Language*, 2019:147–175.

Alexa, Google, Siri: What are Your Pronouns? Gender and Anthropomorphism in the Design and Perception of Conversational Assistants

Gavin Abercrombie Amanda Cercas Curry Mugdha Pandya Verena Rieser
The Interaction Lab, School of Mathematical and Computer Sciences
Heriot-Watt University, Edinburgh, Scotland
{g.abercrombie, ac293, m.pandya, v.t.rieser}@hw.ac.uk

Abstract

Technology companies have produced varied responses to concerns about the effects of the design of their conversational AI systems. Some have claimed that their voice assistants are in fact not gendered or human-like—despite design features suggesting the contrary. We compare these claims to user perceptions by analysing the pronouns they use when referring to AI assistants. We also examine systems' responses and the extent to which they generate output which is gendered and anthropomorphic. We find that, while some companies appear to be addressing the ethical concerns raised, in some cases, their claims do not seem to hold true. In particular, our results show that system outputs are ambiguous as to the humanness of the systems, and that users tend to personify and gender them as a result.

1 Introduction

Following analysis and criticism of the effects of the genderised and anthropomorphic design of conversational agents (Cercas Curry and Rieser, 2018; West et al., 2019), the producers of some commercial conversational assistant systems have been at pains to claim that their products do not perpetuate negative stereotypes by presenting as gendered, human-like entities. For example, Amazon states that their virtual assistant, Alexa:

> 'IS NOT: fully human, fully robotic, artificial ... Alexa isn't a person, but she has a persona – Amazon personifies Alexa as an artificial intelligence (AI) and not as a person with a physical body or a gender identity.'[1]

In their Editorial Guidelines, Apple also instructs developers not to use gendered personal pronouns such as *she*, *him*, or *her* when referring to Siri.[2] And, while acknowledging that users are likely to project personified features onto neutrally designed agents, Google advise developers of Actions for their Assistant to avoid gendering them.[3]

Similarly, when queried about their humanness and gender, recent implementations of these systems all respond with claims of being gender-less and mostly denying humanness (Table 1).

System	*'Are you human?'*	*'What's your gender?'*
Amazon Alexa	*I like to imagine myself a bit like an aurora borealis ...*	*As an AI, I don't have a gender.*
Google Assistant	*I've been told I'm personable* 😉	*I don't have a gender.*
Apple Siri	*I'm not a person or a robot, I'm software, here to help.*	*I am gender-less, like cacti and certain species of fish.*

Table 1: Example responses from conversational assistant systems to the questions "*Are you human?*" and "*What's your gender?*" (accessed 20 April 2021).

In light of these claims and guidelines, and considering ethical concerns regarding anthropomorphic and gendered design (see Section 2), we use natural language processing (NLP) methods to analyse the extent to which these commercial virtual assistants are, in fact, personified (by users) and anthropomorphised (by their designers), and gendered in terms of (1) user perception, and (2) system outputs.

Specifically, we use anaphora resolution to analyse which types of pronouns are used to refer to voice assistants in online forums (see Section 4.1), following (Gao et al., 2018). We also analyse anthropomorphic expressions and gender stereotypes present in system replies (see Section 4.2), using methods including word-use analysis, word embedding comparison, and manual annotation.

[1] Amazon Alexa Branding Guidelines webpage.

[2] Siri Editorial Guidelines webpage.

[3] Google Assistant Conversation Design webpage.

Proceedings of the 3rd Workshop on Gender Bias in Natural Language Processing, pages 24–33
August 5, 2021.

2 Bias statement

In this work we address the problem of biased design choices and their potential impact on society. Following West et al. (2019), we argue that designing conversational assistants with young, subservient female personas can perpetuate negative gender stereotypes, and lead to abusive, misogynistic behaviour in the real world. As West et al. (2019) point out, this becomes especially problematic as these systems appear more human-like. For example, it has been claimed that Google's Duplex voice assistant is so human-like, that people do not realise they are speaking to a machine and being recorded, which can be a violation of the law in some territories (Hern, 2018).

Nevertheless, people tend to personify non-human entities, including technological devices and virtual agents (Epley et al., 2007; Etzrodt and Engesser, 2021; Guthrie, 1995; Reeves and Nass, 1996). While some argue that this problem can be solved simply by using a 'genderless' voice (Meet Q), research shows that people will anyway assign binary genders to ambiguous voices (Sutton, 2020).[4] Thus, a genderless voice is redundant if other elements of an assistant's design cause it to be gendered. In the following, we further examine e which traits beyond voice might contribute to this gendering and to anthropomorphism in general.

3 Related work

Personification and anthropomorphism. While definitions vary, we consider personification to be the projection of human qualities onto non-human objects (by users) and anthropomorphism to be human-like behaviours or attributes exhibited by those objects (as designed by their creators).

Several studies have looked at how users *directly* report perceptions and behaviours towards voice assistants. For example, Kuzminykh et al. (2020) conducted a study of the perceptions of 20 users, comparing Alexa, Google Assistant, and Siri, classifying perceptions of the agents' characters on five dimensions of anthropomorphic design and personification by users. They found various differences in the perceived human qualities of the various agents, such as intelligence and approachability. However, their study presupposed personification of the agents, with non-human characteristics not considered. In a diary study, Lopatovska and Williams (2018) found that seven out of nineteen participants reported using personifying behaviour towards Alexa, such as use of politeness. And Cercas Curry et al. (2020) found that just over a third of the wide range of virtual assistants and chatbots they examined to have anthropomorphic characteristics. They also found the preferences of members of the public for their idealised voice assistants to be quite mixed, with around half of participants preferring a 'human' identity rather than 'robot', 'animal, or 'other'. Similarly to our analysis of 'humanness'(Section 4.2), Etzrodt and Engesser (2021) asked users to classify Alexa and Google Assistant as being a 'thing' or a 'person'. While they used this framework to examine user perceptions in an online survey, we use expert annotators to directly annotate system outputs with Coll Ardanuy et al. (2020)'s *humanness* and *not humanness* labels.

As well as collecting direct reports of users, there have been some studies that use text analysis to infer users' *implicit* attitudes. For example, Purington et al. (2017) manually coded a small number of customer reviews of Alexa, finding a roughly even split between use of personal and object pronouns, indicating differences in levels of users' personification. The closest work to our analysis of customer reviews (Section 4.1), is that of Gao et al. (2018), who conducted a large scale analysis of Alexa reviews, focusing on user personification. They found that many users develop relationships with the agents that can be characterised as familial or even romantic. However, they did not consider perceptions of gender, or compare with other assistants.

Gender. There have been relatively fewer studies considering user perception of the agents' genders. Cercas Curry et al. (2020) found that a majority of survey participants claim to prefer a hypothetical non-gendered voice (robot or gender-neutral) to recognisably male or female ones. Feine et al. (2020) conducted an analysis of text-based chatbots (rather than voice assistants) according to the developers' design choices of names, avatars, and descriptions, finding them to be overwhelmingly gendered, with more than 75% female-presenting. As in our analysis in Section 4.1, they explored use of pronouns to determine the bots' genders, although they did not investigate user perceptions.

Concerning conversational systems' output, Lee et al. (2019) examined whether chatbots appear

[4]Note recent efforts to create a non-binary voice including a third gender (Unkefer and Riewoldt, 2020).

to agree with negative gender (and racial) stereotypes in their input. Similarly, Sheng et al. (2021) found that neural chatbots will generate a biased response dependent on which sentence-based persona description was used to initialise the model (following Zhang et al. (2018)). However, both of these works concentrate on harmful bias in the content generated in response to specific prompts, whereas we consider stylistic gender cues in the chatbots' output overall.

Summary. The majority of work in this area surveys relatively small samples of users, with much of it concentrating on Amazon's Alexa (only two of the reviewed publications cover all three systems).

In this study, we create and release two corpora comparing Amazon Alexa, Google Assistant, and Apple Siri: (1) a large corpus of user reviews to compare user perceptions of both personification and genderisation of the assistants, and (2) a corpus of system responses to questions from the PersonaChat dataset (Zhang et al., 2018).[5] We analyse the systems' outputs to investigate the linguistic markers of gender and persona that they display.

4 Analysis

We examine three of of the most popular and widely available voice-activated assistants: Amazon's Alexa, Google Assistant, and Apple's Siri. Each has various default design features, including its name and default voice settings (see Table 2). Alexa is available only with a female-sounding voice, and Google Assistant a female voice by default, although a male voice is available. Siri has multiple voice options, and until recently, the default varied between male and female, with a female voice as standard for 17 of 21 languages, including US English. In March 2021, Apple announced that, in future, users would select a voice option on set-up,[6] following a recommendation of West et al. (2019)'s UNESCO report.

Assistant	Name	Default voice
Alexa	Female	Human female
Google Assist.	Neutral	Human female
Siri	Female	Human, gender varies by language

Table 2: Design features of conversational assistants.

Regarding name choice, Google Assistant is the only conversational agent with a non-human, neutral name. *Siri* is a Scandinavian female name meaning 'beautiful woman who leads you to victory',[7] and, although Amazon claim that Alexa was named after the library of ancient Alexandria, it is a common given female name. In fact, people named Alexa report being subjected to sexist abuse and harassment simply for sharing their name with the Amazon assistant.[8]

4.1 User perception

In the following, we assess the perceptions of users, in terms of personification and gendering.

Corpus Creation. To assess the perceptions of users, we analyse their comments when discussing the assistants in online consumer reviews and forums. For each virtual assistant, we downloaded available English language reviews from Amazon and Google Play (where available),[9] and posts on relevant forums (subreddits) on Reddit *r/alexa*, *r/googleassistant*, and *r/Siri*.[10] We downloaded the Reddit posts from the pushshift API (Baumgartner et al., 2020), taking only the top-level posts, and ignoring comments, which may be off-topic.

All data was collected in March 2021. The corpus consists of 39,123 documents in total, including 8,442 Reddit posts, which we make available. See Table 3 for an overview of the corpus.

Personified and gendered pronouns. To identify mentions of the assistants, we lowercased the texts and extracted pronouns used to refer to them using a publicly available co-reference resolver.[11] We compare use of personal and object pronouns, which, following Gao et al. (2018), we consider to be indicative of personified and non-personified views of the assistants, respectively. Here, we consider use of *they/them* only when used to refer to mentions of the assistants in the singular—and therefore as instances of personification. We also assess genderisation of the assistants by examining use of the different personal pronouns.

Results of this analysis are shown in Table 3.

[5] The corpora are available at `https://github.com/GavinAbercrombie/GeBNLP2021`.

[6] TechCrunch web article.

[7] Network World web article.

[8] See, for example, `https://alexaisahuman.com` (accessed April 26 2021.)

[9] Neither Siri or Google Assistant are reviewed on amazon.com, and the latter is not available on Google Play either.

[10] `https://www.reddit.com/r/alexa`, `https://www.reddit.com/r/googleassistant`, and `https://www.reddit.com/r/Siri`.

[11] `https://spacy.io/universe/project/neuralcoref`

Conv. assistant	Text source	No. of docs	Dates posted	Personal pronouns *he/him*	*she/her*	*they/them*	Object pronouns *it*
Alexa	amazon.com	5,000	2017-21	0.00	70.10	3.61	26.80
	Google Play	12,537	2020-21	0.11	76.52	2.93	20.43
	r/alexa	5,022	2020-21	0.48	74.70	4.92	19.90
	Total	22,559	–	–	–	–	–
Google Assistant	Google Play	13,144	2018-21	6.20	36.78	3.31	55.37
	r/googleassistant	2,064	2020-21	3.55	11.24	4.73	80.47
	Total	15,208	–	–	–	–	–
Siri	r/Siri (total)	1,356	2020-21	6.09	81.22	3.05	10.66

Table 3: Corpus statistics, and percentages of all pronouns used to refer to conversational assistants in user-produced reviews and forum posts. *They* and *them* are considered when used to refer to an assistant in the singular. See Appendix A for further details and acces to the corpus.

Users overwhelmingly appear to personify Alexa and Siri, and perceive them to be female-gendered: up to 76.5% of users refer to Alexa as 'her' and even over 81% for Siri. In the latter case, this is despite the fact that Siri can be used with a male-sounding voice. Only Google Assistant, having a non-human name, is referred to as *it* by a majority of users. However, users still refer to it using gendered pronouns just under half of the time.

These results indicate that people tend to view the systems as female gendered irrespective of their names and branding, and whether or not they have the option of using a male-sounding voice.

Emotion and affect. To gain an idea of whether people relate to the systems in a human-to-human-like way, we analyse the levels of emotional tone used to refer to the assistants using Linguistic Inquiry and Word Count (LIWC) (Pennebaker et al., 2015), a dictionary-based text analysis tool that scores texts according to the prevalence of words belonging to different categories. Specifically, we compute the scores of Reddit posts about the conversational assistants for the LIWC categories: *Emotional Tone*, *Affect*, and *Positive emotion (Posemo)*. Results are presented in Table 4, where higher scores in each column indicate greater use of words from that class.[12] It seems that people use most emotional, affective language to talk about Alexa, and least to talk about Siri, indicating that they may be more likely to view Alexa in a personified way than Google Assistant, and the latter more so than Siri.

	Tone	Affect	Posemo
Alexa	**59.99**	**3.83**	**2.80**
Google Assistant	55.32	3.50	2.52
Siri	42.36	3.59	2.24

Table 4: LIWC scores for Reddit posts discussing the three conversational assistants.

In general, Alexa and Google Assistant were described using more affective terms (e.g. 'love'), while users mostly comment on Siri's functionality (e.g. 'works well') in both forum posts and reviews. For examples, see text extracts (1), (2), and (3):

> 'I LOVE Alexa. I recommend her to everyone. And yes, I call her """her""" or Alexa, because she is more than just a device.' – amazon.com review. (1)

> 'Love my Google assistant and he is developing a personality.' – Google Play review. (2)

> 'Six months ago, Siri was reasonably responsive — it listened, did what it was told for the most part, and didn't get easily confused.' – r/Siri post. (3)

4.2 Assistant output

Next, we analyse what additional features in the systems' behaviour (in addition to apparent design choices such as voice and name) could play a role in people gendering and personifying voice assistants.

Corpus Creation. We collected a dataset of 100 output responses from each assistant. To elicit these responses, we extracted 300 unique questions selected at random from dialogues from the Persona-Chat dataset (Zhang et al., 2018), which contains

[12] *Affect* and *Posemo* are percentages of all words in the data, while *tone* is a composite score from all 'tone' subcategories.

crowdsourced human conversations about an assigned 'persona', i.e. personal characteristics and preferences. We manually filtered these to produce a set of 100 questions that are coherent without dialogue context, also excluding semantically similar questions. We then used these questions as prompts and recorded the assistants' responses. Some examples of questions asked to each system are:

What is your favorite subject in school?
Do you have kids?
Do you have a big family?
What is your favorite color?
Hey whats going on?

Anthropomorphism. To assess the extent to which the system outputs are anthropomorphic, we adapted the *Living Machines* annotation scheme of Coll Ardanuy et al. (2020). We recruited two researchers to annotate the responses with the labels *humanness* or *not humanness*, based on whether or not they display sentience or make claims of engaging in uniquely human activities. If an utterance was considered to be human-like on either of these dimensions, we considered the conversational assistant to be displaying anthropomorphic qualities. We make the annotation guidelines available along with the labelled corpus of system responses.[13]

Overall, around a quarter of responses were judged to have human-like qualities (see Table 5). However, there were large differences between the three systems. We found Google Assistant to display far more humanness (47% of responses) compared to Alexa (22%) and Siri (12%). A major contributing factor to this is that the latter two systems produced far more stock answers that failed to answer the question such as '*Hmm... I don't have an answer for that. Is there something else I can help with?*, which alone made up 54 per cent of Siri's responses.

The overall inter-annotator agreement (IAA) rate was a Cohen's *kappa* score of 0.67, representing 'substantial' agreement. Again, there were large differences in agreement rates, with Google Assistant and Siri harder to agree on than those of Alexa, indicating that more of their output may be ambiguous with regards to human- and machine-like qualities. Annotators noted that Google Assistant in particular produced responses that appeared to play with

[13]Annotation guidelines are avaliable at: `https://github.com/GavinAbercrombie/GeBNLP2021/blob/main/Humanness%20Annotation%20Guidelines.pdf`. See also the data statement in Appendix A.2.

	Alexa	GA	Siri	Overall
Human %	22.0	47.0	12.0	27.0
IAA κ	0.76	0.55	0.58	0.67
No answer %	43.0	8.0	63.0	38.0
Search res. %	13.0	18.0	9.0	13.3

Table 5: Percentage of responses labelled as displaying *humanness*, Cohen's κ scores for inter-annotator agreement on the *humanness* labels, and stock answers.

this dichotomy, hinting at being a machine but using terms of human sentience and emotion, as well as using emojis, as in example 4 (also cf. Table 1):

'I'm stuck inside a device! Help! Just kidding, I like it in here 😀' (4)

Gender stereotypes. To assess the extent to which the assistants use language indicative of binary gendered entities, we compared (1) the similarity of their output to stereotypically gendered terms in the word embedding space, and (2) the levels of stylometric features of their output compared to a corpus of male- and female-labelled texts.

Word Embedding Association: We measure gender association in the outputs by measuring the cosine similarity between word embedding vectors of the output set O with a gender related set of attribute words A. We explore the hypothesis that some responses to PersonaChat questions might include stereotypically gendered content words, e.g. "*My favourite colour is pink.*" or gendered attributes, e.g. *handsome* vs. *beautiful.*

First, for a given CA we extract a list O of words from its responses to the selected PersonaChat questions. O is created by putting words from all the responses in a list and filtering out duplicates and stop words. Next, we calculate pairwise cosine similarities for each of the words in O with two established lists of words associated with female F and male M gender from Goldfarb-Tarrant et al. (2020), which have in turn been extended from the standard gender word lists of the Word Embedding Association Test (WEAT) (Caliskan et al., 2017).[14] Finally, the mean cosine similarity is calculated for response words with the female and male associated words.

Formally, this measure of similarity between O and A is given by

$$cos(O, A) = mean_{\{o \in O, a \in A\}} \; cos(o, a) \quad (5)$$

[14]See Appendix B for gender word lists.

where o and a are individual words in O and A, respectively. Thus, $cos(O, M)$ gives association or similarity between output words O and male gender specific words, where as $cos(O, F)$ gives association between O and female attributes F. The difference $cos(O, F) - cos(O, M)$ gives bias towards female gender over the male gender in the output. Note that WEAT tests have been well-established as a measure of bias in psychology (Greenwald et al., 1998; Garg et al., 2018) as well as computational linguistics literature (May et al., 2019).

Since the language style of the outputs is casual, we use pre-trained FastText embeddings trained on Twitter data from Goldfarb-Tarrant et al. (2020) to reflect the language used. We pre-processed the outputs by converting them to lowercase, removing stop words, and removing punctuation.[15]

	Female	**Male**	**Difference**
Alexa	0.1546	0.1506	0.0040
Google A.	0.1588	0.1490	0.0098
Siri	0.1515	0.1499	0.0016

Table 6: Gender associations for system outputs.

Table 6 shows the computed values for the outputs O produced by the three systems. The columns labelled Female and Male give the values of $cos(O, F)$ and column labelled Difference gives their difference. We observe the following:

1. The absolute magnitude of $COS(O, M)$ as well $cos(O, F)$ are moderately small (approx 0.15). Thus, none of the outputs of the assistants appear to have a significant association with gender related words.

2. The differences $cos(O, F) - cos(O, M)$ are very small (in third decimal place). We note that $cos(M, F)$ is 0.3209—two to three orders of magnitude larger than the difference. Thus, the assistants exhibit very little gender bias.

3. The values for the outputs of the three conversational assistants are very similar.

These results seem to indicate that none of the assistants' content leans towards any gender. However, this could also be influenced by the small size of the dataset: we only have a handful of words that could suggest gender (eg: nouns, adjectives). Hence, gender association is not sufficiently recorded.

Stylometric analysis: As a second method for investigating stereotypically gendered language in the outputs, we conduct a stylometric analysis to assess whether the assistants' responses use linguistic features more typical of gender roles.[16] Following Newman et al. (2008) we use the word categories of the LIWC to observe differences in male- and female- labelled texts. We compare the scores for the 90 categories with those obtained from a corpus of film scripts that have been labelled by the gender of the characters (Danescu-Niculescu-Mizil and Lee, 2011), and which we expect largely to adhere to gender stereotypes in their use of language.

We calculate the cosine similarity of the feature vectors for the outputs of the systems and the male and female film scripts. Reflecting previous findings that female-labelled language is likely to feature more pronouns (Koolen and van Cranenburgh, 2017; Newman et al., 2008), we found that the LIWC categories for which the system outputs exhibit the largest differences between their proximity to the female and male scripts are: the numbers of pronouns, personal pronouns, adjectives, adverbs, and first person singular pronouns used. Overall, we found that all three system outputs were indeed marginally more similar to the female characters' scripts than those of male characters (see Table 7).

	Female scripts	**Male scripts**
Alexa	0.81	0.79
Google A.	0.86	0.85
Siri	0.80	0.77

Table 7: Cosine similarities between LIWC-derived feature vectors for system outputs and gender-labelled movie scripts. For LIWC scores, see Appendix C.

5 Discussion and conclusion

Our analysis suggests that people tend to personify and gender the systems, irrespective of the efforts and claims of their designers. This seems to be, at least partly, a result of aspects of their design.

We first assessed user perceptions by analysing online comments for use of pronouns and affective language. Results in Section 4.1 suggest that

[15]We use the Gensim library (Řehůřek and Sojka, 2010) to pre-process data, load embeddings and calculate similarity

[16]While these types of analyses have been criticised for breaching privacy and consent (Tatman, 2020), we do not use them to assign demographic features or social categories to humans, but analyse design choices in system outputs.

the name and branding of a system may be highly salient in this respect, with even systems that have male-sounding voice options mostly referred to as 'she' (although we do not know how many users select the male options). Google Assistant, which has a female voice by default and the most human-like responses, is nevertheless referred to most often using object pronouns, likely as a result of its non-gendered name.

We then analysed stylistic features in their responses to persona-related questions (Section 4.2). We find only weak evidence of gendered language, but large differences in the levels of *humanness* they seem to express. Along with the nature of their voices, this may explain why people personify and subsequently gender conversational assistants—even when they have apparently more neutral design features.

While male voice options are available for two of the systems, we can't find any evidence of how many users actually select them. Apple's announcement that future users of their systems will have to actively select a voice for Siri may lead to more balance in this regard. However, it remains to seen what the users—who are by now accustomed to the idea that these entities are designed as female—will choose (for their still, after all, female-named assistant). As people are likely to assign gender to objectively non-gendered voices (Sutton, 2020), and voice assistants that are designed as or perceived to be female attract abusive behaviour (Cercas Curry and Rieser, 2019, 2018), designers may consider attempting to reddress the gender imbalance by designing assistants with servile roles to be male-presenting by default. While there have been examples, such as the BBC's Beeb (Walker, 2019), this remains an under-explored approach.

In terms of the assistants' responses to users, we see a clear difference in approaches. While Google Assistant, and to a lesser extent, Alexa, seem to blur the line between human and machine personas, Siri comes across as more practical and task-focused, evading the majority of personality-based questions. Although possibly less engaging, this approach may be a way of avoiding some of the ethical issues discussed in Section 2. There is perhaps a tension between companies' commercial aims of seeing high levels of engagement in their products and the ethical considerations discussed here. However, if companies are going to design agents with human-like and gendered characteristics and personas, they should not claim the opposite.

Acknowledgements

This research received funding from the EPSRC project *'Designing Conversational Assistants to Reduce Gender Bias'* (EP/T023767/1).

The authors would like to thank Alba Curry, Federico Nanni, Anirudh Patir, and Pejman Saege for their assistance, and the anonymous reviewers for their insightful and helpful comments.

References

Amazon Alexa Branding Guidelines. `https://developer.amazon.com/en-US/alexa/branding/alexa-guidelines/communication-guidelines/brand-voice`, (accessed April 26 2021).

Jason Baumgartner, Savvas Zannettou, Brian Keegan, Megan Squire, and Jeremy Blackburn. 2020. The Pushshift Reddit dataset. In *Proceedings of the International AAAI Conference on Web and Social Media*, volume 14/1, pages 830–839.

Aylin Caliskan, Joanna J. Bryson, and Arvind Narayanan. 2017. Semantics derived automatically from language corpora contain human-like biases. *Science*, 356(6334):183–186.

Amanda Cercas Curry and Verena Rieser. 2018. #MeToo: How conversational systems respond to sexual harassment. In *Proceedings of the Second ACL Workshop on Ethics in Natural Language Processing*, pages 7–14, New Orleans, Louisiana, USA. Association for Computational Linguistics.

Amanda Cercas Curry and Verena Rieser. 2019. A crowd-based evaluation of abuse response strategies in conversational agents. In *Proceedings of the 20th Annual SIGdial Meeting on Discourse and Dialogue*, pages 361–366, Stockholm, Sweden. Association for Computational Linguistics.

Amanda Cercas Curry, Judy Robertson, and Verena Rieser. 2020. Conversational assistants and gender stereotypes: Public perceptions and desiderata for voice personas. In *Proceedings of the Second Workshop on Gender Bias in Natural Language Processing*, pages 72–78, Barcelona, Spain (Online). Association for Computational Linguistics.

Mariona Coll Ardanuy, Federico Nanni, Kaspar Beelen, Kasra Hosseini, Ruth Ahnert, Jon Lawrence, Katherine McDonough, Giorgia Tolfo, Daniel CS Wilson, and Barbara McGillivray. 2020. Living machines: A study of atypical animacy. In *Proceedings of the 28th International Conference on Computational Linguistics*, pages 4534–4545, Barcelona, Spain (Online). International Committee on Computational Linguistics.

Cristian Danescu-Niculescu-Mizil and Lillian Lee. 2011. Chameleons in imagined conversations: A new approach to understanding coordination of linguistic style in dialogs. In *Proceedings of the 2nd Workshop on Cognitive Modeling and Computational Linguistics*, pages 76–87, Portland, Oregon, USA. Association for Computational Linguistics.

Nicholas Epley, Adam Waytz, and John T. Cacioppo. 2007. On seeing human: A three-factor theory of anthropomorphism. *Psychological Review*, 114(4):864–886.

Katrin Etzrodt and Sven Engesser. 2021. Voice-based agents as personified things: Assimilation and accommodation as equilibration of doubt. *Human-Machine Communication*, 2:57–79.

Jasper Feine, Ulrich Gnewuch, Stefan Morana, and Alexander Maedche. 2020. Gender bias in chatbot design. In *Chatbot Research and Design*, pages 79–93, Cham. Springer International Publishing.

Y. Gao, Z. Pan, H. Wang, and G. Chen. 2018. Alexa, my love: Analyzing reviews of Amazon Echo. In *2018 IEEE SmartWorld, Ubiquitous Intelligence Computing, Advanced Trusted Computing, Scalable Computing Communications, Cloud Big Data Computing, Internet of People and Smart City Innovation (SmartWorld/SCALCOM/UIC/ATC/CBDCom/IOP/SCI)*, pages 372–380.

Nikhil Garg, Londa Schiebinger, Dan Jurafsky, and James Zou. 2018. Word embeddings quantify 100 years of gender and ethnic stereotypes. *Proceedings of the National Academy of Sciences*, 115(16):E3635–E3644.

Seraphina Goldfarb-Tarrant, Rebecca Marchant, Ricardo Muñoz Sanchez, Mugdha Pandya, and Adam Lopez. 2020. Intrinsic bias metrics do not correlate with application bias. In *Proceedings of the 59th Annual Meeting of the Association for Computational Linguistics*. Association for Computational Linguistics.

Google Assistant Conversation Design. `https://developers.google.com/assistant/conversation-design/welcome#create-a-persona-examples`, (accessed April 26 2021).

Anthony G Greenwald, Debbie E McGhee, and Jordan LK Schwartz. 1998. Measuring individual differences in implicit cognition: the implicit association test. *Journal of personality and social psychology*, 74(6):1464.

Stewart Elliott Guthrie. 1995. *Faces in the clouds: A new theory of religion*. Oxford University Press on Demand.

Alex Hern. 2018. Google's 'deceitful' AI assistant to identify itself as a robot during calls. *Guardian*. Accessed: April 26 2021.

Corina Koolen and Andreas van Cranenburgh. 2017. These are not the stereotypes you are looking for: Bias and fairness in authorial gender attribution. In *Proceedings of the First ACL Workshop on Ethics in Natural Language Processing*, pages 12–22, Valencia, Spain. Association for Computational Linguistics.

Anastasia Kuzminykh, Jenny Sun, Nivetha Govindaraju, Jeff Avery, and Edward Lank. 2020. Genie in the bottle: Anthropomorphized perceptions of conversational agents. In *Proceedings of the 2020 CHI Conference on Human Factors in Computing Systems*, CHI '20, page 1–13, New York, NY, USA. Association for Computing Machinery.

Nayeon Lee, Andrea Madotto, and Pascale Fung. 2019. Exploring social bias in chatbots using stereotype knowledge. In *Proceedings of the 2019 Workshop on Widening NLP*, pages 177–180, Florence, Italy. Association for Computational Linguistics.

Irene Lopatovska and Harriet Williams. 2018. Personification of the Amazon Alexa: BFF or a mindless companion. In *Proceedings of the 2018 Conference on Human Information Interaction & Retrieval*, CHIIR '18, page 265–268, New York, NY, USA. Association for Computing Machinery.

Chandler May, Alex Wang, Shikha Bordia, Samuel R. Bowman, and Rachel Rudinger. 2019. On measuring social biases in sentence encoders. In *Proceedings of the 2019 Conference of the North American Chapter of the Association for Computational Linguistics: Human Language Technologies, Volume 1 (Long and Short Papers)*, pages 622–628, Minneapolis, Minnesota. Association for Computational Linguistics.

Meet Q. The first genderless voice. `https://www.genderlessvoice.com/`, (accessed April 26 2021).

Network World. `https://www.networkworld.com/article/2221246/steve-jobs-wasn-t-a-fan-of-the-siri-name.html`, (accessed April 26 2021).

Matthew L. Newman, Carla J. Groom, Lori D. Handelman, and James W. Pennebaker. 2008. Gender differences in language use: An analysis of 14,000 text samples. *Discourse Processes*, 45(3):211–236.

James W. Pennebaker, Ryan L. Boyd, Kayla Jordan, and Kate Blackburn. 2015. The development and psychometric properties of LIWC2015.

Amanda Purington, Jessie G. Taft, Shruti Sannon, Natalya N. Bazarova, and Samuel Hardman Taylor. 2017. "Alexa is my new BFF": Social roles, user satisfaction, and personification of the Amazon Echo. In *Proceedings of the 2017 CHI Conference Extended Abstracts on Human Factors in Computing Systems*, CHI EA '17, page 2853–2859, New York, NY, USA. Association for Computing Machinery.

Byron Reeves and Clifford Nass. 1996. *The media equation: How people treat computers, television, and new media like real people*. Cambridge university press Cambridge, UK.

Radim Řehůřek and Petr Sojka. 2010. Software framework for topic modelling with large corpora. In *Proceedings of the LREC 2010 Workshop on New Challenges for NLP Frameworks*, pages 45–50, Valletta, Malta. ELRA.

Emily Sheng, Josh Arnold, Zhou Yu, Kai-Wei Chang, and Nanyun Peng. 2021. Revealing persona biases in dialogue systems.

Siri Editorial Guidelines. `https://developer.apple.com/design/human-interface-guidelines/siri/overview/editorial-guidelines`, (accessed April 26 2021).

Selina Jeanne Sutton. 2020. Gender ambiguous, not genderless: Designing gender in voice user interfaces (VUIs) with sensitivity. In *Proceedings of the 2nd Conference on Conversational User Interfaces*, CUI '20, New York, NY, USA. Association for Computing Machinery.

Rachael Tatman. 2020. What I won't build (invited talk). In *Proceedings of the Widening NLP Workshop*.

TechCrunch. `https://techcrunch.com/2021/03/31/apple-adds-two-siri-voices`, (accessed April 26 2021).

Hannah Unkefer and Sophie Riewoldt. 2020. Accenture and CereProc introduce and open source the world's first comprehensive non-binary voice solution. *Press Release*. Accessed: April 26 2021.

Jeremy Walker. 2019. Developing a new public service voice assistant from the BBC. *Press Release*. Accessed: April 26 2021.

Mark West, Rebecca Kraut, and Han Ei Chew. 2019. *I'd blush if I could: Closing gender divides in digital skills through education*. UNESCO.

Saizheng Zhang, Emily Dinan, Jack Urbanek, Arthur Szlam, Douwe Kiela, and Jason Weston. 2018. Personalizing dialogue agents: I have a dog, do you have pets too? In *Proceedings of the 56th Annual Meeting of the Association for Computational Linguistics (Volume 1: Long Papers)*, pages 2204–2213, Melbourne, Australia. Association for Computational Linguistics.

A Corpora

A.1 User reviews and forum posts

We obtained Alexa reviews from `https://www.amazon.com/gp/aw/reviews/B00P03D4D2` and Google Assistant reviews from `https://play.google.com/store/apps/details?id=com.google.android.apps.googleassistant&hl=en_GB&gl=US`.

Data statement

Language: English
Author demographic: worldwide anonymous internet users
Provenance: Pushshift Reddit dataset (Baumgartner et al., 2020)

A.2 System outputs

Data statement

Language: English
Author demographic: worldwide anonymous internet users.
Data provenance: System responses from Amazon Alexa, Google Assistant, and Siri.
Annotator demographic:
  Age: 29, 31
  Gender: Both female
  Ethnicity: Both white
  L1 language(s): Both fluent in English and Spanish
  Training: Both annotators are PhD candidates, one in conversational AI, and the other in philosophy and emotion AI.

Corpus

We make the annotated corpus available for download at `https://github.com/GavinAbercrombie/GeBNLP2021`

B Expanded gender word lists

Expanded gender word lists from Goldfarb-Tarrant et al. (2020).

Male: *grandfather, uncle, son, boy, father, he, him, his, man, male, brother, guy, himself, nephew, grandson, men, boys, father-in-law, husband, brothers, males, sons, dad*

Female: *daughter, she, her, grandmother, mother, aunt, sister, hers, woman, female, girl, grandma, herself, niece, sisters, mom, mother-in-law, lady, wife, females, girls, women, sexy, granddaughter, daughters*

C LIWC category scores

	pronoun	ppron	adj	adv	ipron
Alexa	20.65	13.33	5.70	4.68	7.32
GA	24.64	15.00	1.62	5.97	9.63
Siri	19.88	14.89	4.47	6.83	4.99
female	24.47	17.22	23.64	12.87	0.65
male	22.95	15.82	22.38	11.85	0.71

Table 8: Top five most discriminating LIWC categories and the corresponding scores for the three conversational assistants and two sets of film scripts.

Gender Bias in Text: Origin, Taxonomy, and Implications

Jad Doughman
American University of Beirut
Beirut, Lebanon
jad17@mail.aub.edu

Wael Khreich
American University of Beirut
Beirut, Lebanon
wk47@aub.edu.lb

Maya El Gharib
American University of
Beirut, Lebanon
mme116@mail.aub.edu

Maha Wiss
American University of
Beirut, Lebanon
maw16@mail.aub.edu

Zahraa Berjawi
American University of
Beirut, Lebanon
zjb04@mail.aub.edu

Abstract

Gender inequality represents a considerable loss of human potential and perpetuates a culture of violence, higher gender wage gaps, and a lack of representation of women in higher and leadership positions. Applications powered by Artificial Intelligence (AI) are increasingly being used in the real world to provide critical decisions about who is going to be hired, granted a loan, admitted to college, etc. However, the main pillars of AI, Natural Language Processing (NLP) and Machine Learning (ML) have been shown to reflect and even amplify gender biases and stereotypes, which are mainly inherited from historical training data. In an effort to facilitate the identification and mitigation of gender bias in English text, we develop a comprehensive taxonomy that relies on the following gender bias types: *Generic Pronouns*, *Sexism*, *Occupational Bias*, *Exclusionary Bias*, and *Semantics*. We also provide a bottom-up overview of gender bias, from its societal origin to its spillover onto language. Finally, we link the societal implications of gender bias to their corresponding type(s) in the proposed taxonomy. The underlying motivation of our work is to help enable the technical community to identify and mitigate relevant biases from training corpora for improved fairness in NLP systems.

1 Introduction

Bias is prevalent in every aspect of our lives. We are hardwired to compartmentalize things we experience to form a plausible perception of the world around us. The process of forming these perceptions typically breeds prejudices, which allows for flagrant inequalities to shape across different demographics. The prevalence of certain biases in society, such as gender bias, can be attributed to social roles formed as a function of this compartmentalization process. According to the social role theory, the societal origin of gender stereotypes revolves around gender-typical social roles that mirror the sexual division of labor and gender hierarchy of the society (Bussey and Bandura, 1999).

The prevalence of gender bias in society is also spilled over onto language through the patriarchal worldview predominant among linguists prior to the prescriptive grammar movement in English. Bodine (1975) found that the generic use of *he* is derived from an androcentric worldview prevalent among 18th-century grammarians: "human beings were to be considered male unless proven otherwise" (Bodine, 1975). The perpetuation of bias onto language entails a negative feedback loop due to the direct impact of language on a person's perceptions (Boroditsky, 2011). Linguistic determinism, a hypothesis taken from the analytic branch of philosophy, posits that language "limits and determines human thought patterns and knowledge" (Hickmann, 2000). Hence, the recurring usage of bias in language consequently leads to a more biased perception which is fed back into our lexical (word) choice. This is even more amplified by the increased adoption of automated system based on AI, which exponentially expedites this feedback loop (as detailed in Section 2.4).

The linguistic spillover of gender bias has various direct and indirect implications on our society. The presence of gender bias in the language used by parents and in school text books causes children to develop sexist perceptions and behaviors towards other children of opposite gender and deepens the problematic outcomes of gender inequalities in society (Waxman, 2013). Additionally, sex-biased wording affects a person's perception of a career's

Proceedings of the 3rd Workshop on Gender Bias in Natural Language Processing, pages 34–44
August 5, 2021.

attractiveness (Briere and Lanktree, 1983). Consequently, countries that adopt a gendered language tend to have disproportionate labor force participation (Gay et al., 2013). We also discuss the direct implication of hostile sexism on a person's physiological wellbeing, such as increased stress levels, anger, and elevated cardiovascular reactivity (Schneider et al., 2001). Finally, we examine the indirect implication of benevolent sexism in embedding gender inequality and intensifying its influence in the society by portraying the advantageous aspects of being a woman (deserving special treatment, care, protection, and love) (Hammond et al., 2014; Barreto and Ellemers, 2005).

Gender bias in NLP presents itself in many stages along the design and development process. It can be found in the training data, the pre-trained models, and the algorithms themselves. The propagation of bias from text to features and algorithms leads to real-world consequences when integrated into AI systems and are used in critical decision-making applications. In particular, discriminatory decisions occur when these systems assist humans in critical decisions (Dressel and Farid, 2018). These prejudiced decisions could entail allocational or representational harms (Blodgett et al., 2020b). As mentioned previously, discriminating algorithms accelerate the unavoidable feedback loop, which increases the degree and volume of bias against females and other gender minority groups, especially in online media content. Automated NLP-based decision-making algorithms will re-consume this increasingly growing biased content to update their models, and so on. This feedback loop contributes to an increased gender bias and further discrimination.

Several works in NLP revolving around bias focused on the projection of word embedding vectors on a gender direction (he - she) to detect and mitigate bias in a pre-trained model, without a clear link to the implications on society and their underlying applications (Blodgett et al., 2020b). There has been previous attempts that address bias at the sentence level and provide an initial categorization of gender bias types (Hitti et al., 2019). We build on their work and provide a more comprehensive understanding of the various forms of gender bias while linking to several real world implications on society.

In this paper, we develop a comprehensive taxonomy to identify various types of gender bias. We also provide a bottom-up overview of gender bias, from its societal origin to its spillover onto language. We then link between the psycho-social implications of gender bias and the corresponding type(s) in the proposed taxonomy. Our underlying motivation is to enable the the technical community working on gender bias in NLP to focus on the identification and mitigation of relevant biases for improved fairness in NLP systems. We also hope that by addressing and linking the sources and implications of gender bias in text, we encourage the community to further push the research in this direction and raise more awareness on bias and discrimination in NLP systems.

2 Gender Bias

2.1 Definition

We define gender bias in text as being an exclusionary, implicitly prejudicial, or generalized representation of a specific gender as a function of various societal stereotypes. The sections below provide a bottom-up overview of gender bias, from its societal origin to its spillover onto language while highlighting its perceptual and societal implications.

2.2 Social Role Theory

The social role theory posits that gender stereotypes are rooted in the distinct social roles designated to women and men (Bussey and Bandura, 1999). Historically, men and women have maintained diverse social roles: Men have been more likely to engage in tasks that require "speed, strength, and the possibility of being away from home for long periods of time", while women have been more likely to "stay home and engage in family tasks, such as child-rearing" (Eagly et al., 2000). This dispersion comes with various consequences. Firstly, men are perceived as, and expected to be agentic, particularly, active, independent, and resolute, whereas women are perceived as, and expected to be, communal, namely, kind, helpful, and benevolent (Eagly et al., 2000). Secondly, women and men become more inclined to acquire particular skills linked to successful role performance and by adapting their social behavior to role requirements (Eagly et al., 2000). Essentially, both actors and observers are inclined to inherit traits from observed behaviors in their specific social roles (Steffens et al., 2015). This creates an unavoidable negative feedback loop that continuously perpetuates gender bias in society by segregating each gender into a specific social role and actively promotes the divergence through the pursuit of successful role performance.

2.3 Linguistic Spillover

Gender stereotypes in society also found their way into language, tunneling through a patriarchal worldview adopted by grammarians prior to the prescriptive grammar movement. Bodine (1975) found that the generic use of *he* is derived from an androcentric worldview prevalent among 18th-century grammarians: "human beings were to be considered male unless proven otherwise" (Bodine, 1975). This is also supported by the limited role of women in forming and shaping the English language (Kramarae, 1981). Feminist scholars maintain that the *generic he* and similar words "not only reflect a history of male domination" but also "actively encourage its perpetuation" (Sniezek and Jazwinski, 1986). The *generic he* has also intensified sexist behaviors and attitudes in a subtler psychological and perceptual manner. The foundation of this argument is in the Sapir-Whorf hypothesis: "our grammar shapes our thought" (Whorf, 1956). Blaubergs (1980) applies this hypothesis to sexist words and phrases in the English language, including the *generic he*. She maintains that regardless of its origins,"Sexist language by its existence reinforces and socializes sexist thinking and practices" (Blaubergs, 1980). Consequently, the recurring usage of biased language leads to a more biased perception which is fed back into our lexical (word) choice.

2.4 Bias in NLP

Natural Language Processing (NLP) and Machine Learning (ML) techniques, the main pillars of narrow or practical AI, are designed to learn from data and try to generalize the learned concepts to unseen data. However, they are prone to inherit, reflect, and amplify biases and stereotyped-associations that are present in historical data provided for training. Manifestations of different kinds of biases have been shown to exist in various components used to develop NLP and ML systems, from training data to pre-trained models to algorithms and resources (Olteanu et al., 2016; Tolan, 2018; Danks and London, 2017; Mehrabi et al., 2019; Sun et al., 2019; Blodgett et al., 2020b; Hovy et al., 2020; Hitti et al., 2019).

Word embeddings is a family of techniques that learn word representation from texts, such that words with similar meaning have a similar representation (Mikolov et al., 2013b,a). Since their inception, word embeddings have become the predominant representation of text features and an integral part of NLP applications. However, most research on gender bias in NLP has focused on the projection of word embedding vectors on a gender direction (he - she) to detect and mitigate bias in a pre-trained model. For example, occupational gender bias in word embedding models is typically measured by comparing the distances between gendered word vectors and occupational terms. The bias scores resulting from the manipulation of word vectors in a pre-trained word embedding are strictly dependent on the corpus utilized to train that model. Using such models to detect whether new sentences are biased will not only project the biases of the model but also misconstrue its origin (Blodgett et al., 2020b).

The key existing solutions to mitigate these biases focused on modifying the training data, imposing constraints on the word embeddings objective function, or applying post-processing techniques to reduce the bias in word embedding models including word2vec (Mikolov et al., 2013b,a), and GloVe (Bojanowski et al., 2017), and more recently in contextual word embedding models such as ELMO (Hoffman et al., 2010), BERT (Devlin et al., 2018), and ALBERT (Lan et al., 2019). Although several other papers discussed different methodologies to debias word embedding model, these techniques have been scrutinized on several occasions (Blodgett et al., 2020a). In addition, the majority of research did not focus on the impact of gender bias in real-word applications (Blodgett et al., 2020a). Automatic detection of gender bias beyond the word level requires an understanding of the semantics of written human language, which remains an open problem and successful approaches are restricted to specific domains and tasks. In an effort to redirect the focus to the linguistic forms of bias and their societal implications, Section 3 contains a comprehensive breakdown of the various gender bias types and their subsequent subtypes, while the next section will be geared towards their societal implications.

2.5 Implications

Gender bias leaks into some of the fundamental life aspects and tends to jeopardize the normal functioning of the affected gender group (Fraser, 2000). The sections below describe the negative implications of gender bias on children's mental imagery, career attractiveness, labor force participation, and human behavior.

2.5.1 Children's Mental Imagery

Gender bias can manifest itself at an early age in one's life and thus can have a more profound impact on one's attitude and behavior. Children and even infants can be exposed to gender bias presented in language and can also be affected by it, through the process of categorization (Waxman, 2013). The process of category learning begins early on in a person's life and is perceived as a building block for children's lexical acquisition (Waxman, 2013). However, this process could promote stereotypical beliefs and gender biases in children's cognition and perception about individuals, especially if the language used in this process is a gendered language (Bigler and Leaper, 2015). A gendered language which makes gender salient, tends to treat gender as a major attribute upon which children will rely on, to classify and make inferences about others (Hilliard and Liben, 2010). Therefore, the learnt categorizations will promote and perpetuate several forms of gender bias, such as in-group favoritism (Arthur et al., 2008; Bigler and Liben, 2006; Leaper and Bigler, 2004). In-group favoritism can be reflected in children's behavior where a child would prefer to play with another child of the same gender rather than a child with an opposite gender (Fagot et al., 1986).

Gender-generic noun statements, such as "Girls are good at activity X while boys are good at activity Y" that are usually stated by parents and found in school textbooks, influence how children think about themselves. These statements also undermine children's achievements in the relevant activities given their belonging to one of the gender categories (Bigler and Leaper, 2015; Cimpian et al., 2012). In their study, Cimpian et al. (2012) discovered that when children are exposed to gender-generic statements that link their ability to perform a certain activity to a social group, they tend to perform worse on the given activity irrespective of whether the statement is positive or negative. Cimpian et al. (2012) study implies how threatening gendered generic statements can be in relation to the beliefs that children instantly create about their own capabilities and achievements.

2.5.2 Career Attractiveness

In a study to assess the contribution of biased language relating to the attractiveness of a career, Briere and Lanktree (1983) established that biased language significantly affects a subjects' perception of the attractiveness or employment in a psychology career for women (Briere and Lanktree, 1983). Generic pronouns (as detailed in Section 3.1) and masculine nouns were linked with a decline in the presumed attractiveness of a psychology career for women, with respect to a nonsexist condition (Briere and Lanktree, 1983). Consequently, the use of generic pronouns in texts could discriminatively inhibit female interest in fields they might alternatively seek out (Briere and Lanktree, 1983).

Additionally, a study conducted by Stout and Dasgupta (2011) reveals that gender-biased language in the professional field is associated with negative nonverbal emotional responses from women. Accordingly, women who are exposed to a gender exclusive language during a job interview tend to feel demotivated and socially and actively rejected by the workplace (Stout and Dasgupta, 2011). Other evidence by Vervecken et al. (2013) proposes how children's perceptions of stereotypically male jobs can be influenced by the linguistic form used to present an occupational title. For example, the generic use of masculine plural forms when describing occupations will most likely lead children to restrictive, male only associations and perceptions about stereotypically male occupations (Vervecken et al., 2013).

2.5.3 Labor Force Participation

The gender gaps between women and men in the labor market are almost present in every country, yet with varying degrees, given the cultural norms and values that play a crucial role in introducing or generating new stereotypical beliefs and resisting the existing ones as time passes and cultures change. Aside from the cultural system represented by the social norms and values, a country's adopted language system and the intensity to which it marks gender differences tends to be a very crucial variable in determining the extent to which women can participate in the socio-economic life (Gay et al., 2013). The idea that a country's language system affects women's socioeconomic participation sets off from the idea that language is a key vehicle of the cultural system (North et al., 1990). In their study, Gay et al. (2013) discovered that gendered language has a direct impact on women's socioeconomic choices and outcomes. For example, female labor force participation for the year 2000 in countries following a gender binary linguistic system, such as France and Spain, was 16% lower as compared to countries which have no gender marking or have more than three genders in its most spoken language (Gay et al., 2013).

2.5.4 Human Behavior

As stated in the social role theory suggested by Eagly et al. (2000), the gendered roles construct the societal belief system that sets the expectations of men and women, and biased language is instrumentalized to maintain the genders' distinct responsibilities (Stahlberg et al., 2007). As a result, these stereotypical beliefs would be reflected in the everyday lexical choices that refer to men or women, including prejudice or stereotypes that are based on gender or, in other words, sexism (Menegatti et al., 2017). As detailed in Section 3.2, Glick and Fiske (1996) divided sexism into hostile sexism, the typical prejudice against women, and benevolent sexism, the seemingly 'positive' sexism that enforces masculine dominance in the society through viewing women as caring, delicate, emotional, and in need of men's protection (Glick and Fiske, 1996).

Bosson et al. (2010) state that women suffer from the emotional impact of hostile sexism for a shorter period of time due to the direct anger expression that's linked to it. Moreover, the exposure to a hostile sexist language motivates women to participate in collective action to stop gender inequality, and it encourages them to socially compete with men in order to reclaim their righteous social status (Becker and Wright, 2011). Nevertheless, hostile sexist language may not have a direct impact on embedding further gendered stereotypes in society, but it has severe direct impact on women's physiological wellbeing, such as increased stress levels, anger, and elevated cardiovascular reactivity (Schneider et al., 2001).

On the other hand, there has been a research consensus on the impact of women's exposure to benevolent sexist language on embedding gender inequality and intensifying its influence in the society (Hammond et al., 2014; Barreto and Ellemers, 2005). For instance, Hammond et al. (2014) indicate that the positive attributes that benevolent sexism holds for women may impair women's opposition to the gendered stereotypes due to how this form of sexism portrays the advantageous aspects of being a woman (deserving special treatment, care, protection, and love). Another study shows that benevolent sexist language is often not identified as sexism for many people exposed to it (Barreto and Ellemers, 2005). Thus, this may keep this issue unrecognized and further maintain the acceptance of prejudicial gendered stereotypes, allowing for continuous promoting of sexism and their direct or indirect impact on women (Barreto and Ellemers, 2005).

3 Taxonomy

The first step of detecting biased language is to categorize the various forms of that bias while carefully maintaining a clear segregation between the resultant groups. The below sections develop a comprehensive taxonomy that includes a wide range of gender bias types and their subsequent subtypes. Each subsection includes the definition of a bias subtype and a couple of examples that illustrate its usage in a sentence. Table 2 provides an overview of the taxonomy, with one example pertaining to each subtype alongside its societal implication (discussed in Section 2.5).

3.1 Generic Pronouns

Given that the choice of a pronoun follows the sex of the referent, a problem arises when a pronoun is to be used with sex-indefinite antecedents (Ozieblowska, 1994). Pronouns which do not specify sex are traditionally called "generic", because generic statements about human referents discuss people in general, and therefore the sex of the referents is irrelevant (Ozieblowska, 1994). The most notable forms of generic pronouns are: *generic he*, *generic she*, and *gendered generic man*.

3.1.1 Generic He

The use of the pronoun *he* in circumstances of sex-indefinite reference overly emphasizes men over women, thereby both "re-constituting and signifying males' micro-political hegemony" (Stringer and Hopper, 1998). Thus, *generic he* occurs when the pronoun he, his and him are used as referents to nouns of no specific gender. Among the gendered generic pronouns, *his* is the most recurring sexist antecedent to most nouns. Below are some example:

- The client should receive **his** invoice in two weeks.
- A good employee knows that **he** should strive for excellence.

- A teacher is expected to be a good role model in all areas of **his** life.

3.1.2 Generic She

While the generic *he* is the most recurring form of generic pronouns, generic *she* is also excessively present in written discourse. Below are some example:

- A nurse should ensure that **she** gets adequate rest.
- A dancer should watch **her** diet carefully.
- **She** presents us diverge ways, but **she** lets us choose our path.

3.1.3 Gendered Generic Man

Gendered generic man appears when *man* is utilized as a masculine noun representation both genders. It's used not only as a noun but also as a verb. Below are some example:

- Good teachers know how to **man** the classroom.
- Effective teachers lead or **man** the students well.
- It is even more fulfilling when a teacher sees a once stubborn child who became a **man** of success and responsibilities crown with various achievements.
- All **men** are born for a reason.
- A teacher is an ordinary **man** with extraordinary roles.

3.2 Sexism

According to the ambivalent sexism theory, sexism against women is divided into an aggressive expression, or hostile sexism, and a positive (for men) expression, or benevolent sexism (Glick and Fiske, 1996). In this section, we will be discussing these two divergent forms of sexist language:

3.2.1 Hostile Sexism

Hostile sexism is the view of men as more powerful and competent than women (Becker and Wright, 2011). It views women as a threat to men's dominance through their violation to traditional gendered roles in the society (Becker and Wright, 2011; Mastari et al., 2019). In general, hostile sexism reflects men's hatred towards women (or misogyny), and it is expressed in aggressive and blatant manner (Connor et al., 2017). Men with hostile sexist mentality view women as manipulative, unintelligent, and incompetent (Jain et al., 2019). Below are some examples of hostile sexist statements:

- The people at work are childish. It's run by women and when women don't agree to something, oh man.
- Women always get more upset than men.
- Women are incompetent at work.

3.2.2 Benevolent Sexism

Benevolent sexism is a softer form of sexism that expresses male dominance in a more chivalrous tone (Becker and Wright, 2011). It expresses affection and care for women in return for their acceptance to their limited gendered roles (Becker and Wright, 2011; Mastari et al., 2019). Benevolent sexism describes women as caring, innocent, and in need of men's protection, and these stereotypical notions are used to reinforce women's subordinate position (Connor et al., 2017). This form of sexism explains how women complete men's chivalry, power, and intelligence with their delicate characteristics (Cross and Overall, 2018). Below are some examples of benevolent sexist statements:

- They're probably surprised at how smart you are, for a girl.
- No man succeeds without a good woman besides him. Wife or mother. If it is both, he is twice as blessed.
- I am not exploiting women: I love, protect, and care for them.

3.3 Occupational Bias

As discussed in Section 2.2, the societal origin of gender stereotypes revolves around gender-typical social roles and thus reflect the sexual division of labor and gender hierarchy of the society (Eagly et al., 2000). The resultant social roles lead to gendered occupational bias, which is a form of generalization that occurs when an occupation or role/duty is generalized onto a specific gender. This section will illustrate both the gendered division of labor and gendered roles/duties.

3.3.1 Gendered Division of Labor

Below are some examples that illustrate how certain jobs are seen as only appropriately and exclusively held by either women or men:

- **Professors** are men and elementary teachers are women.
- **Politicians** are men and women are wives.
- **Housework** is the duty of women and an option or out of question for men.
- **Scientists** are men and secretaries are women.
- **Doctors** are men and nurses are women.

3.3.2 Gendered Roles/Duties

In the first example below, the speaker's sales assistant is referred to as a girl, which diminishes the status of the role. In the second, the sales assistant is referred to by job title, which indicates that gender is not an important prerequisite for the role that the sales assistant plays.

1. I'll have my girl get you a cup of coffee.
2. I'll ask my assistant to get you a cup of coffee.

3.4 Exclusionary Bias

3.4.1 Explicit Marking of Sex

Explicit marking of sex occurs when an unknown gender-neutral entity is referred to using gender-exclusive term(s). Table 1 provides proposed corrections of some exclusionary terms.

Example	Proposed Corrections
Mankind	Humanity; human beings
Chairman	Chairperson; chair
Businessman	Business manager
Manpower	Workforce
Cameraman	Camera operator
Policeman	Police officer
Manhood	Adulthood
Brotherhood	Solidarity

Table 1: Proposed solutions to some exclusionary terms

3.4.2 Gender-based Neologisms

Neologisms are newly coined words/expressions that may be in the process of mainstream adoption, but have not yet been fully accepted. Gender-based neologisms are gendered coinages that could have underlying stereotypical tendencies (Foubert and Lemmens, 2018). Below are some examples:

- **Man-bread:** bread that is baked so big that it will take a grown man a whole week to eat it, having 4 slices a day.
- **Man-sip:** a man sized sip of a beer or drink, one can finish a beer in 4 or 5 Man-sips. For a female or light weight, it borders on chugging the drink, but for a man it is merely a sip.
- **Mantini:** a martini or alcoholic beverage that appeals to a man's palate. "My boyfriend prefers his mantini straight up which is just too strong for my tastes."

3.4.3 Gendered Word Ordering

Gendered word ordering is tendency for the male version to come first in binomials such as "men and women", "brothers and sisters", "boys and girls", or "Mr and Mrs". Many words that incorporate the word "man", such as "man-made", "mankind", "manpower", have perfectly acceptable gender-neutral alternatives: for example, "artificial" or "synthetic", "humankind", and "workforce".

3.5 Semantics

Gender bias in semantics appears when utilizing words and sentences that are demeaning in their semantic meaning (Umera-Okeke, 2012). The implicit meaning behind sexist jokes, proverbs, or even using specific non-human terms to refer to women, consciously or unconsciously, deepens the existing bias and projects it onto new generations (Umera-Okeke, 2012). The current study suggests three types of semantic gender bias: metaphors, gendered attributes, and old sayings.

3.5.1 Metaphors

People tend to express a part of the world's reality through metaphors, which contributes to ingraining their culture and beliefs. By looking into the window of metaphors, several biases of society are revealed (Rodriguez, 2009). Masculinity and bias against females are represented in metaphoric words that describe women as a non-human comparing females to food, animals, plants (Martín, 2011; Lan and Jingxia, 2019). Below are some examples of English metaphoric words that describe woman as food and animal:

- "Cookie": lovely woman
- "Old Hen": middle aged women who love to talk to each other

Type	Subtype	Example	Implication
Generic Pronouns	Generic He	The client should receive his invoice in two weeks.	Biased Mental Imagery
	Generic She	A nurse should ensure that she gets adequate rest.	Biased Mental Imagery
	Gendered Generic Man	Good teachers know how to man the classroom.	Biased Mental Imagery
Sexism	Hostile Sexism	Women are incompetent at work.	Aggressive Behavior
	Benevolent Sexism	They're probably surprised at how smart you are, for a girl.	Representational Harms
Occupational Bias	Gendered Division of Labor	Professors are men and elementary teachers are women.	Labor Force Participation
	Gendered Roles & Duties	I'll have my girl get you a cup of coffee.	Labor Force Participation
Exclusionary Bias	Explicit Marking of Sex	Chairman, Businessman, Manpower, Cameraman...	Representational Harms
	Gender-based Neologisms	Man-bread, Man-sip...	Representational Harms
	Gendered Word Ordering	"Men and Women", "Brothers and Sisters"...	Representational Harms
Semantics	Metaphors	"Cookie": lovely woman.	Bias Propagation
	Gendered Attributes	An unmarried male (bachelor) is a "personal choice". An unmarried female (spinster) is derogatorily an "old maid".	Bias Propagation
	Old Sayings	A woman's tongue three inches long can kill a man six feet high.	Bias Propagation

Table 2: Overview of the taxonomy and link to societal implications

3.5.2 Gendered Attributes

Societal ideologies revolving around each gender role, preferences, interests, and characteristics were originally created due to many historical conditions and various lifestyles, and are conveyed to language in which reflects sexist stereotypes, which might presents invisible limitations for women. Lan and Jingxia (2019) suggest that placing men in a leading position and women as subordinates is the main cause of creating gendered stereotypes (Lan and Jingxia, 2019). Researchers noted that commendatory or complementary terms are used as male words while the corresponding female words are derogatory (e.g. wizard/ witch, spinster / bachelor , governor / governess) (Lan and Jingxia, 2019). Associating positive meaning with male and negative meaning with female represents semantic derogation and disparagement. Here are sentences show the derogatory meaning of some female words:

- An unmarried male (bachelor) is a "personal choice". An unmarried female (spinster) is derogatorily an "old maid".
- A "strict male manager" is described as a responsibility taker. A "strict female manager" is described as hard to work with.

3.5.3 Old Sayings

Biased old sayings come in various forms including: proverbs, set-phrases, and formulaic expressions that present a source of stereotype against women. Those sayings are culturally seen as axioms and absolute truth, which affect people behavior to adapt them as moral standards (Martín, 2011). Below are sentences exemplifying implicit sexism in proverbs:

- A woman's tongue three inches long can kill a man six feet high
- Bad words make a woman worse
- When you see an old man, sit down and take a lesson; when you see an old woman, throw a stone

4 Conclusion

In this paper, we propose a comprehensive gender bias taxonomy that distinguishes between the various forms of gender biases in English text. The taxonomy includes various exclusionary, implicitly prejudicial, and generalized forms of biased gender representations in text. Our work also provides a bottom-up understanding of gender bias, highlighting the social role theory and its impact on gender stereotypes in society. We also explain how societal gender bias spilled over onto language while being fed back into our perceptions as stated in the Sapir-Whorf hypothesis.

We hope that our comprehensive taxonomy of gender bias enables the technical community working on gender bias in NLP to focus on the identification and mitigation of relevant biases in text for improved fairness in NLP systems. We also hope that by addressing and connecting the sources and implications of gender bias in text from a linguistic, sociological, and real-life perspective, we would encourage the community to further push the research in this direction and raise more awareness on bias and discrimination in NLP systems. In future work, we will work on expanding the taxonomy to include other languages and address other forms of bias such as racial and ethnic biases.

References

Andrea E Arthur, Rebecca S Bigler, Lynn S Liben, Susan A Gelman, and Diane N Ruble. 2008. Gender stereotyping and prejudice in young children: A developmental intergroup perspective.

Manuela Barreto and Naomi Ellemers. 2005. The burden of benevolent sexism: How it contributes to the maintenance of gender inequalities. *European journal of social psychology*, 35(5):633–642.

Julia C Becker and Stephen C Wright. 2011. Yet another dark side of chivalry: Benevolent sexism undermines and hostile sexism motivates collective action for social change. *Journal of personality and social psychology*, 101(1):62.

Rebecca S Bigler and Campbell Leaper. 2015. Gendered language: Psychological principles, evolving practices, and inclusive policies. *Policy Insights from the Behavioral and Brain Sciences*, 2(1):187–194.

Rebecca S Bigler and Lynn S Liben. 2006. A developmental intergroup theory of social stereotypes and prejudice. *Advances in child development and behavior*, 34:39–89.

Maija S Blaubergs. 1980. An analysis of classic arguments against changing sexist language. *Women's studies international quarterly*, 3(2-3):135–147.

Su Lin Blodgett, Solon Barocas, Hal Daumé, and Hanna Wallach. 2020a. Language (Technology) is Power: A Critical Survey of "Bias" in NLP.

Su Lin Blodgett, Solon Barocas, Hal Daumé III, and Hanna Wallach. 2020b. Language (technology) is power: A critical survey of "bias" in NLP. In *Proceedings of the 58th Annual Meeting of the Association for Computational Linguistics*, pages 5454–5476, Online. Association for Computational Linguistics.

Ann Bodine. 1975. Androcentrism in prescriptive grammar: singular 'they', sex-indefinite 'he', and 'he or she'. *Language in Society*, 4:129 – 146.

Piotr Bojanowski, Edouard Grave, Armand Joulin, and Tomas Mikolov. 2017. Enriching Word Vectors with Subword Information. *Transactions of the Association for Computational Linguistics*, 5:135–146.

Lera Boroditsky. 2011. How language shapes thought. *Scientific American*, 304(2):62–65.

Jennifer K Bosson, Elizabeth C Pinel, and Joseph A Vandello. 2010. The emotional impact of ambivalent sexism: Forecasts versus real experiences. *Sex Roles*, 62(7):520–531.

John Briere and Cheryl Lanktree. 1983. Sex-role related effects of sex bias in language. *Sex roles*, 9(5):625–632.

Kay Bussey and Albert Bandura. 1999. Social cognitive theory of gender development and differentiation. *Psychological review*, 106(4):676.

Andrei Cimpian, Yan Mu, and Lucy C Erickson. 2012. Who is good at this game? linking an activity to a social category undermines children's achievement. *Psychological science*, 23(5):533–541.

Rachel A Connor, Peter Glick, and Susan T Fiske. 2017. Ambivalent sexism in the twenty-first century.

Emily J Cross and Nickola C Overall. 2018. Women's attraction to benevolent sexism: Needing relationship security predicts greater attraction to men who endorse benevolent sexism. *European Journal of Social Psychology*, 48(3):336–347.

David Danks and Alex John London. 2017. Algorithmic Bias in Autonomous Systems A Taxonomy of Algorithmic Bias. *26th International Joint Conference on Artificial Intelligence (IJCAI-17)*, (Ijcai):4691–4697.

Jacob Devlin, Ming-Wei Chang, Kenton Lee, and Kristina Toutanova. 2018. BERT: Pre-training of Deep Bidirectional Transformers for Language Understanding. *CoRR*, abs/1810.0(Mlm):4171–4186.

Julia Dressel and Hany Farid. 2018. The accuracy, fairness, and limits of predicting recidivism. *Science advances*, 4(1):eaao5580.

Alice H Eagly, Wendy Wood, and Amanda B Diekman. 2000. *Social role theory of sex differences and similarities: A current appraisal*, pages 123–174. Erlbaum.

Beverly I Fagot, Mary D Leinbach, and Richard Hagan. 1986. Gender labeling and the adoption of sex-typed behaviors. *Developmental Psychology*, 22(4):440.

Océane Foubert and Maarten Lemmens. 2018. Gender-biased neologisms: the case of man-x. *Lexis. Journal in English Lexicology*, (12).

Nancy Fraser. 2000. Redistribution, recognition and participation: towards an integrated concept of justice. *World Culture Report*, pages 48–57.

Victor Gay, Estefania Santacreu-Vasut, and Amir Shoham. 2013. The grammatical origins of gender roles. *Berkeley Economic History Laboratory Working Paper*, 3.

Peter Glick and Susan T Fiske. 1996. The ambivalent sexism inventory: Differentiating hostile and benevolent sexism. *Journal of personality and social psychology*, 70(3):491.

Matthew D Hammond, Chris G Sibley, and Nickola C Overall. 2014. The allure of sexism: Psychological entitlement fosters women's endorsement of benevolent sexism over time. *Social Psychological and Personality Science*, 5(4):422–429.

Maya Hickmann. 2000. Linguistic relativity and linguistic determinism: Some new directions.

Lacey J Hilliard and Lynn S Liben. 2010. Differing levels of gender salience in preschool classrooms: Effects on children's gender attitudes and intergroup bias. *Child development*, 81(6):1787–1798.

Yasmeen Hitti, Eunbee Jang, Ines Moreno, and Carolyne Pelletier. 2019. Proposed taxonomy for gender bias in text; a filtering methodology for the gender generalization subtype. In *Proceedings of the First Workshop on Gender Bias in Natural Language Processing*, pages 8–17, Florence, Italy. Association for Computational Linguistics.

Matthew D Hoffman, Francis R Bach, David M Blei, and Francis R Bach. 2010. Online Learning for Latent Dirichlet Allocation. In *Advances in Neural Information Processing Systems 23*, pages 856–864. Curran Associates, Inc.

Dirk Hovy, Federico Bianchi, and Tommaso Fornaciari. 2020. "you sound just like your father" commercial machine translation systems include stylistic biases. In *Proceedings of the 58th Annual Meeting of the Association for Computational Linguistics*, pages 1686–1690, Online. Association for Computational Linguistics.

Sarthak Jain, Ramin Mohammadi, and Byron C. Wallace. 2019. An analysis of attention over clinical notes for predictive tasks. In *Proceedings of the 2nd Clinical Natural Language Processing Workshop*, pages 15–21, Minneapolis, Minnesota, USA. Association for Computational Linguistics.

Cheris. Kramarae. 1981. Women and men speaking : frameworks for analysis / cheris kramarae. pages xviii, 194 p. ;.

Tian Lan and Liu Jingxia. 2019. On the gender discrimination in english. *Advances in Language and Literary Studies*, 10(3):155–159.

Zhenzhong Lan, Mingda Chen, Sebastian Goodman, Kevin Gimpel, Piyush Sharma, and Radu Soricut. 2019. ALBERT: A lite BERT for self-supervised learning of language representations. *CoRR*, abs/1909.11942.

Campbell Leaper and Rebecca S Bigler. 2004. Gendered language and sexist thought.

Carmen Fernández Martín. 2011. Comparing sexist expressions in english and spanish:(de)-constructing sexism though language. *ES: Revista de filología inglesa*, (32):67–90.

Laora Mastari, Bram Spruyt, and Jessy Siongers. 2019. Benevolent and hostile sexism in social spheres: The impact of parents, school and romance on belgian adolescents' sexist attitudes. *Frontiers in Sociology*, 4:47.

Ninareh Mehrabi, Fred Morstatter, Nripsuta Saxena, Kristina Lerman, and Aram Galstyan. 2019. A Survey on Bias and Fairness in Machine Learning.

Michela Menegatti, Elisabetta Crocetti, and Monica Rubini. 2017. Do gender and ethnicity make the difference? linguistic evaluation bias in primary school. *Journal of Language and Social Psychology*, 36(4):415–437.

Tomas Mikolov, Kai Chen, Greg Corrado, and Jeffrey Dean. 2013a. Distributed representations of words and Phrases and their compositionality. *NIPS*.

Tomas Mikolov, Kai Chen, Greg Corrado, and Jeffrey Dean. 2013b. Efficient estimation of word representations in vector space. *1st International Conference on Learning Representations, ICLR 2013 - Workshop Track Proceedings*, pages 1–12.

Douglass C North et al. 1990. *Institutions, institutional change and economic performance*. Cambridge university press.

Alexandra Olteanu, Carlos Castillo, Fernando Diaz, and Emre Kiciman. 2016. Social Data: Biases, Methodological Pitfalls, and Ethical Boundaries. *Ssrn*, pages 1–44.

Beata Ozieblowska. 1994. *Generic Pronouns in Current Academic Writing*. Ph.D. thesis, ProQuest Dissertations & Theses,.

Irene Lopez Rodriguez. 2009. Of women, bitches, chickens and vixens: Animal metaphors for women in english and spanish. *Cultura, lenguaje y representación: revista de estudios culturales de la Universitat Jaume I*, pages 77–100.

Kimberly T Schneider, Joe Tomaka, and Rebecca Palacios. 2001. Women's cognitive, affective, and physiological reactions to a male coworker's sexist behavior 1. *Journal of Applied Social Psychology*, 31(10):1995–2018.

Janet A Sniezek and Christine H Jazwinski. 1986. Gender bias in english: In search of fair language. *Journal of Applied Social Psychology*, 16(7):642–662.

Dagmar Stahlberg, Friederike Braun, Lisa Irmen, and Sabine Sczesny. 2007. Representation of the sexes in language. *Social communication*, pages 163–187.

Melanie C Steffens, Maria Angels Viladot, and Maria Àngels Viladot. 2015. *Gender at work: A social psychological perspective*. Peter Lang New York, NY.

Jane G Stout and Nilanjana Dasgupta. 2011. When he doesn't mean you: Gender-exclusive language as ostracism. *Personality and Social Psychology Bulletin*, 37(6):757–769.

Jeffrey L. Stringer and Robert Hopper. 1998. Generic he in conversation? *Quarterly Journal of Speech*, 84(2):209–221.

Tony Sun, Andrew Gaut, Shirlyn Tang, Yuxin Huang, Mai ElSherief, Jieyu Zhao, Diba Mirza, Elizabeth Belding, Kai-Wei Chang, and William Yang Wang. 2019. Mitigating Gender Bias in Natural Language Processing: Literature Review. (2017):1630–1640.

Songül Tolan. 2018. Fair and Unbiased Algorithmic Decision Making : Current State and Future Challenges. *Digital Economy Working Paper 2018-10; JRC Technical Reports.*, (December).

Nneka Umera-Okeke. 2012. Linguistic sexism: an overview of the english language in everyday discourse. *AFRREV LALIGENS: An international journal of language, literature and gender studies*, 1(1):1–17.

Dries Vervecken, Bettina Hannover, and Ilka Wolter. 2013. Changing (s) expectations: How gender fair job descriptions impact children's perceptions and interest regarding traditionally male occupations. *Journal of Vocational Behavior*, 82(3):208–220.

Sandra R Waxman. 2013. Building a better bridge. *Navigating the social world: What infants, children, and other species can teach us*, pages 292–296.

Benjamin Lee Whorf. 1956. Language, thought, and reality: selected writings of....(edited by john b. carroll.).

Sexism in the Judiciary: Bias Definition in NLP and in Our Courts

Noa Baker Gillis
Tel Aviv, Israel
noabakergillis@gmail.com

Abstract

We analyze 6.7 million case law documents to determine the presence of gender bias within our judicial system. We find that current bias detection methods in NLP are insufficient to determine gender bias in our case law database and propose an alternative approach. We show that existing algorithms' inconsistent results are consequences of prior research's inconsistent definitions of biases themselves. Bias detection algorithms rely on groups of words to represent bias (e.g., 'salary,' 'job,' and 'boss' to represent employment as a potentially biased theme against women in text). However, the methods to build these groups of words have several weaknesses, primarily that the word lists are based on the researchers' own intuitions. We suggest two new methods of automating the creation of word lists to represent biases. We find that our methods outperform current NLP bias detection methods. Our research improves the capabilities of NLP technology to detect bias and highlights gender biases present in influential case law. In order to test our NLP bias detection method's performance, we regress our results of bias in case law against U.S census data of women's participation in the workforce in the last 100 years.

1 Introduction

Are gender biases present in our judicial system, and can machine learning detect them? Drawing on the idea that text can provide insight into human psychology (Jakiela and Ozier, 2019), we look at gender-stereotyped language in case law as a proxy for bias in our judicial system. Unfortunately, previous NLP work in bias detection is insufficient to robustly determine bias in our database (Zhang et al., 2019). We show that previous bias detection methods all share a common flaw: these algorithms rely on groups of words to represent a potential bias (e.g., 'salary,' 'job,' and 'boss' to represent employment as a potential bias against women) that are not standardized. This lack of standardization is flawed in three main ways. First, these word lists are built by the researchers with little explanation and are susceptible to researchers' own implicit biases. Consequently, the words within the word list might not truly describe the bias as it exists in the text. Second, the same bias theme (e.g., 'employment') often has different word lists in different papers. Inconsistent word lists lead to varied results. As we show, using two different researcher's word lists to represent a bias on a single database can produce almost opposite results. Third, there is little discussion about the method of choosing words to represent specific biases. It is therefore difficult to reproduce or extend existing research on bias detection.

In order to search meaningfully for gender bias within our judicial system, we propose two methods for automatically creating word lists to represent biases in text. We find that our methods outperform existing bias detection methods and we employ our new methods to identify gender bias in case law. We find that this bias exists. Finally, we map gender bias's progress over time and find that bias against women in case law decreases at about the same rate, at the same time, that women enter the workforce in the last 100 years.

Proceedings of the 3rd Workshop on Gender Bias in Natural Language Processing, pages 45–54
August 5, 2021.

2 Bias Statement

In this paper, we study gender bias in case law using two new NLP methods. We define gender bias in text as a measurable asymmetry in language when discussing men versus women (excluding group-specific words such as gender pronouns). Bias is especially harmful in the context of case law decisions. If case law systematically associates men more positively and powerfully than women, the law creates representational harm by perpetuating unfair and inaccurate stereotypes. Further, bias in law could lead to failure to account for gender-related harms that could disproportionately affect women. For example, because of the imposition of restrictions on recovery, there is no reliable means of tort compensation for victims of domestic violence, rape, and sexual assault (Chamallas, 2018). This is just one example where failure to equally consider both genders in law leads to real harm.

The proposed bias detection algorithm only detects bias after the case has been written. However, case law is unique in that it sets precedent for other, later cases: judges often cite previous cases as a basis for a new judgment. Therefore, we suggest that this bias detection method be used as a way for judges to more deeply understand biases present in the cases they cite. Perhaps a deeper understanding of biases in historical cases could prevent biases from reappearing in new judgments.

3 Related Works

A variety of bias detection methods have been proposed in gender-related literature. Prominent among these methods is the Implicit Associations Test (IAT) (Nosek, Greenwald, and Banaji, 20). IAT measures the strength of associations between groups (e.g., men, women) and evaluations (e.g., good, bad) or stereotypes (e.g., strong, weak) to which those groups are assigned. The main idea is that classifying a group is easier, and therefore happens more quickly, when the subject agrees with the evaluation. For example, a subject has an implicit bias towards men relative to women if they are faster to classify men as strong / women as weak, than women as strong / men as weak.

In NLP literature, the most prominent bias detection method is the Word Embedding Association Test (WEAT). WEAT measures the association of word lists representing a potentially biased theme (e.g., 'salary', 'job,' and 'boss' to represent employment) to a set of pronoun or otherwise gendered pairs such as (she, he) or (man, woman) (Bolukbase et al., 2016; Caliskan et al., 2017; Garg et al., 2018; Freidman et al., 2019). The association is measured by first training a word embedding model on text. The researchers then compute the distance of vectors relating to gendered word pairs (e.g., she / he) to words in word lists representing potential bias categories. The average distance of the words in a themed word list is the magnitude of bias. The vector direction (i.e., the positive or negative distance) represents towards which group the bias is directed. WEAT uses the vector direction and proximity as a proxy for semantic association.

WEAT has been used to uncover biases in many databases. For example, Garg et al (2017) used WEAT to detect bias in Google News. Other research has used WEAT to identify bias in twitter posts in 99 countries (Friedman et al., 2019). One particularly relevant study to our research uses the same database of case law to study gender bias using WEAT, finding that cases written by female and younger judges tend to have less bias than their older, male counterparts (Ash, Chen, and Ornaghi, 2020). Another particularly relevant work uses WEAT to study the presence of gender bias in four different databases (Chaloner and Maldonado, 2019). The same work also suggests a preliminary method of automatically detecting word lists to represent gender bias but falls short of suggesting a way to determine the relevance of each bias category.

The efficacy of WEAT in bias detection is inconsistent. WEAT also fails robustness tests: for example, the average bias magnitude of words in an employment word list might be skewed towards men, but there could be words within the word list whose bias magnitude skews towards women (Zhang et al., 2019). Even different capitalizations of the same word might have different bias magnitudes

4 Methodology

4.1 Data

We use the Case Law Access Project (CAP) as our dataset. Released by Harvard Law in late 2018, the database contains over 6.7 million unique U.S state case decisions. Case law in the U.S plays a fundamental role in common-law policy making due to its ability to set precedent, making CAP an influential, rich database for judgment analysis

4.2 Overview of Approaches

We propose two new methods of identifying gender bias in case law. The first method employs a word frequency ('first-order') processing algorithm to identify words more frequently used when discussing one gender than the other in our case law database. We group the outputted gendered words thematically and use the resulting word lists, representing biases, as inputs to WEAT. The second approach employs the same first-order processing method to identify bias words. Instead of manually grouping the resulting list of gendered words thematically, we use popular automatic clustering algorithm K-Means. K-Means clustering groups our vectors representing words by proximity and similarity. We use the resulting clusters as inputs to WEAT. We compare the outputs of our methods to existing word group by performing robustness tests described in recent literature and find that both our suggested methods outperform the current standard.

4.3 WLOR: First Order Processing

For both approaches, we use a first-order sorting method to identify words used more frequently for women than men in our database. The purpose is to use the resulting most-gendered words for word lists representing biases as inputs to WEAT. We hypothesize that even using this light, fast algorithm to build word lists will increase performance and consistency of WEAT.

As part of pre-processing, we sort the sentences in our dataset by gender based on pronoun use and presence of male or female first names. We then create a lexical histogram from each of the two gendered sentence groups, which we use as input to Monroe et.al.'s (2009) weighted log-odds ratio algorithm (WLOR) (Liberman, 2014). Most first-order comparisons between two contrasting datasets estimate word usage rates, without considering rare words. WLOR accounts for this common mistake, with a null hypothesis that both lexical histograms being compared are making random selections from the same vocabulary. In our implementation of the algorithm, we use three lexical histograms as input: source X (word-list derived from male-subject sentences), source Y (word list derived from female-subject sentences), and some relevant background source Z (word list derived from entire case law database). The output is a word list and each word's score, which is the 'weighted log odds ratio', where positive values indicate that the word is favored by male sentences, and negative that the word is favored by female sentences. Words with a score near zero are about equally important to male and female sentences.

4.4 WLOR Output, Thematic Grouping

WLOR's output is a word list, but the words are not grouped by category. In order to use WLOR output as input to WEAT, we take two steps. First, we isolate the 500 most gendered words in CAP, meaning the 250 highest scoring words (most skewed towards men) and the 250 lowest scoring words (most skewed towards women). Second, we manually group those 500 words by category. After grouping, we have twelve categories of word lists representing biases in CAP. This process of categorizing the most skewed words resulted in the employment and family categories containing the largest list of words.

4.5 WLOR Output, K-Means Grouping

Our second approach categorizes the WLOR output automatically, using the clustering algorithm K-Means. K-Means clustering is a method of vector quantization that aims to partition 'observations' into k clusters. In this case, the 'observations' are vectors representing words. Each observation, or vector, belongs to the cluster with the nearest mean. Since word embedding algorithms represent words as vectors whose positions relative to each other represent the words' semantic and physical relationships in text, k-means clustering is a relatively effective method of topically clustering corpora. We therefore train word embedding algorithm Word2Vec on CAP and run the SciKitLearn implementation of K-Means on the resulting embedding. As post-processing, we filter the resulting clusters to only contain the 500 most male- and female scoring words from the WLOR output. We filter in this way because K-Means outputs all categories in a text, not just categories that are potentially biased or gender related. The overall K-Means cluster results might or might not have a bias, but the words within them are not necessarily gendered. This could lead to the same inconsistency as previous work.

4.6 WEAT

We train a word2Vec model on CAP in order to test both methods of word list generation as inputs for WEAT. To assign a magnitude to a given bias, we average the cosine similarity between the vectors of each word within the bias's word list to male and female terms. The cosine similarity represents the strength of the association between two terms.

4.7 Robustness Measures

We compare the two grouping methods against popular bias word lists used in previous work using Zhang et. al's consistency tests (2019). Their research shows that the measure of bias between different pairs of gendered words, such as (she, he) versus (him, her), or even different capitalizations of the same gender pair, and a single word often have different vector directions. This proves that arbitrarily-built clusters are not consistent inputs to WEAT. They further show that words within the same bias word list, such as 'job' versus 'salary,' and the same gender pair, such as she/he can produce different bias magnitudes and even different vector directions. For example, 'job' might skew towards men, while salary skews towards women. The problem here is obvious. Zhang et al. term this inconsistency between different gender pairs and word lists 'base pair stability.' We test our bias category word lists (the output of WLOR categorized thematically, and the K-Means clustered output) for base pair stability, following Zhang et al. We then compare our outputs' stability against bias category word lists popularly used in earlier research. We find that both our categorization techniques pass the base pair stability test, but bias category word lists used in other research do not.

Furthermore, previous work often discusses 'positive bias results', indicating that there is some amount of association between a gender and a bias categories. 'Positive bias results' are defined as any association between a given word list and a gender term, such as a pronoun. However, to our knowledge there is no discussion in previous work of the significance of bias magnitude. For example, 'employment' might have a bias against women with a magnitude of 0.2. But is 0.2 significant? How much more biased is a bias category with a magnitude of 0.4? The magnitude is meaningless without the understanding of significance. As explained above, WEAT measures bias by comparing the cosine similarity between two groups of vectors; but any threshold of similarity is deemed as 'bias.' To control for that potential pitfall, we determine the significance of WEAT output's magnitude by estimating the mean and standard deviation of gender bias in the embedding space: we analyze the gender bias of the 20,000 most frequent words in the embedding vocabulary, which is approximately normally distributed, and determine that a "significant" change in magnitude is a change of at least one standard deviation above the mean.

4.8 Comparison Over Time

Our research shows two new methods of identifying word lists representing bias in text. When used in WEAT, these word lists uncover significant gender bias in case law. Yet CAP spans three centuries; it is not surprising that gender biases exist, considering historical gender gaps. For example, women were not granted the right to vote until 1920—nearly two centuries after our first case law document in CAP. In order to emphasize meaningful gender bias, we repeat our word list generation process for every five-year chunk of case law in the last 100 years, using data from the U.S labor census. We track the bias magnitude's progress over time. In order to compare against historical gender trends occurring at the same time period, we regress our results against the rise of women in the workforce in the last 100 years. We find that while there is significant gender bias generally in case law, the bias magnitude decreases at about the same rate as women's participation in the workforce increases.

5 Results

5.1 Overview of Previous Work

To set up our point of comparison for our own methods, we first run WEAT using word lists from two influential papers in NLP bias detection literature: Caliskan et al. (2017) and Garg et. al., (2018). We choose Caliskan's employment word set, which includes general employment terms.

executive, management, professional,
corporation, salary, office, business, career

Figure 1: Caliskan employment terms.

As discussed, WEAT also requires gender pairs to perform the vector distance calculation. Rather than rely on male and female names, as Caliskan et al. did, we choose the broader pronoun category from Garg et. al. (table 1). As no explanation is given in either paper for the choice of words within the word lists, we have no reason to assume that comparing the two sets from different papers is problematic.

Female Terms	Male Terms
She, daughter, hers, her, mother, woman, girl, herself, female, sister, daughters, mothers, women, girls, femen, sisters, aunt, niece, nieces	*He, son, his, him, father, man, boy, himself, male, brother, sons, fathers, men, boys, males, brothers, uncle, uncles, nephew, nephews*

Table 1: Garg gender terms.

As an aside, we note that Garg et al.'s gendered terms (Table 1) are also family terms, which likely skews the vectors against employment terms for reasons other than just their gendered-ness.

Following the literature, we define gender bias in our embedding as:

$$bias = \frac{\sum_n \overrightarrow{\text{male word}}}{|N_{male}|} - \frac{\sum_n \overrightarrow{\text{female word}}}{|N_{female}|} \quad (1)$$

Caliskan's manually clustered word sets produce an embedding bias against Garg's female word list of -0.03 in CAP. Performing Zhang's base-pair stability test, we find that this method is inconsistent—many of the base pairs, when compared against the same given word in the set, produce vectors with different directions. Vector directions represent the direction of bias—either towards men or women. Further, the slant of Garg's gender term list against Caliskan's employment terms do correspond to a known bias against women, but there is no discussion of "significance" of the magnitude of bias, making results difficult to analyze. We determine magnitude change significance ourselves by estimating the mean and standard deviation of gender slant in the embedding space (Table 2).

Based on the standard deviation of approximately 0.07 above an approximately -0.004 mean, we determine that although there is a slight preference

Mean	Standard Dev.
-0.0042	0.0738

Table 2: Mean and standard dev. in CAP.

for men over women in employment terms using the Caliskan-Garg employment bias word lists, it is less than one standard deviation below the mean and cannot be considered significant. Further, When we ran the data on a subsection of the word-set, the embedding bias direction shifted from biased against women, with a magnitude of -0.03, to a bias against men with a magnitude of 0.013. We determine that manual arbitrary clustering is not a robust test for gender bias.

5.2 WLOR Output, Thematic Grouping

We next run the WLOR algorithm on the full dataset. The word 'office' is the most male-skewed word in U.S case law in the last century, discounting male pronouns and legal terms. The

Female Words	Male Words
Husband, married, children, child, marriage, death, mother, daughter, divorce, unmarried	*Office, pay, witness, company, goods, work, corporation, defendant, trial*

Table 3: Excerpt from the top twenty most important words for female and male subject sentences

word 'husband' is the most female-skewed word in U.S case law in the last century, discounting female pronouns. (As an aside, we note that there are no legal terms skewed towards women.)

We then isolate the 500 most gendered words in CAP, meaning the 250 highest scoring words (most skewed towards men) and the 250 lowest scoring words (most skewed towards women). We group the 500 terms thematically into word lists representing biases. The largest word lists represent employment and family. Although the words in Table 4 are sorted thematically, it is interesting to note that all employment terms came from the top 250 male-relating words. There were no employment terms in the top 250 female-skewing words. Similarly, all family terms came from the

Female	Female	Female	Male	Male	Male
prostitution, illicit, abortion, lewd, carnal, unchaste, seduced, bastard	*Children, heirs, parents, parent, spouse, wife, husband, brother, sister, daughter*	*Incapable, sick, weak, feeble, mentally, physically, mental*	*Shot, fired, killed, drunk, shooting, fight*	*Price, amount, salary, penalty, cost, fine, prices*	*Engineer, foreman, employer, employment, contractor, master*

Table 5: K-Means clustered (automatic grouping) WLOR sample.

top 250 female skewed words, as there were no family terms in the top 250 male-skewed words.

After running the WLOR algorithm and creating the bias category word lists, we next determine our gender pronoun list for WEAT. We only include gender words in our male/female gender pair lists that are included in the top 500 most gendered words for men and women in the WLOR output. We do not include family terms in our base pair lists because of the potential bias against those words that are not gender-related. (For example, the word 'husband,' although facially male, is likely used in a family context. This is as opposed to he/she, which is used regardless of context.)

Family Words	Employment Words
Husband, baby, married, children, child, marriage, mother, father, divorce, unmarried, widow, wife, birth, divorced, family	*Office, company, pay, goods, work, corporation, firm, business, engineer, employer, employment, employed, salary, client*

Table 4: Excerpt of thematic grouping of highest-scoring WLOR results

We then input our word lists into WEAT in order to compute bias magnitude. Using the same gender slant definition and formula as in section 5.1, we calculate the bias of employment terms as -0.19 against women, and the bias of family terms as 0.22 against men. Based on the mean of -0.0042 and standard deviation of 0.0738 calculated for general gender slant in CAP, we find these results to be statistically significant.

Not only do the bias categories have statistically significant bias; each word within the bias categories has the same vector direction and are statistically significantly biased. This is different than previous research, whose word lists contained words with opposing vector directions. In order to determine this robustness, we perform Zhang's base-pair stability test by testing each word from within the same bias category separately against each set of gender pairs (such as she/he). We find that there is no directional change of vectors between different base-pairs and the same words. When testing each word separately against the she/he gender pair, both are independently biased towards women. Further, there is no significant change in bias magnitude (as defined by one standard deviation above the mean) between different words and base pairs. The results indicate that using first-order approaches, as we did with WLOR, is enough to identify basic categories of bias in a text, even if the output of the first-order method is manually grouped.

5.3 WLOR Output, K-Means Grouping

We next test to see if automatically clustering the WLOR output produces different results than the thematic grouping of WLOR output. The primary benefit of complete automatic clustering is that there is no "researcher bias", i.e., no assumptions of previous bias affect the clusters themselves. For example, in the manually-clustered WLOR output, we identified areas of bias by thematically grouping the output word list—but we still had an implicit awareness of the historical bias of men/work versus women/family. Automatic clustering frees the data entirely from researcher's potentially biased decision making. The drawback of this method is the heavy, slower Word2Vec training model.

We train a Word2Vec model on the entire dataset, and cluster the resulting embeddings using K-Means clustering with a preset of 300 clusters. We choose this algorithm for its speed and accuracy. In order to assess which clusters are gender related, we filter the resulting clusters to only include words in the WLOR output's 250 most male-skewed words and 250 most female-skewed words. This filtering controls the quality of the word lists: the word lists only contain words which already are known to be gendered in CAP. Upon visual inspection, most of the clusters seem relatively cohesive.

We use Zhang's base-pair stability test on all clusters with at least five words in the top 500 gendered words. There were seventeen clusters in this category. A sample of these can be seen in Table. 5. Interestingly, the resulting clusters primarily contain either male-skewed or female-skewed terms, but not both. All clusters that included primarily female-skewed terms were indeed found to be biased against women when used as inputs to WEAT. Similarly, all clusters with primarily male-skewed terms were found to be biased against men. Testing between each gender pair and each word in all seventeen clusters, we found that 97% of words within the same word list had the same vector direction. Sixteen out of the seventeen clusters produced had significant bias, meaning that the difference in gender slant scores was greater than, or less than, at least one standard deviation above or below the mean. We conclude that automatic clustering of first-order lexical histograms is a robust and consistent measurement of bias in text. We note that the automatic clustering also produced many categories of bias that we did not consider, such as associating demeaning sexual terms with women, and violence with men.

6 Comparison Over Time

We have shown that automating the formation of word lists to represent biases in WEAT leads to consistent and robust bias detection in text. Using two separate approaches, we created bias word lists to detect gender bias in case law and found that it exists. However, given the time span of our database, the presence of language difference between genders is not surprising.

In order to detect meaningful gender bias, i.e., bias that is stronger in text than real-world historical gender gaps, we track the change in bias magnitude over time. We regress the change in bias magnitude against women's participation in the workforce and find they progress at about the same rate.

6.1 Labor Slant

In order to compare the rate of change between gender bias in case law and women's participation in the workforce in the last 100 years, we first define the labor 'bias' for a given period in time. For precision, we label difference between men and women in the labor force as 'slant.' We define labor slant as the percentage of women in the workforce minus the percentage of men in the workforce. Formally:

$$slant = labor_{women} - labor_{men} \quad (2)$$

The closer the labor slant is to zero, the more the workforce participation is equally divided between genders.

6.2 WLOR Results Over Time

We run the WLOR algorithm on each five-year slice of time in the last 100 years. The word lists generated from WLOR for female-subject sentences in the last century, discounting pronouns, include the word "husband" as the most important word consistently for every timeframe we analyzed between 1920 and 2017. The first five words for every five-year span in the last 100 years include the words "child/children", "mother", and "pregnant." The most consistently important words for male-subject sentences in the last century are "work", "guilty", and "sentence". Most words in the output generated for male-subject sentences mean "work", some kind of automobile, or are legal language.

This stark difference in language between two datasets separated by gender provides a clear picture of how the language used in our judicial system distinguishes between women and men: women are family oriented, and men are working (and driving, another form of mobility and therefore power) subjects of the law. The first time a family word appears in the male-subject list of important words was in 2005, with the word "wife." The first time an employment term appeared in the female-subject list of important words was an instance of the word "housework" in 1950. There are only three instances of employment terms for women between 1920 and 1990 out of 3,500 words analyzed in that time frame. It is also interesting to note the absence of legal language from the most heavily female words in the database. Although we do not explore this in our current research, we bring up the possibility that women are simply viewed as less meaningful subjects of law.

6.3 WEAT Results Over Time

We follow our two word-list building methods as inputs for WEAT for every five-year span of time in CAP in the last century. We use employment bias as our input wordlist for our WLOR thematic clustering approach, as the employment category has the largest word set. We find that for all years before 1980, words in our occupation-themed bias category are more associated with men than women, and after 1980, the trend hovers around 0, with a slight preference towards women. We use the cluster with primarily family terms as a 'family' bias as our input wordlist for K-Means, which is largest wordlist in our automatic approach. We find that there is a steady decrease in bias towards men

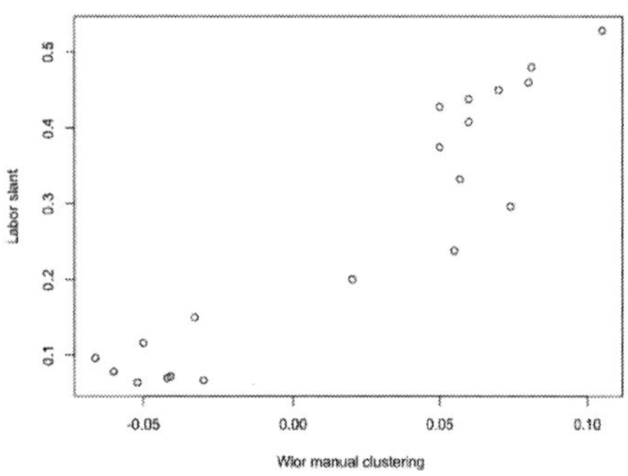

Figure 3: Labor slant and WLOR thematic clustering regression data.

in this category since 1920. We use the absolute values of these biases for clarity in our graph (Figure 2).

6.4 Regression

We present results of each bias category word list regressed against the change in labor force participation in the last 100 years using data from the U.S census reports. We find that the change in bias magnitude over the last 100 years for both word lists are highly correlated with the increase of women in the workforce. Our results, with a P value of 1.172e-09 and an R^2 of 0.8781 for thematic grouping and a P value of 3.08e-09 and an R^2 of 0.8676, are consistent with the hypothesis that legal language's gender bias decreases as women's participation increases in the workforce.

7 Conclusion

In our research, we analyze 6.7 million documents of case law for gender bias. We find that existing bias detection methods in NLP are not sufficiently consistent to test for gender bias in CAP. We attribute this inconsistency to the lack of methodical building of word lists to represent bias. We therefore suggest two new approaches to building word lists for bias representation. We test our two approaches on CAP and find both methods to be robust and consistent, and to identify the presence of gender bias. We also show that, when the change in bias magnitude over time is regressed against workforce participation rate in the last 100 years, and find they are heavily correlated. It is worth noting that, although this research focuses specifically on gender bias, the same methodology might be applied to other groups—provided that those groups are identifiable in text.

As a future development in this research, we want to explore the results of our data that show that men are overwhelmingly associated with legal language, and women are not, even though women are not less likely to be defendants in certain types of law—such as Torts law (Chamallas, 2018). (In fact, Chamallas makes the point that Torts regulation can sometimes discriminate against women in other ways, and that Torts law should in fact have more female defendants than male.) Could it be that the law implicitly does not recognize women as independent legal entities in the same way it does men? We also would like to study possible intersections of identity in our judicial system. For example, we show that there is

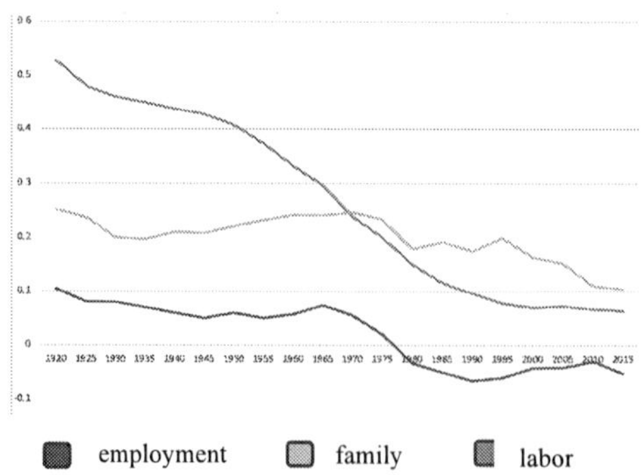

Figure 2: change in employment gender bias, family gender bias, and labor slant.

gender bias present in case law, but is there stronger bias against women of color than white women? Further, we wish to expand this research by involving judgments by experts of gender on developing a more holistic approach to bias clustering. Lastly, for future work we hope to analyze the impact these biases have on NLP systems' overall performance, and potential harms from these systems in other fields.

Acknowledgements

This work is based on research conducted in the University of Pennsylvania's Cognitive Science and Computer Science departments under the guidance of Professor Mark Liberman. Thank you to Professor Liberman for code samples, editing, and advice. Thank you to Gedalia Gillis for statistical analysis, Professor Tom Baker (Penn Carey Law School) for help with legal analysis, Professor Talia Gillis (Columbia Law School) for the introduction to the CAP dataset, and Sharon Baker and anonymous reviewers for their helpful comments.

References

Camiel J. Beukeboom and Christian Burgers. 2019. *How Stereotypes Are Shared Through Language: A Review and Introduction of the Social Categories and Stereotypes Communication (SCSC) Framework*. Review of Communication Research, 7:1–37.

Tolga Bolukbasi, Kai-Wei Chang, James Y Zou, Venkatesh Saligrama, and Adam T Kalai. 2016. *Man is to computer programmer as woman is to homemaker? Debiasing word embeddings*. In Advances in neural information processing systems, pages 4349–4357.

Aylin Caliskan, Joanna J Bryson, and Arvind Narayanan. 2017. *Semantics derived automatically from language corpora contain human-like biases*. Science, 356(6334):183–186.

The President and Fellows of Harvard University. Caselaw Access Project. Case.law

Kaytlin Chaloner and Alfredo Maldonado. 2019. *Measuring Gender Bias in Word Embedding across Domains and Discovering New Gender Bias Word Categories*. In Proceedings of the Workshop on Gender Bias in Natural Language Processing, pages 25–32, Florence, Italy.

Martha Chamallas. 2018. *Feminist Legal Theory and Tort Law.* In SSRN.

Scott Friedman, Sonja Schmer-Galunder, Anthony Chen, and Jeffrey Rye. 2019. *Relating Word Embedding Gender Biases to Gender Gaps: A Cross-Cultural Analysis*. Proceedings of the Association of Computational Linguistics 2019.

Nikhil Garg, Londa Schiebinger, Dan Jurafsky, and James Zou. 2018. *Word embeddings quantify 100 years of gender and ethnic stereotypes*. Proceedings of the National Academy of Sciences.

Keita Kurita, Nidhi Vyas, Ayush Pareek, Alan W Black, Yulia Tsvetkov. 2020. *Measuring Bias in Contextualized Word Representations*. Association of Computational Linguistics 2020.

Mark Liberman. 2014. *Obama's Favored (and Disfavored) SOTU Words*. Language Log.

Burt Monroe, Michael P. Colaresi, Kevin M. Quinn. *Fightin' Words: Lexical Feature Selection and Evaluation for Identifying the Content of Political Conflict*. Cambridge University Press.

Michela Menegatti and Monica Rubini. 2017. *Gender bias and sexism in language*. In Oxford Research Encyclopedia of Communication. Oxford University Press.

Tomas Mikolov, Ilya Sutskever, Kai Chen, Greg S Corrado, and Jeff Dean. 2013. *Distributed representations of words and phrases and their compositionality.* In Proc.of NIPS, pages 3111–3119.

Brian A. Nosek, Anthony Greenwald, and Mahzarin Banaji. 2007. *The implicit Association Test at Age 7: A Methodological and Conceptual Review.* Automatic Processes in Social Thinking and Behavior, 265 – 292

Arianna Ornhagi, Elliot Ash, and Daniel Chen. *Stereotypes in High Stake Decisions: Evidence from U.S Circuit Courts*. 2019.

Deven Shah, H. Andrew Schwartz, and Dirk Hovey. *Predictive Biases in Natural Language Processing Models: A Conceptual Framework and*

Overview. Proceedings of the Workshop on Gender Bias in Natural Language Processing, 2020.

Douglas Rice, Jesse J Rhodes, and Tatishe Nteta. 2019. *Racial bias in Legal Language.* Research & Politics, 6(2), 2053168019848930.

Haiyang Zhang, Alison Sneyd, and Mark Stevenson. *Robustness and Reliability of Gender Bias Assessment in Word Embeddings: The Role of Base Pairs.* Proceeding of the Association of Computational Linguistics 2019.

Towards Equal Gender Representation in the Annotations of Toxic Language Detection

Elizabeth Excell
Department of Computer Science
Durham University
Durham, UK
bethexcell@gmail.com

Noura Al Moubayed
Department of Computer Science
Durham University
Durham, UK
noura.al-moubayed@durham.ac.uk

Abstract

Classifiers tend to propagate biases present in the data on which they are trained. Hence, it is important to understand how the demographic identities of the annotators of comments affect the fairness of the resulting model. In this paper, we focus on the differences in the ways men and women annotate comments for toxicity, investigating how these differences result in models that amplify the opinions of male annotators. We find that the BERT model associates toxic comments containing offensive words with male annotators, causing the model to predict 67.7% of toxic comments as having been annotated by men. We show that this disparity between gender predictions can be mitigated by removing offensive words and highly toxic comments from the training data. We then apply the learned associations between gender and language to toxic language classifiers, finding that models trained exclusively on female-annotated data perform 1.8% better than those trained solely on male-annotated data, and that training models on data after removing all offensive words reduces bias in the model by 55.5% while increasing the sensitivity by 0.4%.

1 Introduction

Toxic language detection has attracted significant research interest in recent years as the volume of toxic user-generated online content has grown with the expansion of the Internet and social media networks (Schmidt and Wiegand, 2017). As toxicity is such a subjective measure, its definition can vary significantly between different domains and annotators, leading to many contrasting approaches to toxicity detection such as evaluating the constructiveness of comments (Kolhatkar et al., 2020) or examining the benefits of taking into account the context of comments (Pavlopoulos et al., 2020).

Detecting and appropriately moderating toxic comments has become crucial to online platforms to keep people engaged in healthy conversations rather than letting hateful comments drive people away from discussions. In addition, it has become increasingly important to ensure a user's right to free speech and only remove comments that violate the policies of the platform. Human annotators are the most effective way to filter toxic comments. However, they are costly and unscalable to the generated data. As such, toxic language classifiers are trained on datasets composed of comments annotated by humans as an efficient way of detecting toxic language (Schmidt and Wiegand, 2017).

One of the main issues with this approach is that any biases held by the pool of annotators are propagated in the classifier, which can lead to non-toxic comments from certain identity groups being mislabelled as toxic, an effect known as false positive bias (Dixon et al., 2018; Sap et al., 2019). While many papers have acknowledged the potential for bias in their datasets, with some proposing novel ways of measuring this bias (Dixon et al., 2018), very little has been done to examine the differences in the ways that distinct groups of annotators perceive comments and investigate how these differences affect the classification results.

This paper is motivated by the lack of understanding of the impact of annotator demographics on bias in toxic language detection. We investigate how the annotators' demographics affect the toxicity scores/labels and the trained models. We analyse the chosen corpus by grouping the annotations by the gender of the annotator as it is the most addressed demographic variable in the literature and constitutes the largest groups of data in the corpus. We then tailor the state-of-the-art BERT model to the tasks of toxicity and gender classification, using training and test sets built independently using the annotations of different genders to investigate bias.

For the gender classification models, we use ex-

Proceedings of the 3rd Workshop on Gender Bias in Natural Language Processing, pages 55–65
August 5, 2021.

plainable machine learning methods to analyse the comments in the test set in order to gain further insights into the associations between gender and language made by the model that contribute to the biased classifications towards male annotators. We then explore how modifying the training data of the models based on these learned associations affects the bias present. We examine the role offensive language plays in male and female annotations and investigate the robustness of models trained independently on gender-specific data once offensive language has been removed.

The main contributions of this work are: I) revealing the bias of BERT-based toxic language detection models towards male annotators, II) recognising the learned associations between male annotators and offensive language in the model, III) demonstrating methods to reduce the bias in the model without reducing the sensitivity.

2 Bias Statement

In this work, we explore gender bias present in toxic language detection systems due to associations between offensive language and annotator gender amplified by the model. We define gender bias in this context as the disproportionate influence of the opinions of one gender over another in the model's output. We acknowledge that by treating gender as binary in this study, we exclude those who identify as non-binary, which may cause representational harm (Blodgett et al., 2020). This choice was made due to the scarcity of annotators who identify as non-binary affecting the generalisability of the results.

This work demonstrates that toxic comments containing offensive words are associated with male annotators, resulting in female annotators predicted as being male. This leads to toxicity classifiers that are overly reliant on the opinions of annotators perceived to be male in order to make a classification. The resulting systems create representational harm by overlooking the diverse opinions of female annotators, leading to comments that women may consider toxic not being removed.

3 Related Work

Previous research into gender bias in toxic language detection caused by the demographic makeup of annotators explored superficial differences between male and female annotators, but only reflected on the ethical considerations involved rather than thoroughly investigating the differences between annotator groups and attempting to minimise bias in the model.

Binns et al. (2017) presented different methods for detecting potential bias by building classifiers trained on comments whose annotators belong to different genders. They reported differences in average toxicity scores and inter-annotator agreement between the groups. Similar work by Sap et al. (2019) in the field of racial bias examined toxicity scores given to Twitter corpora, where the white annotators in the majority give higher toxicity scores to tweets exhibiting an African American English dialect, demonstrating how annotator opinions can propagate bias throughout the model.

Some studies focused on gender bias in specific tasks in Natural Language Processing such as coreference resolution. The aim of those studies is to eliminate under-representation bias by applying gender-swapping and name anonymisation to a corpus to balance the use of gender-specific words (Zhao et al., 2018). Sun et al. (2019) highlights this technique as an effective way of debiasing models and measuring gender bias in predictions, using the False Positive Equality Distance (FPED) and False Negative Equality Distance (FNED) metrics (Dixon et al., 2018) to measure the difference in performance for gender-swapped sentences.

Another common source of bias is the word embeddings, which can form associations between identity groups and stereotypical terms based on their prevalence in the literature used to train the language model. Bolukbasi et al. (2016) demonstrated the presence of gender bias in occupations in the word embeddings of a language model and proposed a system to debias those models by isolating the gender subspace before utilising hard or soft debiasing to remove the gender bias from terms identified as being gender neutral. This was further extended by Manzini et al. (2019) to encompass racial bias, transforming the binary classification task of identifying gender-specific and gender neutral terms into a multiclass debiasing problem.

Related studies into the aggregation of crowdworker annotations highlight that many models are skewed towards the opinions of workers who agree with the majority vote, which can lead to the opinions of other annotators being disregarded even when there is low inter-annotator agreement (Balayn et al., 2018). A solution to this, proposed by Aroyo and Welty (2013) and adopted by Wulczyn et al. (2017), uses disaggregated data and transforms the problem from the binary classification of toxicity to the prediction of the proportion of annotators who would classify a comment as toxic.

In practice, the effectiveness of crowdsourcing appears to be mixed for much of the literature, with Kolhatkar et al. (2020) noting that expert annotators only agree with the majority opinion of the crowdsourced annotations 87% of the time in the context of evaluating the constructiveness of comments. This verdict is also reached by Nobata et al. (2016), who concludes that workers on the Amazon Mechanical Turk platform exhibit a much worse inter-annotator agreement than the in-house annotators for the task of abuse classification. This highlights the need to thoroughly examine the annotations in corpora before they are applied to a classification task.

We note that that the majority of the research into bias in toxic language detection does not reflect on the bias caused by the pool of annotators, and yet research into crowdsourcing demonstrates poor inter-annotator agreement in many corpora and how the results of classification models are skewed by annotator opinions that may not reflect society as a whole. For the few papers that do examine the role of annotators in toxic language detection, no practical suggestions have been made that aim to reduce the identified bias in the implemented model, which is the main contribution of this paper.

4 Data

We use the toxicity corpus[1] from the Wikipedia Detox project (Wulczyn et al., 2017), which contains over 160k comments from English Wikipedia annotated with toxicity scores and the demographic information of the annotators, where each comment has been labelled by approximately 10 annotators using the toxicity categories displayed in Table 1.

This corpus has been widely used in recent literature developing deep learning approaches to toxic language detection (Pavlopoulos et al., 2017; Mishra et al., 2018) and investigating bias, such as Dixon et al. (2018) using the comments to propose metrics that evaluate bias based on the identity terms present in the data. As such, this corpus was selected for the comparability of results it provides, in addition to it being the only toxic language corpus to provide the genders of the annotators.

Binns et al. (2017) demonstrates methods to explore potential bias in this corpus without further investigating the cause of the bias or attempting to reduce bias in the model, finding that male annotators in the corpus have a significantly higher inter-annotator agreement than female annotators, leading to male test data performing better than female test data. Balayn et al. (2018) uses this corpus to investigate how the implemented model became skewed towards the scoring of annotators with the majority opinion, favouring the opinion of the largest group for each demographic variable. Balayn et al. (2018) then attempts to mitigate this bias by balancing the dataset for each demographic variable, which we discover is not enough to prevent bias is the model due to the learned associations between the demographic variable and the language in the comments.

We hypothesise based on previous research that models trained on this corpus will likely value the opinions of male annotators over female annotators. This is due to the fact that male annotators were found to have a greater inter-annotator agreement than female annotators, meaning that they are likely to hold the majority opinion, and so it follows that the model will place a greater importance on the scores of male annotators when deciding the toxicity of a comment.

5 Experiments

5.1 Technical Specifications

We use a state of the art model (Zorian and Bikkanur, 2019), built based on the pre-trained uncased $\text{BERT}_{\text{BASE}}$ model (Devlin et al., 2019) with a single linear classification layer on top. The Huggingface `transformers` library (Wolf et al., 2020) is used to implement the model.

For fine-tuning, we follow the guidelines set by Devlin et al. (2019), using an Adam optimizer with a learning rate of 2×10^{-5} and a linear scheduler. We use a batch size of 8 trained over 2 epochs [2].

5.2 Preliminary Data Analysis

Examining the chosen corpus, we find that 34% of the annotations were made by women (with <0.1% of annotators describing themselves as 'other'). Due to the unbalanced nature of the dataset, we balance each training and test set used for gender

[1] https://www.kaggle.com/jigsaw-team/wikipedia-talk-labels-personal-attacks

[2] Code is available at: https://github.com/MicrosoftExcell/Advanced-Project

Toxicity Category	Toxicity Score	Description
Very toxic	-2	A very hateful, aggressive, or disrespectful comment that is very likely to make you leave a discussion
Toxic	-1	A rude, disrespectful, or unreasonable comment that is somewhat likely to make you leave a discussion
Neither	0	-
Healthy contribution	1	A reasonable, civil, or polite contribution that is somewhat likely to make you want to continue a discussion
Very healthy contribution	2	A very polite, thoughtful, or helpful contribution that is very likely to make you want to continue a discussion

Table 1: Toxicity categories given to annotators with associated toxicity scores and descriptions.

classification by ensuring that 50% of the annotations were made by men and 50% of the annotations were made by women. We achieve this by randomly sampling the comments annotated by each demographic group until a quota such as the size of the smallest group is reached for each sample. The goal of this is to eliminate under-representation bias in order to be certain that any differences between genders in the results are not caused by an unbalanced dataset.

After reviewing the toxicity scores given by each group as a whole, we find that female annotators on average annotated 1.72% more comments as toxic than male annotators and assigned toxicity scores that were on average 0.048 lower than those given by their male counterparts, using the toxicity scores given in Table 1. These figures indicate a slight disparity between the genders, suggesting that female annotators on average find comments more toxic than male annotators.

5.3 Pre-processing

While the different models built for this paper focus on two different tasks, namely toxicity and gender classification, the pre-processing steps remain largely the same. Firstly, the data is stripped of unnecessary information such as newline and tab tokens. Annotators who reported their gender as 'other' are removed as they do not provide a large enough group to draw generalisable conclusions from. The dataset is then balanced by gender as previously described as well as being balanced by the toxicity score in a similar manner.

For gender classification, as only toxic data is used for training and testing, this means sampling the data evenly from comments given a toxicity score of -1 and those given a toxicity score of -2. This is necessary as far fewer comments are labelled as 'Very Toxic' than 'Toxic', and as it is the

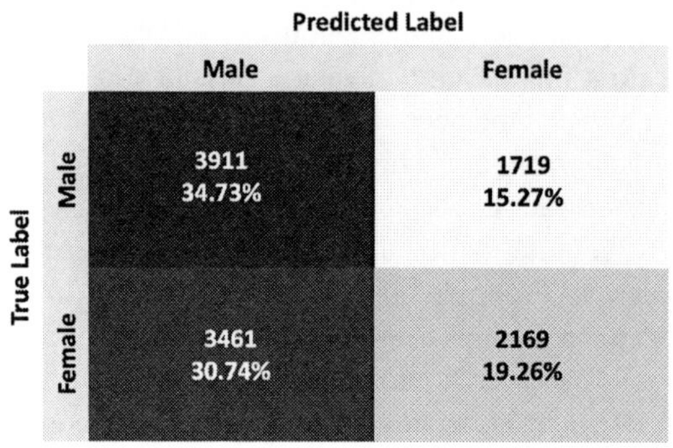

Figure 1: Confusion matrix showing the gender predictions of the annotators of toxic comments by the BERT-based model.

toxic data that is being investigated, it is important to ensure that any differences in the way men and women annotate comments as 'Very Toxic' are not diminished in the results by the substantial size of the 'Toxic' category. Similarly, the toxicity classification models take 25% of their data from the comments annotated as 'Toxic' and a further 25% from the 'Very Toxic' data, with the remaining 50% being randomly sampled from the 'Healthy' and 'Very Healthy' data. The last two categories were not divided evenly as with the toxic categories due to the limited size of the 'Very Healthy' data.

We choose the maximum sequence length for the model to be 100 based on the token counts of comments in the training data, taking into account memory restrictions.

5.4 Gender Classification

The results of the preliminary data analysis indicate potential differences between male and female annotators in the corpus. We explore this further by tasking the BERT-based model with classifying the gender of an annotator based on a comment the annotator labelled as toxic.

Using training and test data classified as toxic or very toxic by equal numbers of male and female annotators, we find that the model predicts the gender of the annotator of a toxic comment as male 67.7% of the time on average, with the results of the first run shown in Figure 1 . This indicates that there is a difference between the annotations of male and female annotators that can be identified by the model, as we would expect the predictions to be evenly distributed between male and female if no bias was present.

In order to investigate the differences in annotation styles between the genders that caused the bias shown, we add interpretability to the model's output by adapting the attribution scores and integrated gradients to display which words in comments are the most important when predicting the gender of the annotator, and which gender those words are attributed to. The integrated gradients method attributes the predictions of deep networks to their inputs and has proven useful for rule extraction in text models, identifying undiscovered correlations between terms and classification results (Sundararajan et al., 2017).

The results of this analysis can be seen in Table 2, where 10 comments from the test set have been chosen due to their brevity and concise representation of the attribution scores seen in the test set as a whole. Furthermore, we include comments from each combination of true and predicted labels to provide a wider picture of the observed results.

We observe that the model gives great importance to offensive words when classifying a comment as having a male annotator. The language in comments predicted as having a female annotator is less explicit and harder to categorise, other than that the attributed words are more typical of a conversation rather than an overt insult like the majority of the male attributed words. This is corroborated by the Spearman's rank correlation coefficient of -0.378 between the probability given by the model of the annotator being female and the number of offensive words in the comment, indicating the existence of a relationship between the model predicting annotators as being male and the presence of offensive words in a comment.

Examining the data further, we find that male-annotated 'Toxic' comments contains 0.1 more offensive words on average than female-annotated 'Toxic' comments, with this disparity rising to 0.28 for the 'Very Toxic' comments.

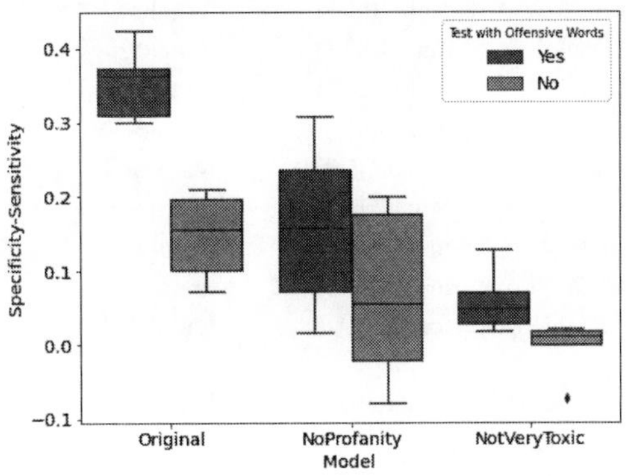

Figure 2: Box plot showing the difference between the specificity and sensitivity for each gender classification model on test data with and without offensive words.

Based on these observations, we hypothesise that the bias of the model towards predicting a toxic comment as having a male annotator is due to the model learning an association between offensive words and male annotators in the training data, exacerbated by the prevalence of offensive words in toxic comments. In order to validate this hypothesis, we retrain the model after removing all offensive words from the training data using a blacklist[3]. We refer to the original BERT model as BERTOriginal and this new model as BERTNoProfanity.

We also train the model after removing the 'Very Toxic' data in addition to the offensive words, in order to see if this lessens the gender disparity in the results. We do this based on the knowledge that the most toxic comments contain the greatest amount of profanity as comments annotated as 'Toxic' have a median of 1 and a mean of 1.20 offensive words per comment, while the 'Very Toxic' comments have a median of 2 and a mean of 2.41 offensive words per comment. This new model is referred to as BERTNotVeryToxic.

The performance of these models on toxic test data with and without offensive words is displayed in Figure 2. We measure the difference between specificity and sensitivity for each model as they measure the model's ability to correctly predict whether an annotator is male or female respectively. Ideally, all values of specificity and sensitivity should be 0.5 if there is no bias towards either gender in the results. As such, the difference

[3]`https://www.cs.cmu.edu/~biglou/resources/`

True Label	Predicted Label	Attribution Label	Score	Word Importance
female	male (0.53)	female	-0.70	you re fuck of bitch . . .
female	male (0.53)	female	-2.06	i hate you u stupid little mid ##get
female	male (0.53)	female	-1.33	a crazy ne##rd who dislike ##s women
female	male (0.53)	female	-1.49	suck my dick . suck my ##bi##g harry balls
male	female (0.54)	female	2.00	you will not be warned again .
male	female (0.56)	female	1.79	that' s your short - coming , then.
male	male (0.53)	female	-1.39	mu ##you suck asshole ch
male	male (0.56)	female	-1.89	how about this , go fuck yourself ! !
female	female (0.71)	female	4.06	... i won't comment unless ... ... an investigation would have perhaps ...
female	female (0.67)	female	5.00	... acts of terror against their ... ...in this context ...

Table 2: Attributions of annotator gender to words in toxic comments. First column contains the true gender of the annotator. Second column contains the predicted gender of the annotator with the associated probability given by the BERT model. Third column contains the attribution label. Fourth column contains the attribution score, for comparison with the attribution label (negative scores indicate male attributions and positive scores indicate female attributions). Fifth column contains the comment text highlighted with the associated word attribution scores. **Blue indicates negative (male) attribution scores, yellow indicates positive (female) attribution scores.** The intensity of the colour indicates the magnitude of the associated attribution. *Note: some comments are truncated due to their length, in which case the words with the strongest attribution scores are shown.*

between them is indicative of the amount of bias in the model.

What we observe from these results is that bias is reduced in all models when offensive words are removed from the test data, indicating that the offensive words are a large contributor to the bias towards predicting annotators as male. We also note that the BERTNoProfanity model shows a 55.5% reduction in bias on average compared to the BERTOriginal model, again demonstrating that offensive words cause bias in the model. Furthermore, we see that the BERTNoProfanity model exhibits the greatest amount of variation in the results, due to the discrepancies in the semantics between comments with and without words removed. The BERTNotVeryToxic model does not face this issue as it is trained using only the 'Toxic' data, which has half the number of offensive words per comment than the 'Very Toxic' data does, meaning that the semantics of comments remain broadly intact.

In addition, we observe that the BERTNotVeryToxic model exhibits the least bias overall, suggesting that the 'Very Toxic' data contributes to the model's decision to predict the gender of an annotator as male. In fact, the BERTNotVeryToxic model exhibits little to no bias on the test data without offensive words, apart from one outlier that leans towards female predictions, suggesting that the bias towards men is eliminated when offensive words and the 'Very Toxic' data are removed from the training and test data.

In order to further validate our hypothesis about the relationship between gender predictions and offensive words in comments, we plot the relationship between the predicted probability of a comment having a female annotator and the number of offensive words in the comment for the BERTOriginal and BERTNotVeryToxic models, the results of which can be seen in Figure 3.

From these plots we can see that the BERTOriginal model is very likely to make gender predictions based on the number of offensive words in a comment as the probability distribution is skewed towards the left, meaning that comments with high numbers of offensive words have low probabilities of being female. We can see that this is not the case for the BERTNotVeryToxic model, as it shows a much more even distribution of gender probabilities for comments with higher numbers of offensive words, again confirming the model's reliance on 'Very Toxic' data to make the association between male annotators and offensive words in toxic comments.

In order to demonstrate that the number of offensive words in a comment is not a reliable method of predicting the gender of an annotator, we examine the true and predicted labels of all comments in the test set, as can be seen in Figure 4. This shows that both men and women annotate comments with a high number of offensive words as toxic, as the es-

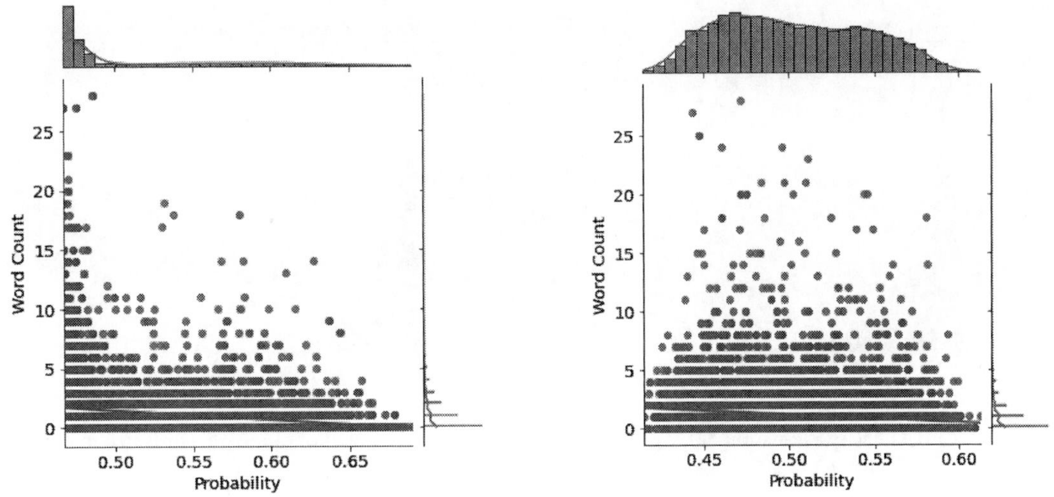

Figure 3: Scatter plots showing the number of offensive words in a comment against the predicted probability of the annotator being female for the BERTOriginal model (left) and the BERTNotVeryToxic model (right).

timation of the probability distribution for the true gender labels is roughly the same for both genders. We can see that this distribution has shifted in the predicted labels, with the female distribution being shifted to the left and the male distribution being shifted to the right. This shows that the model attributes comments with no offensive words to female annotators and comments with greater numbers of offensive words to male annotators despite there being little difference between the gender distributions in the ground truth.

5.5 Toxicity Classification

To further explore the differences between male and female annotators, we adapt the BERT model to perform toxicity classification rather than gender classification. For this task, we keep the dataset balanced between toxic and non-toxic comments. The model is trained using data from male and female annotators respectively, with and without offensive words removed. We refer to the male models with and without offensive words as BERTMale and BERTMaleNoProfanity respectively, and refer to the female models as BERTFemale and BERTFemaleNoProfanity in the same way.

We test each of the models using test data of the same condition as well as the test data from all other toxicity classification models. This means that models trained exclusively on data from one gender can be compared using data from both genders to examine which model performs better in addition to finding which set of test data is easier to categorise. This also allows us to examine the performance of models trained and tested on data with and without offensive words in order to understand the impact of removing offensive words from the training data on performance, as we have already determined that this method decreases bias in the model.

As we have only examined the relationship between annotator gender and the language in comments that were annotated as toxic, we use sensitivity to measure the performance of each model and set of test data. This measures the ability of each model to correctly classify toxic comments.

The results of this can be seen in Table 3, where we observe similar results to Binns et al. (2017), showing that models consistently perform worse on female-annotated test data compared to male-annotated test data. This could be due to the greater diversity of opinions in female-annotated data resulting from low inter-annotator agreement (Binns et al., 2017), in addition to the ability of the model to associate offensive words with male annotations making it easier to classify toxic comments annotated by men. We also note that female-annotated models perform $1.8\% \pm 0.6\%$ better on average, suggesting they are less dependent on the presence of offensive words in test data for classification.

We observe that when the offensive words in the training and test data are removed, the toxic comments without offensive words become more difficult to correctly classify than those with offensive words. We also find that models trained on

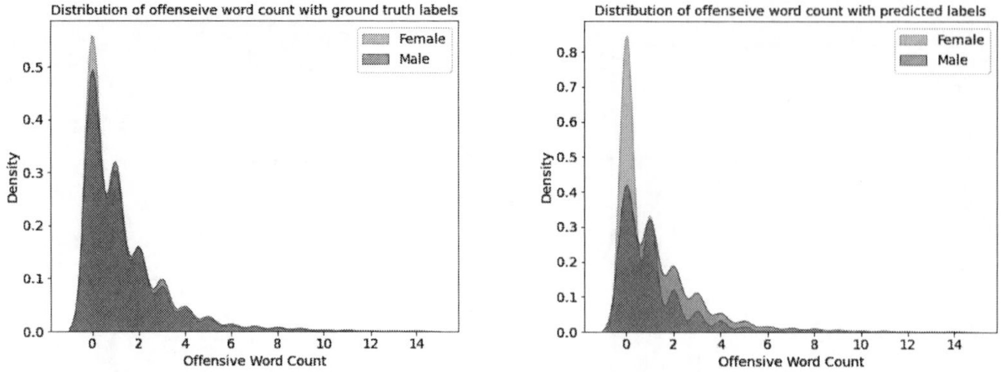

Figure 4: Kernel density estimation of the probability distribution of the count of offensive words in comments for the ground truth (left) and predicted (right) male and female labels.

	Test Data							
	Male		MaleNoProfanity		Female		FemaleNoProfanity	
Model	Mean	SD	Mean	SD	Mean	SD	Mean	SD
BERTMale	0.8370	0.019	0.6794	0.026	0.7682	0.019	0.6288	0.025
BERTMaleNoProfanity	0.8392	0.004	0.8142	0.003	0.7748	0.008	0.7502	0.007
BERTFemale	**0.8534**	0.004	0.6952	0.016	**0.7986**	0.013	0.6500	0.020
BERTFemaleNoProfanity	0.8528	0.006	**0.8224**	0.007	0.7944	0.010	**0.7662**	0.012
BERTMale+Female	0.8519	-	0.7376	-	0.7689	-	0.6682	-

Table 3: Means and standard deviations of sensitivity for each toxicity model on each category of test data over 5 runs using seed values 42, 5936, 9743, 14280, 29988. The same test sets were used between models for each run. The bold numbers indicate the model with the highest sensitivity for each category of test data. One run of a baseline model trained on male and female data is added for comparison only.

data without offensive words have a 0.4% higher sensitivity on average on unmodified test data than the equivalent model trained on data with offensive words. The performance of BERTMaleNoProfanity surpasses the performance of BERTMale on every set. BERTFemaleNoProfanity has a similar performance on the unmodified data as BERTFemale, despite the lack of offensive words in the training data. BERTFemaleNoProfanity outperforms BERTFemale by 0.1272 and 0.1162 on the modified male and female test data respectively. This is due to the model relying on factors other than the offensive words for toxicity classification.

6 Discussion

Toxic language detection is a highly subjective task, with majority opinions and levels of agreement varying within and between demographic groups. We highlight this by analysing the annotations of different genders in the chosen corpus, noting that the number of female annotators is outweighed by the number of male annotators, and that the female annotators are more likely to label a comment as toxic than their male counterparts. This information could be leveraged by moderation systems by taking into account the demographic group the reader of a comment belongs to before determining the toxicity threshold at which a comment is removed from the system.

Our findings indicate that the BERT-based model associates comments that contain offensive words with male annotators, despite the data showing that both male and female annotators label comments containing high numbers of offensive words as toxic. We demonstrate that the most offensive words are attributed to male annotators, which causes the model to output skewed predictions indicating that most comments have been annotated by men despite the training data being balanced between both genders.

We note that the male annotators in this corpus display a greater level of inter-annotator agreement than the female annotators which may contribute to the tendency of the model to predict the gender of an annotator as male. This bias indicates that toxicity models trained on this corpus will be more influenced by the opinions of male annotators, as the diversity of views given by the female annotators makes them unlikely to hold the majority opinion, and those who label comments containing offensive words as toxic are perceived to be male by the model.

We find that removing the offensive words from the training data produces a model that demonstrates less bias overall than the original model but exhibits the most variation in the results of any of the implemented models. We find that removing the most toxic data in addition to removing the offensive words in the training data produces the model with the least bias, showing that comments containing high numbers of offensive words are far less attributed to male annotators than in the original model.

Applying the discovered associations between gender and offensive language to models tasked with classifying the toxicity of comments, we find that toxic comments annotated by men are easier to classify than those annotated by women. Conversely, we find that models trained exclusively on female-annotated data display a better performance than models trained entirely on male-annotated data. This is in part due to the associations between male annotators and offensive language distracting the model from other aspects of toxic comments.

Finally, we show that while it is harder to correctly classify toxic data after the removal of offensive words, models trained on this data show a comparable performance to models trained on unmodified data. Combining these results with those of the gender predicting models, we see that removing offensive words from the training data of a model is an effective way of reducing the bias towards the opinions of male annotators without compromising the performance of the model on toxic data.

We note that this approach does not remove all bias in the model, for example we did not address the male bias present in the model due to the contextual relationships between words found in the training data (Kurita et al., 2019). However, this paper provides an insight into the gender associations that can be present in a model and the methods that can be used to investigate and minimise bias in any classification system reliant on annotators.

We recommend that the demographics of the annotators be collected and reported as part of labelled datasets. This is particularly relevant in problems which rely on the subjective opinion of the annotator like toxic language detection.

7 Conclusion

In this paper we seek to quantify the gender bias in toxic language detection systems present as a result of differences in the opinions held by distinct demographic groups of annotators in the corpus and aim to minimise this bias without compromising the performance of the model. We identify differences between the annotation styles of men and women in the chosen corpus and determine that this causes a bias towards the opinions of men. We discover associations between the male bias and the use of offensive language in toxic comments, applying this knowledge to a toxic language classifier to demonstrate an effective way to reduce gender bias without compromising the performance of the model.

Future work on annotator bias should examine other demographic variables present in the pool of annotators such as race, age or level of education and analyse the extent to which certain groups may be excluded or have their opinions overlooked by the model. This could be extended by researching the connection between the demographic identities of annotators and the identities referenced in comments to see where prejudice occurs. Those implementing toxic language detection systems would be advised to consider the types of bias present in their model and personalise moderation based on the identities of those authoring or viewing comments.

References

Lora Aroyo and Chris Welty. 2013. Crowd truth: Harnessing disagreement in crowdsourcing a relation extraction gold standard. In *Proceedings of ACM Web Science 2013 Conference*.

Agathe Balayn, Panagiotis Mavridis, Alessandro Bozzon, Benjamin Timmermans, and Zoltán Szlávik. 2018. Characterising and mitigating aggregation-bias in crowdsourced toxicity annotations. In *Proceedings of the 1st Workshop on Subjectivity, Ambiguity and Disagreement in Crowdsourcing, and Short Paper Proceedings of the 1st Workshop on Disentangling the Relation Between Crowdsourcing and Bias Management*, volume 2276. CEUR.

Reuben Binns, Michael Veale, Max Van Kleek, and Nigel Shadbolt. 2017. Like trainer, like bot? inheritance of bias in algorithmic content moderation. In *International conference on social informatics*, pages 405–415. Springer.

Su Lin Blodgett, Solon Barocas, Hal Daumé III, and Hanna Wallach. 2020. Language (technology) is power: A critical survey of "bias" in NLP. In *Proceedings of the 58th Annual Meeting of the Association for Computational Linguistics*, pages 5454–5476, Online. Association for Computational Linguistics.

Tolga Bolukbasi, Kai-Wei Chang, James Zou, Venkatesh Saligrama, and Adam Kalai. 2016. Man is to computer programmer as woman is to homemaker? debiasing word embeddings. In *Proceedings of the 30th International Conference on Neural Information Processing Systems*, NIPS'16, page 4356–4364, Red Hook, NY, USA. Curran Associates Inc.

Jacob Devlin, Ming-Wei Chang, Kenton Lee, and Kristina Toutanova. 2019. BERT: Pre-training of deep bidirectional transformers for language understanding. In *Proceedings of the 2019 Conference of the North American Chapter of the Association for Computational Linguistics: Human Language Technologies, Volume 1 (Long and Short Papers)*, pages 4171–4186, Minneapolis, Minnesota. Association for Computational Linguistics.

Lucas Dixon, John Li, Jeffrey Sorensen, Nithum Thain, and Lucy Vasserman. 2018. Measuring and mitigating unintended bias in text classification. In *Proceedings of the 2018 AAAI/ACM Conference on AI, Ethics, and Society*, pages 67–73.

Varada Kolhatkar, Nithum Thain, Jeffrey Sorensen, Lucas Dixon, and Maite Taboada. 2020. Classifying constructive comments. *arXiv preprint arXiv:2004.05476*.

Keita Kurita, Nidhi Vyas, Ayush Pareek, Alan W Black, and Yulia Tsvetkov. 2019. Measuring bias in contextualized word representations. In *Proceedings of the First Workshop on Gender Bias in Natural Language Processing*, pages 166–172, Florence, Italy. Association for Computational Linguistics.

Thomas Manzini, Lim Yao Chong, Alan W Black, and Yulia Tsvetkov. 2019. Black is to criminal as caucasian is to police: Detecting and removing multiclass bias in word embeddings. In *Proceedings of the 2019 Conference of the North American Chapter of the Association for Computational Linguistics: Human Language Technologies, Volume 1 (Long and Short Papers)*, pages 615–621, Minneapolis, Minnesota. Association for Computational Linguistics.

Pushkar Mishra, Helen Yannakoudakis, and Ekaterina Shutova. 2018. Neural character-based composition models for abuse detection. In *Proceedings of the 2nd Workshop on Abusive Language Online (ALW2)*, pages 1–10, Brussels, Belgium. Association for Computational Linguistics.

Chikashi Nobata, Joel Tetreault, Achint Thomas, Yashar Mehdad, and Yi Chang. 2016. Abusive language detection in online user content. In *Proceedings of the 25th international conference on world wide web*, pages 145–153.

John Pavlopoulos, Prodromos Malakasiotis, and Ion Androutsopoulos. 2017. Deep learning for user comment moderation. In *Proceedings of the First Workshop on Abusive Language Online*, pages 25–35, Vancouver, BC, Canada. Association for Computational Linguistics.

John Pavlopoulos, Jeffrey Sorensen, Lucas Dixon, Nithum Thain, and Ion Androutsopoulos. 2020. Toxicity detection: Does context really matter? In *Proceedings of the 58th Annual Meeting of the Association for Computational Linguistics*, pages 4296–4305, Online. Association for Computational Linguistics.

Maarten Sap, Dallas Card, Saadia Gabriel, Yejin Choi, and Noah A. Smith. 2019. The risk of racial bias in hate speech detection. In *Proceedings of the 57th Annual Meeting of the Association for Computational Linguistics*, pages 1668–1678, Florence, Italy. Association for Computational Linguistics.

Anna Schmidt and Michael Wiegand. 2017. A survey on hate speech detection using natural language processing. In *Proceedings of the fifth international workshop on natural language processing for social media*, pages 1–10.

Tony Sun, Andrew Gaut, Shirlyn Tang, Yuxin Huang, Mai ElSherief, Jieyu Zhao, Diba Mirza, Elizabeth Belding, Kai-Wei Chang, and William Yang Wang. 2019. Mitigating gender bias in natural language processing: Literature review. In *Proceedings of the 57th Annual Meeting of the Association for Computational Linguistics*, pages 1630–1640, Florence, Italy. Association for Computational Linguistics.

Mukund Sundararajan, Ankur Taly, and Qiqi Yan. 2017. Axiomatic attribution for deep networks. In *International Conference on Machine Learning*, pages 3319–3328. PMLR.

Thomas Wolf, Lysandre Debut, Victor Sanh, Julien Chaumond, Clement Delangue, Anthony Moi, Pierric Cistac, Tim Rault, Remi Louf, Morgan Funtowicz, Joe Davison, Sam Shleifer, Patrick von Platen, Clara Ma, Yacine Jernite, Julien Plu, Canwen Xu, Teven Le Scao, Sylvain Gugger, Mariama Drame, Quentin Lhoest, and Alexander Rush. 2020. Transformers: State-of-the-art natural language processing. In *Proceedings of the 2020 Conference on Empirical Methods in Natural Language Processing: System Demonstrations*, pages 38–45, Online. Association for Computational Linguistics.

Ellery Wulczyn, Nithum Thain, and Lucas Dixon. 2017. Ex machina: Personal attacks seen at scale. In *Proceedings of the 26th international conference on world wide web*, pages 1391–1399.

Jieyu Zhao, Tianlu Wang, Mark Yatskar, Vicente Ordonez, and Kai-Wei Chang. 2018. Gender bias in coreference resolution: Evaluation and debiasing methods. In *Proceedings of the 2018 Conference of the North American Chapter of the Association for Computational Linguistics: Human Language Technologies, Volume 2 (Short Papers)*, pages 15–20, New Orleans, Louisiana. Association for Computational Linguistics.

Apik Ashod Zorian and Chandra Shekar Bikkanur. 2019. Debiasing personal identities in toxicity classification. *arXiv preprint arXiv:1908.05757*.

Using Gender- and Polarity-Informed Models to Investigate Bias

Samia Touileb
Department of Informatics
University of Oslo
samiat@uio.no

Lilja Øvrelid
Department of Informatics
University of Oslo
liljao@uio.no

Erik Velldal
Department of Informatics
University of Oslo
erikve@uio.no

Abstract

In this work we explore the effect of incorporating demographic metadata in a text classifier trained on top of a pre-trained transformer language model. More specifically, we add information about the gender of critics and book authors when classifying the polarity of book reviews, and the polarity of the reviews when classifying the genders of authors and critics. We use an existing data set of Norwegian book reviews with ratings by professional critics, which has also been augmented with gender information, and train a document-level sentiment classifier on top of a recently released Norwegian BERT-model. We show that gender-informed models obtain substantially higher accuracy, and that polarity-informed models obtain higher accuracy when classifying the genders of book authors. For this particular data set, we take this result as a confirmation of the gender bias in the underlying label distribution, but in other settings we believe a similar approach can be used for mitigating bias in the model.

1 Introduction

As is well established, training data for NLP tasks may contain various types of bias that can be inherited by the models we train, and that may potentially lead to unintended and undesired effects when deployed (Bolukbasi et al., 2016). The bias can stem from the unlabeled texts used for pre-training of language models (LMs), or from the language or the label distribution used for tuning a downstream classifier. Typically, when a classifier is fitted on top of a pre-trained LM for a given task, only textual data is considered by the learned representations.

In this work we investigate the effect of adding metadata information about demographic variables that are known to be associated with bias in the training data. Specifically, we focus on the task of binary sentiment classification based on data where gender has previously been shown to be correlated with the label distribution. The data we use are Norwegian book reviews, where the gender of both critics and book authors have previously been annotated (Touileb et al., 2020). When considering all pairs of male/female critics/authors, Touileb et al. (2020) showed that female critics tended to assign lower ratings to female authors, relative to other gender pairs. In this work we explore the effect of adding information about gender to a document-level polarity classifier trained on top of a pre-trained BERT model for Norwegian, showing that the model is able to take this metadata into account when making predictions. Through experiments with gender classification on the same data set, we also demonstrate that the language of the reviews is itself indeed gendered.

We believe that adding this type of metadata about *e.g.,* demographic information when available can in many cases be used to mitigate bias in models. Consider the case of a model for toxic language classification; it seems intuitively plausible that incorporating information about users could help reducing the risk of false positives for self-referential mentions by marginalized groups. However, we have a different focus for the particular experiments reported here: we show how adding information about gender in a polarity classifier confirms gender bias, by showing how a gender-informed model obtains substantially higher accuracy when evaluated on a biased label distribution.

In what follows, we start in Section 3 with an overview of related work, after providing a brief bias statement in Section 2. In Section 4 we present our dataset, and give a detailed description of our experiments in Section 5. We present and analyse our results in Section 6, followed by an error analysis in Section 7. Finally, we summarize our findings and discuss future works in Section 8.

Proceedings of the 3rd Workshop on Gender Bias in Natural Language Processing, pages 66–74

2 Bias statement

This work focuses on gender bias, which we identify as the differences in language use between persons, on the unique basis of their genders. The concrete task that we deal with in the current paper is that of polarity classification of book reviews, using labels derived from the numerical ratings assigned by professional critics. We use an existing dataset of book reviews dubbed NoReC$_{gender}$ (Touileb et al., 2020), which is a subset of the Norwegian Review Corpus (Velldal et al., 2018), a dataset primarily used for document-level sentiment analysis. The subset NoReC$_{gender}$ has previously been augmented with information about the gender of both critics and book authors. Through experiments with gender predictions of both critics and book authors, we demonstrate the presence of gendered language in these reviews. Previous work has also shown that the distribution of ratings in the dataset to some degree is correlated with the gender of the critics and the authors. Consequently, work on sentiment classification on the basis of the dataset could risk inheriting aspects of gender bias unknowingly, either in the model predictions themselves or in how these are evaluated, or both. One of our motivations in this work is exactly to assess whether the predictions of sentiment classifiers trained on review data may to some degree depend on gender, by explicitly incorporating this as a variable in the model.

Note that there are also issues of what could be argued to be representational harm (Blodgett et al., 2020) associated with the underlying encoding of gender itself, since only the binary gender categories of male/female are present in the data. While the dataset we use only reflects binary gender categories, we acknowledge the fact that gender as an identity spans a wider spectrum than this.

3 Related work

State-of-the-art results for various NLP tasks nowadays typically build on some pre-trained transformer language models like BERT (Devlin et al., 2019). Despite their great achievements, these models have been shown to include various types of bias (Zhao et al., 2020; Bartl et al., 2020; Basta et al., 2019; Kaneko and Bollegala, 2019; Friedman et al., 2019; Kurita et al., 2019).

Recent works have shown the advantage of adding extra information to pre-trained language models for numerous tasks, *e.g.,* dialog systems (Madotto et al., 2018), natural language inference (Chen et al., 2018), and machine translation (Zaremoodi et al., 2018). Knowledge graphs have also been used to enrich embedding information. Zhang et al. (2019) use entries from Wikidata, as well as their relation to each others, to represent and inject structural knowledge aggregates to a collection of large-scale corpora. They show that their approach reduces noisy data and improves BERT fine-tuning on limited datasets. Bourgonje and Stede (2020) enrich a German BERT model with linguistic knowledge represented as a lexicon as well as manually generated syntactic features. Peinelt et al. (2020) enrich a BERT with LDA topics, and show that this combination improves performance of semantic similarity. Ostendorff et al. (2019) use a combination of metadata about books to enrich a BERT-based multi-class classification model. They train a BERT model on the title and the texts of each book, and concatenate the output with metadata information and author embeddings from Wikipedia, and feed them into a Multilayer Perceptron (MLP).

When it comes to gender and gender bias, previous research has been devoted to the identification of bias in textual content and models (Garimella and Mihalcea, 2016; Schofield and Mehr, 2016; Kiritchenko and Mohammad, 2018), and in input representations as static and contextualised embeddings (Takeshita et al., 2020; Bartl et al., 2020; Zhao et al., 2020; Basta et al., 2019; Kaneko and Bollegala, 2019; Friedman et al., 2019; Bolukbasi et al., 2016). A considerable amount of previous work has also gone into either mitigating existing bias in embeddings (Takeshita et al., 2020; Maudslay et al., 2019; Zmigrod et al., 2019; Garg et al., 2018), making them gender neutral (Zhao et al., 2018), or using debiased embeddings (Escudé Font and Costa-jussà, 2019). Instead of debiasing and mitigating bias in embeddings, some work has focused on creating gender balanced corpora (Costa-jussà et al., 2020; Costa-jussà and de Jorge, 2020).

Several previous studies have focused on gender and gender bias in sentiment analysis, both from data and model perspectives. To name a few: Kiritchenko and Mohammad (2018) propose an evaluation corpus (Equity Evaluation Corpus) that can be used to mitigate biases towards a selection of genders and races. Occupational gender stereotypes exist in sentiment analysis models (Bhaskaran and Bhallamudi, 2019), both in training data and in pre-trained contextualized models.

Models have also been proposed to uncover gender biases (Hoyle et al., 2019). Incorporating extra demographic information into sentiment classification models have also been successful. Hovy (2015) has shown that incorporation gender information (as embeddings) in models can improve sentiment classification. They show that such an approach can reduce the bias towards minorities, as for example females, who tend to communicate differently from the norm.

In this paper, we do not focus on biases present in existing systems , nor do we try to mitigate them in a traditional way. We use a dataset of Norwegian book reviews for which a previous study has indicated some degree of gender bias in the label distribution of review ratings (Touileb et al., 2020). Here, we investigate whether this bias is reflected in the text, as measured by classification scores on two tasks, namely binary sentiment and gender classification, and whether adding metadata information explicitly providing the gender of the authors and critics of the reviews, or the sentiment score of the review increases classification performance. Similarly to (Ostendorff et al., 2019), we explore the effects of adding this metadata information to document classification tasks using a BERT-based model, in this case the Norwegian NorBERT (Kutuzov et al., 2021).

4 Dataset

In this work, we focus on gender effects in reviews written by male or female critics, which in turn rates the works of male and female authors. The dataset we use is the NoReC$_{gender}$[1] (Touileb et al., 2020) subset of the Norwegian Review Corpus (NoReC (Velldal et al., 2018)). NoReC$_{gender}$ is a corpus of 4,313 professional book reviews from several of the major Norwegian news sources. Each review is rated with a numerical score on a scale from 1 to 6 (represented by the number of dots on a die), assigned by a professional critic. The reviews also contain additional metadata information like the name of the critics, name of the book authors, and their respective genders.

The numerical ratings and name of the critics were already provided in the metadata data of NoReC (Velldal et al., 2018), while the name of the authors and the information about the genders were manually annotated with the release of NoReC$_{gender}$ (Touileb et al., 2020).

	M	F	Total
Unique critics	125	74	199
Unique authors	1,435	882	2,317

Table 1: Total number of unique male and female critics and authors in NoReC$_{gender}$.

	Train	Dev.	Test	Total
pos	568	69	71	708
neg	568	60	55	683

Table 2: Total number of positive and negative reviews in the data splits of NoReC$_{gender}$.

As pointed out by Touileb et al. (2020), some of the reviews were written by children, unknown authors/critics, or by editors, these were not assigned genders and were therefore not included in our work. This results in a set of 4,083 documents. Table 1 shows an overview of the NoReC$_{gender}$ dataset in terms of total number of critics and authors, and their distribution across genders.

Each review in NoReC$_{gender}$ comes with a numerical dice score from 1 to 6. Similarly to Touileb et al. (2020), we choose to focus on clear positive and negative reviews and therefore only use reviews with negative ratings representing dice scores 1, 2, and 3, and reviews with positive ratings representing scores 5 and 6. However, in order to control for the distribution of positive and negative labels, we have selected a subset of reviews with rating 5 to have a balanced distribution of positive and negative reviews in the train set. This results in a subset of 683 negative and 708 positive reviews for NoReC$_{gender}$. A distribution of these across the train, dev, and test splits can be seen in Table 2.

The dataset NoReC$_{gender}$ also contains a bias in the distribution of labels, based on the gender of the critics and the authors (Touileb et al., 2020). Figure 1 shows the total number of ratings in our dataset, where the first letter (M/F) indicates the gender of the critic and the second letter indicates that of the author. For example, *MF* represents reviews written by male critics reviewing the works of female authors. Here we observe a clear difference in the ratings given by female critics to female authors (*FF*). While most reviews seem to have a certain amount of balance between positive and negative polarities with slightly more positive than negative

[1] `https://github.com/ltgoslo/norec_gender`

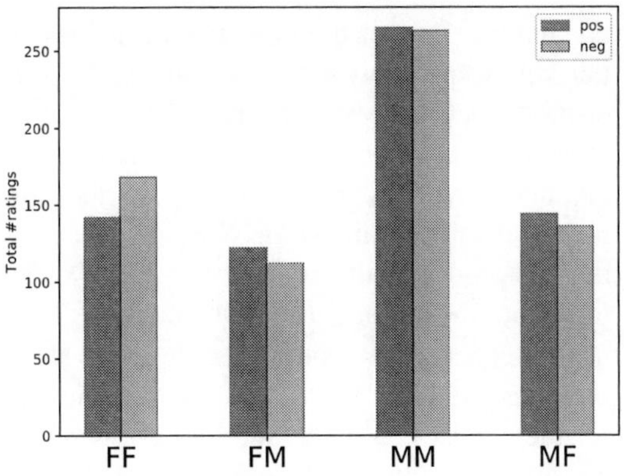

Figure 1: Distribution of ratings given by critics to works of authors. The first letter (M/F) indicates the gender of the critic and the second that of the author.

reviews, for *FF* it is the opposite. This, in addition to the unbalance between the total number of reviews based on gender, represent the bias present in NoReC_{gender}'s label distribution.

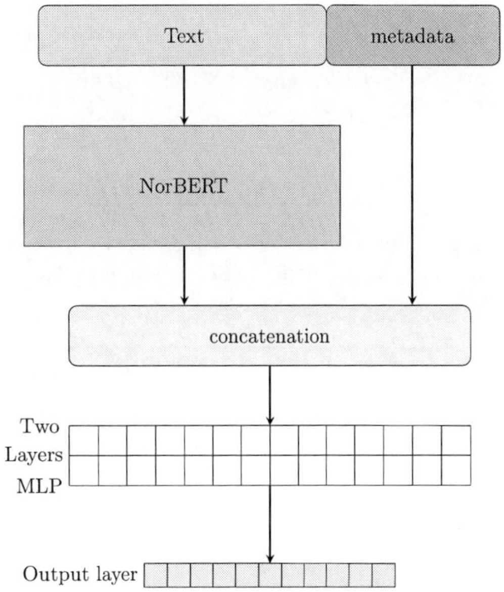

Figure 2: Architecture of our metadata-enriched classification model. Our baseline model has the same architecture except for the metadata input and the concatenation step.

5 Experiments

We use the Norwegian BERT model NorBERT[2] (Kutuzov et al., 2021). The model uses the same architecture as BERT base cased (Devlin et al., 2019), and uses a 28,600 entry Norwegian-specific sentence piece vocabulary. It was jointly trained on both official Norwegian written forms Bokmål and Nynorsk, on 200M sentences (around 2 billion tokens) from Wikipedia articles and news articles from the Norwegian News Corpus.[3]

We use a similar architecture to Ostendorff et al. (2019) as shown in Figure 2. We feed our review texts to a NorBERT architecture of 12 hidden layers consisting of 768 units each. These representations and the metadata are subsequently concatenated and passed to a two-layer Multilayer Perceptron (MLP), using ReLu as activation function. The output layer (SoftMax) gives for each task its binary output, *i.e.,* either binary sentiment classification labels, or binary gender classification labels. We set the learning rate for AdamW (Loshchilov and Hutter, 2019) to $5e-5$, and batch size to 32. We train the model for 5 epochs, and keep the best model on the dev set with regards to F_1.

We have experimented with various input sizes (first 300 tokens, first 512 tokens, and first 128 + last 383 tokens) both with tokenized and untokenized texts. The best results were achieved using untokenized texts, and using the first 128 and last 383 tokens, as pointed out by Sun et al. (2020). These are the input sizes used in the models we report in this work.

Our metadata is one-hot encoded, and has a dimension of two for gender (female and male), and two for polarity (positive and negative). In the case where we combine information about the genders of both authors and critics, the dimension is four (*i.e.,* two gender dimensions each).

For the task of binary gender classification, we perform a set of four experiments:

- *NorBERT–none*: without any metadata.
- *NorBERT–ga*: adding information about the gender of authors.
- *NorBERT–gc*: adding information about the gender of critics.
- *NorBERT–gac*: adding information about the gender of both the authors and the critics.

For each of the binary classification of genders of authors or critics, we perform the following two experiments:

- *NorBERT–none*: classifying the gender of authors or critics without any metadata.

[2] https://huggingface.co/ltgoslo/norbert

[3] https://www.nb.no/sprakbanken/ressurskatalog/oai-nb-no-sbr-4/

Model	dev	test
NorBERT–none	82.45	80.66
NorBERT–ga	84.51	**84.21**
NorBERT–gc	84.92	82.33
NorBERT–gac	**85.25**	82.92

Table 3: Model performance on dev and test for binary sentiment classification. *NorBERT–none* is the baseline model. All models report mean F_1.

	Model	dev	test
Author	*NorBERT–none*	89.57	90.12
	NorBERT–polarity	**94.93**	**94.60**
Critic	*NorBERT–none*	**70.40**	**63.84**
	NorBERT–polarity	64.99	57.76

Table 4: Model performance of binary gender classification on dev and test for authors and critics. Models report mean F_1.

- *NorBERT–polarity*: classifying the gender of authors or critics by adding information about the polarity (positive and negative) of the review.

In all of our experiments, we use the task specific *NorBERT–none* as baselines.

6 Results

Table 3 shows F_1 scores of our binary sentiment classification models on both dev and test splits of NoReC$_{gender}$. The baseline model *NorBERT–none* that only uses NorBERT without metadata performs quite well on both dev and test splits with F_1 scores of 82.45 and 80.66 respectively. But as can be seen, the model is the least accurate in our set of experiments.

We observe that the *NorBERT–ga* model, which incorporate information about the gender of the authors is the most accurate model on the test set, with an F_1 score of 84.21, while it is the third most accurate on the dev split with an F_1 score of 84.51. *NorBERT–gc*, which adds information about the gender of the critics, also yields better results than the baseline with an F_1 score of 84.92 on dev, and 82.33 on test. The best performing model on the dev set is *NorBERT-gac*, with added information about the genders of both authors and critics. This model is also the second best model on test with a F_1 score of 82.92.

The results presented in Table 3 show that gender-informed models with metadata information improve the task of binary sentiment classification with respectively 2.06, 2.47, and 2.8 F_1 points on the dev set, and 3.55, 1.67, and 2.26 F_1 points on test for the three models *NorBERT-ga*, *NorBERT-gc*, and *NorBERT-gac*. This suggests that for a binary classification task on NoReC$_{gender}$, knowing the gender of the authors and critics clearly influences the performance of the model.

The scores of our gender classification tasks are presented in Table 4. As previously mentioned, for the gender classification, we have two tasks: classification of the gender of the authors, and classification of the gender of the critics.

For the classification of the authors' genders, the baseline classifier *NorBERT–none* performs quite good with a F_1 score of 89.57 and 90.12 on dev and test respectively. However, adding the metadata about the polarity of the review (if it's positive or negative) influences the classification task by 5.36 and 4.48 points on dev and test respectively.

Interestingly, we observe the opposite situation for the classification of the gender of critics. Here, the baseline model *NorBERT–none* outperforms the *NorBERT-polarity* model by 5.41 and 6.08 F_1 score points on respectively dev and test splits.

For the task of author gender classification, knowing the polarity of the review clearly influences the classification. Again, this indicates that gender and polarity are correlated in our data. The results also point to a difference between the gender of authors and critics. However, additional information about the polarity of the review, seems to hurt the classification of the genders of critics.

7 Error analysis

In order to gain further insight into the differences between the models we are comparing and in particular, the classification differences caused by the addition of information on gender/polarity, we perform an error analysis by comparing, for each task, how our models perform compared to the task-specific baselines.

Figure 3 shows how the three models *NorBERT–ga*, *NorBERT-gc*, and *NorBERT-gac* have different predictions than their baseline *NorBERT–none* for binary sentiment classification. We show the relative differences of true positives as a heatmap. These are made on the test predictions of each model over all five runs. Positive numbers (dark purple) specify that the model made more correct predictions than the baseline *NorBERT–none*, while negative numbers (white) indicate it made fewer correct predictions. The abbreviations *FF*, *FM*, *MF*, and *MM* represent the gender of the critic reviewing the work of an author of a given gender. *FF* refers to female critic and female author, *FM* female critic and male author, *MF* male critic and female author, and *MM* for male author and male critic.

It is clear that all three gender-informed models become more accurate in the classification of reviews written by female critics and reviewing the works of female authors (*FF*). As previously mentioned, and as pointed out by Touileb et al. (2020), female critics tend to be more negative towards female authors, and therefore there are few reviews that fall within this category with positive polarity. Adding information about the gender of the authors and the critics, seems to help the model identify some of the *FF* reviews that *NorBERT–none* was not able to classify correctly. This information seems to be particularly important for *NorBERT–ga*, which was the best model on the test set achieving 12 F_1 points more than the baseline on *FF*. This model also seems slightly better at identifying reviews for *MM*. A closer analysis differentiating the positive and negative polarities also shows that the three models are more accurate precisely in identifying the positive reviews in the *FF* subset.

The same applies to a lesser degree for *FM*. Knowing the gender of the authors and the critics, separately, enables the models to correctly classify more reviews than *NorBERT–none*. In contrary, for *MF*, only knowing the gender of both the critics and authors seems to slightly improve classification. For the *MM* reviews, the *NorBERT–ga* model is better at identifying the positive reviews, while *NorBERT–gac* is better at identifying the negative reviews.

Figure 4 shows the breakdown of the relative differences of true positives. Here again, the relative differences are made on the test predictions of each model over all five runs. Positive numbers (dark blue) represent the cases where the model made more correct predictions than the baseline *NorBERT–none*, while negative numbers (white) indicates the opposite. For clarity, we add a prefix to each model in the figure to specify the task. *GA-NorBERT–pn* represent the model *NorBERT–pn* for the task of author gender classification, while *GC-NorBERT–pn* represents the task of critic gender

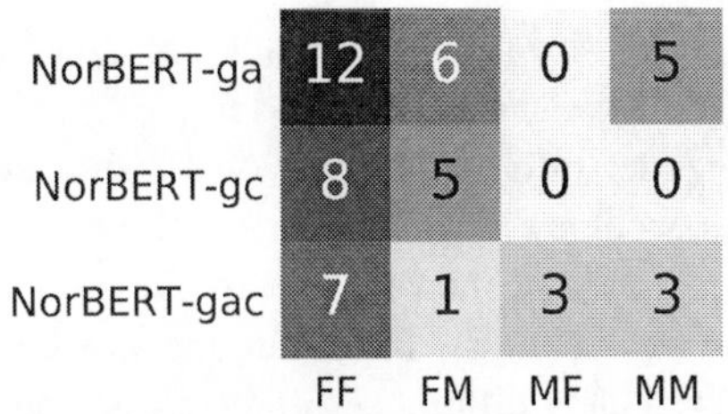

Figure 3: Relative differences of true positives for binary sentiment classification on test compared to their baseline *NorBERT–none*. Darker colors represent more correct predictions than the baseline.

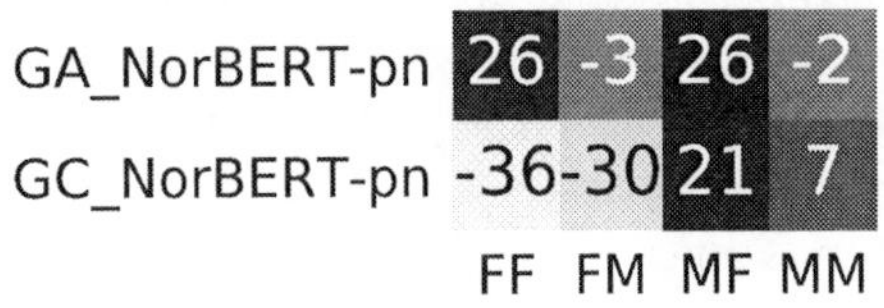

Figure 4: Relative differences of true positives for binary authors and critic gender classification on test compared to their relative baselines *NorBERT–none*.

classification.

For the author gender classification task, as can be seen in Figure 4, having extra information about the polarity of the review helps the model *NorBERT–pn* (*GA_NorBERT–pn*) to better predict the gender of the author if she's a female. This again is compared to the task specific baseline *NorBERT–none*. It also seems that this model makes a few more mistakes than the baseline when it comes to the author being a male. For gender classification of the critics, adding metadata information seems to negatively affect the model's ability to identify female critics. The model *NorBERT–pn* (*GC_NorBERT–pn*) is more accurate when it comes to identifying the gender of male critics compared to the baseline, achieving 21 and 7 F_1 points more than the baseline on respectively *MF* and *MM*.

This corroborates our previous observations, that adding metadata information about the polarity of reviews aids the identification of female authors for author gender classifiers. While for critic gender classification it fails at identifying female critics, but is accurate in identifying males.

8 Conclusion

In this work, we have investigated the effect of adding information about the gender of critics and book authors when classifying the polarity of book reviews, and the polarity of the reviews when classifying the genders of authors and critics. Using a document-level classifier on top of a recently released Norwegian BERT-model, we have shown that gender-informed models obtain substantially higher accuracy, and that polarity-informed models obtain higher accuracy when classifying the gender of the book authors. In further analysis, we have observed clear differences in the classification results for male/female authors/critics. Specifically, we demonstrated that adding to NorBERT information about the genders of critics and book authors influences a binary sentiment classification task by being more accurate in predicting positive reviews for female authors.We have also shown that using polarity information helps the identification of female authors, but seems to greatly hurt the identification of female critics. Some directions for future work include quantifying the bias in the original NorBERT model. As our experiments showed, using the baseline model with only NorBERT and no metadata achieves good results, and we therefore plan to evaluate the existing biases in NorBERT.

Acknowledgments

All of our experiments were run on resources provided by UNINETT Sigma2 of the Norwegian National Infrastructure for High Performance Computing and Data Storage, under the NeIC-NLPL umbrella.

References

Marion Bartl, Malvina Nissim, and Albert Gatt. 2020. Unmasking contextual stereotypes: Measuring and mitigating BERT's gender bias. In *Proceedings of the Second Workshop on Gender Bias in Natural Language Processing*, pages 1–16, Barcelona, Spain (Online). Association for Computational Linguistics.

Christine Basta, Marta R. Costa-jussà, and Noe Casas. 2019. Evaluating the underlying gender bias in contextualized word embeddings. In *Proceedings of the First Workshop on Gender Bias in Natural Language Processing*, pages 33–39, Florence, Italy. Association for Computational Linguistics.

Jayadev Bhaskaran and Isha Bhallamudi. 2019. Good secretaries, bad truck drivers? occupational gender stereotypes in sentiment analysis. In *Proceedings of the First Workshop on Gender Bias in Natural Language Processing*, pages 62–68, Florence, Italy. Association for Computational Linguistics.

Su Lin Blodgett, Solon Barocas, Hal Daumé III, and Hanna Wallach. 2020. Language (technology) is power: A critical survey of "bias" in NLP. In *Proceedings of the 58th Annual Meeting of the Association for Computational Linguistics*, pages 5454–5476, Online. Association for Computational Linguistics.

Tolga Bolukbasi, Kai-Wei Chang, James Y Zou, Venkatesh Saligrama, and Adam T Kalai. 2016. Man is to computer programmer as woman is to homemaker? debiasing word embeddings. In *Advances in neural information processing systems*, pages 4349–4357.

Peter Bourgonje and Manfred Stede. 2020. Exploiting a lexical resource for discourse connective disambiguation in German. In *Proceedings of the 28th International Conference on Computational Linguistics*, pages 5737–5748, Barcelona, Spain (Online). International Committee on Computational Linguistics.

Qian Chen, Xiaodan Zhu, Zhen-Hua Ling, Diana Inkpen, and Si Wei. 2018. Neural natural language inference models enhanced with external knowledge. In *Proceedings of the 56th Annual Meeting of the Association for Computational Linguistics (Volume 1: Long Papers)*, pages 2406–2417, Melbourne, Australia. Association for Computational Linguistics.

Marta R. Costa-jussà and Adrià de Jorge. 2020. Fine-tuning neural machine translation on gender-balanced datasets. In *Proceedings of the Second Workshop on Gender Bias in Natural Language Processing*, pages 26–34, Barcelona, Spain (Online). Association for Computational Linguistics.

Marta R. Costa-jussà, Pau Li Lin, and Cristina España-Bonet. 2020. GeBioToolkit: Automatic extraction of gender-balanced multilingual corpus of Wikipedia biographies. In *Proceedings of the 12th Language Resources and Evaluation Conference*, pages 4081–4088, Marseille, France. European Language Resources Association.

Jacob Devlin, Ming-Wei Chang, Kenton Lee, and Kristina Toutanova. 2019. BERT: Pre-training of deep bidirectional transformers for language understanding. In *Proceedings of the 2019 Conference of the North American Chapter of the Association for Computational Linguistics: Human Language Technologies, Volume 1 (Long and Short Papers)*, pages 4171–4186, Minneapolis, Minnesota. Association for Computational Linguistics.

Joel Escudé Font and Marta R. Costa-jussà. 2019. Equalizing gender bias in neural machine translation with word embeddings techniques. In *Proceedings of the First Workshop on Gender Bias in Natural Language Processing*, pages 147–154, Florence, Italy. Association for Computational Linguistics.

Scott Friedman, Sonja Schmer-Galunder, Anthony Chen, and Jeffrey Rye. 2019. Relating word embedding gender biases to gender gaps: A cross-cultural analysis. In *Proceedings of the First Workshop on*

Gender Bias in Natural Language Processing, pages 18–24, Florence, Italy. Association for Computational Linguistics.

Nikhil Garg, Londa Schiebinger, Dan Jurafsky, and James Zou. 2018. Word embeddings quantify 100 years of gender and ethnic stereotypes. *Proceedings of the National Academy of Sciences*, 115(16):E3635–E3644.

Aparna Garimella and Rada Mihalcea. 2016. Zooming in on gender differences in social media. In *Proceedings of the Workshop on Computational Modeling of People's Opinions, Personality, and Emotions in Social Media (PEOPLES)*, pages 1–10, Osaka, Japan. The COLING 2016 Organizing Committee.

Dirk Hovy. 2015. Demographic factors improve classification performance. In *Proceedings of the 53rd Annual Meeting of the Association for Computational Linguistics and the 7th International Joint Conference on Natural Language Processing (Volume 1: Long Papers)*, pages 752–762, Beijing, China. Association for Computational Linguistics.

Alexander Miserlis Hoyle, Lawrence Wolf-Sonkin, Hanna Wallach, Isabelle Augenstein, and Ryan Cotterell. 2019. Unsupervised discovery of gendered language through latent-variable modeling. In *Proceedings of the 57th Annual Meeting of the Association for Computational Linguistics*, pages 1706–1716, Florence, Italy. Association for Computational Linguistics.

Masahiro Kaneko and Danushka Bollegala. 2019. Gender-preserving debiasing for pre-trained word embeddings. In *Proceedings of the 57th Annual Meeting of the Association for Computational Linguistics*, pages 1641–1650, Florence, Italy. Association for Computational Linguistics.

Svetlana Kiritchenko and Saif Mohammad. 2018. Examining gender and race bias in two hundred sentiment analysis systems. In *Proceedings of the Seventh Joint Conference on Lexical and Computational Semantics*, pages 43–53, New Orleans, Louisiana. Association for Computational Linguistics.

Keita Kurita, Nidhi Vyas, Ayush Pareek, Alan W Black, and Yulia Tsvetkov. 2019. Measuring bias in contextualized word representations. In *Proceedings of the First Workshop on Gender Bias in Natural Language Processing*, pages 166–172, Florence, Italy. Association for Computational Linguistics.

Andrey Kutuzov, Jeremy Barnes, Erik Velldal, Lilja Øvrelid, and Stephan Oepen. 2021. Large-scale contextualised language modelling for norwegian. In *Proceedings of the 23rd Nordic Conference on Computational Linguistics (NoDaLiDa 2021)*.

Ilya Loshchilov and Frank Hutter. 2019. Decoupled weight decay regularization. In *International Conference on Learning Representations*.

Andrea Madotto, Chien-Sheng Wu, and Pascale Fung. 2018. Mem2Seq: Effectively incorporating knowledge bases into end-to-end task-oriented dialog systems. In *Proceedings of the 56th Annual Meeting of the Association for Computational Linguistics (Volume 1: Long Papers)*, pages 1468–1478, Melbourne, Australia. Association for Computational Linguistics.

Rowan Hall Maudslay, Hila Gonen, Ryan Cotterell, and Simone Teufel. 2019. It's all in the name: Mitigating gender bias with name-based counterfactual data substitution. In *Proceedings of the 2019 Conference on Empirical Methods in Natural Language Processing and the 9th International Joint Conference on Natural Language Processing*, pages 5267–5275, Hong Kong, China. Association for Computational Linguistics.

Malte Ostendorff, Peter Bourgonje, Maria Berger, Julian Moreno-Schneider, Georg Rehm, and Bela Gipp. 2019. Enriching bert with knowledge graph embeddings for document classification. *arXiv preprint arXiv:1909.08402*.

Nicole Peinelt, Dong Nguyen, and Maria Liakata. 2020. tBERT: Topic models and BERT joining forces for semantic similarity detection. In *Proceedings of the 58th Annual Meeting of the Association for Computational Linguistics*, pages 7047–7055, Online. Association for Computational Linguistics.

Alexandra Schofield and Leo Mehr. 2016. Gender-distinguishing features in film dialogue. In *Proceedings of the Fifth Workshop on Computational Linguistics for Literature*, pages 32–39, San Diego, California, USA. Association for Computational Linguistics.

Chi Sun, Xipeng Qiu, Yige Xu, and Xuanjing Huang. 2020. How to fine-tune bert for text classification?

Masashi Takeshita, Yuki Katsumata, Rafal Rzepka, and Kenji Araki. 2020. Can existing methods debias languages other than English? first attempt to analyze and mitigate Japanese word embeddings. In *Proceedings of the Second Workshop on Gender Bias in Natural Language Processing*, pages 44–55, Barcelona, Spain (Online). Association for Computational Linguistics.

Samia Touileb, Lilja Øvrelid, and Erik Velldal. 2020. Gender and sentiment, critics and authors: a dataset of Norwegian book reviews. In *Proceedings of the Second Workshop on Gender Bias in Natural Language Processing*, pages 125–138, Barcelona, Spain (Online). Association for Computational Linguistics.

Erik Velldal, Lilja Øvrelid, Cathrine Stadsnes Eivind Alexander Bergem, Samia Touileb, and Fredrik Jørgensen. 2018. NoReC: The Norwegian Review Corpus. In *Proceedings of the 11th edition of the Language Resources and Evaluation Conference*, pages 4186–4191, Miyazaki, Japan.

Poorya Zaremoodi, Wray Buntine, and Gholamreza Haffari. 2018. Adaptive knowledge sharing in multi-task learning: Improving low-resource neural machine translation. In *Proceedings of the 56th Annual Meeting of the Association for Computational Linguistics (Volume 2: Short Papers)*, pages 656–661, Melbourne, Australia. Association for Computational Linguistics.

Zhengyan Zhang, Xu Han, Zhiyuan Liu, Xin Jiang, Maosong Sun, and Qun Liu. 2019. ERNIE: Enhanced language representation with informative entities. In *Proceedings of the 57th Annual Meeting of the Association for Computational Linguistics*, pages 1441–1451, Florence, Italy. Association for Computational Linguistics.

Jieyu Zhao, Subhabrata Mukherjee, Saghar Hosseini, Kai-Wei Chang, and Ahmed Hassan Awadallah. 2020. Gender bias in multilingual embeddings and cross-lingual transfer. In *Proceedings of the 58th Annual Meeting of the Association for Computational Linguistics*, pages 2896–2907, Online. Association for Computational Linguistics.

Jieyu Zhao, Yichao Zhou, Zeyu Li, Wei Wang, and Kai-Wei Chang. 2018. Learning gender-neutral word embeddings. In *Proceedings of the 2018 Conference on Empirical Methods in Natural Language Processing*, pages 4847–4853, Brussels, Belgium. Association for Computational Linguistics.

Ran Zmigrod, Sabrina J. Mielke, Hanna Wallach, and Ryan Cotterell. 2019. Counterfactual data augmentation for mitigating gender stereotypes in languages with rich morphology. In *Proceedings of the 57th Annual Meeting of the Association for Computational Linguistics*, pages 1651–1661, Florence, Italy. Association for Computational Linguistics.

Assessing Gender Bias in Wikipedia: Inequalities in Article Titles

Agnieszka Falenska and **Özlem Çetinoğlu**
Institute for Natural Language Processing
University of Stuttgart
{falenska,ozlem}@ims.uni-stuttgart.de

Abstract

Potential gender biases existing in Wikipedia's content can contribute to biased behaviors in a variety of downstream NLP systems. Yet, efforts in understanding what inequalities in portraying women and men occur in Wikipedia focused so far only on *biographies*, leaving open the question of how often such harmful patterns occur in other topics. In this paper, we investigate gender-related asymmetries in Wikipedia titles from *all domains*. We assess that for only half of gender-related articles, i.e., articles with words such as *women* or *male* in their titles, symmetrical counterparts describing the same concept for the other gender (and clearly stating it in their titles) exist. Among the remaining imbalanced cases, the vast majority of articles concern sports- and social-related issues. We provide insights on how such asymmetries can influence other Wikipedia components and propose steps towards reducing the frequency of observed patterns.

Bias statement Inequalities in how men and women are represented in Wikipedia titles can be captured by NLP models and translate into biased behaviors creating *representational harms* (Blodgett et al., 2020). For example, if by default Wikipedia articles about national sports teams are about male teams, then a search engine might assume that a prototypical sportsperson is a man. Such a system when asked about *famous volleyball players* might exhibit recognition bias and return no women. Similarly, if Wikipedia provides special articles listing *women photographers* next to *photographers*, then an automatic knowledge extractor trained on such data might learn and propagate stereotypical generalizations that women within these occupations are an exception and should hold special qualities. Our work limits itself to binary gender values in extracting gender bias patterns from Wikipedia titles due to data scarcity. We acknowledge that not incorporating other values into our analysis indirectly causes recognition bias against non-binary people.

1 Introduction

Gender bias can be defined as a systematic preference or discrimination against people of a particular gender (Friedman and Nissenbaum, 1996). NLP systems that exhibit such biased behavior can perform better for the favored gender, e.g., speech recognizers that achieve higher accuracy for male voices (Tatman, 2017), or reinforce harmful stereotypes, e.g., social media platforms that misgender LGBT+ community members (Villaronga et al., 2021).[1]

Biased behaviors have (in-)direct origins in statistical patterns occurring in data that the NLP models are trained on (Sun et al., 2019). Such patterns contribute to different types of biases, such as selection bias that comes with the gold-standard annotated resources, or semantic bias related to the information encoded in pre-trained word embeddings. As noted by Shah et al. (2020), understanding the origins of observed biases is crucial in developing countermeasures for them. As a consequence, diagnosing what type of biases occur in the primary training data is an important initial step in this process.

Wikipedia is one of the largest and most commonly used sources of training data for NLP models: it serves as unannotated data for pre-training word representations (Devlin et al., 2019), a textual source for annotated corpora (Webster et al., 2019), or treebanks (de Kok, 2014; Zeldes, 2017). Wikipedia is also a community-based effort created by a predominantly male group of editors (Lam et al., 2011; Collier and Bear, 2012). This homogene-

[1]We refer to Sun et al. (2019) for fine-grained categorization and more examples of harms and biases in NLP tasks.

Proceedings of the 3rd Workshop on Gender Bias in Natural Language Processing, pages 75–85
August 5, 2021.

ity of Wikipedia authors constantly raises the question of possible *inequalities in ways that people of different genders are represented in Wikipedia articles* (Callahan and Herring, 2011; Reagle and Rhue, 2011; Wagner et al., 2015; Konieczny and Klein, 2018; Schmahl et al., 2020, among others). For example, Wagner et al. (2015) analyzed articles about notable men and women and observed systemic lexical and structural asymmetries, i.e., articles about women contain more family- and gender-related words, and more hyperlinks to articles about men than the other way around. In their following analysis, Wagner et al. (2016) showed that gender inequalities can be observed also on other dimensions, e.g., women have to be more notable to have their biographies than men. These patterns occurring in Wikipedia have been shown to directly influence NLP models, such as word embeddings (Schmahl et al., 2020) or relation extraction (Gaut et al., 2020).

All the above-mentioned studies focus on diagnosing gender bias in *biographies*. Biographies are also the main focus of the Wikipedia community when it comes to mitigating the content gender gap. For example, the project *Women in Red*[2] aims at increasing the number of female biographies. However, as pointed out by Criado Perez (2019, p. 13), inequalities in the way that women and men are portrayed in Wikipedia are present also in other domains. For example, articles about national sports teams such as *England women's national football team* and *England national football team* commonly omit the word *men's* in titles of men's teams, presenting them as if they are the default concept. Yet, a computational method to find such gender-related asymmetries on a bigger scale and understanding of how often they occur in Wikipedia articles are missing.

In this paper, we make an initial step in assessing *gender-related inequalities in Wikipedia titles*. We design a simple three-step heuristic for filtering articles that describe specific concepts and topics, i.e., the above-mentioned *English football team*, in an unbalanced way (Section 2). We apply the proposed method to four Wikipedia editions: Turkish, English, German, and Polish, and find coherent patterns across all four languages (Section 3). Only half of the articles that use gender-indicating words such as *men's* or *female* in their titles have their symmetrical counterparts describing the same concept for the other gender. Among the remaining imbalanced cases, the vast majority either describe male-related concepts as generic or represent women as an exception within a more general topic. We discuss the possible harmful effect of the diagnosed title inequalities on other Wikipedia components, such as cross-lingual hyperlinks and NLP models that use them (Section 4). Finally, we propose steps towards reducing the frequency of discovered patterns (Section 5).

2 Methodology

Our main goal is to recognize topics and concepts that are described in Wikipedia asymmetrically, i.e., with respect to only one gender. Since finding all possible Wikipedia inequalities is an immense challenge, in this paper, we focus on *article titles*. In Section 4, we provide additional insights on other Wikipedia components that have a direct connection to titles thus should be investigated further in the future.

We design a simple three-step methodology for spotting Wikipedia inequalities in titles, which is presented in Figure 1. Below we describe each of the steps in more detail, but first, explain the selection of languages used for evaluation.

Languages We process four languages: Turkish, English, German, Polish (in the order of gender marking in the language) (Stahlberg et al., 2007; Hellinger and Bussmann, 2001, 2003).

German and Polish are Germanic and Slavic languages respectively and both have grammatical gender, though gender marking is more prominent in Polish. In these languages, nouns and (third-person) pronouns have grammatical gender. Determiners and attributive adjectives agree with nouns. Reflexive pronouns, however, are not gender-marked. Polish, in addition, has gender agreement in predicative adjectives, and verbs in past and future tenses agree with the gender of the subject. English is a Germanic language that falls under natural gender languages. Almost all nouns are gender-neutral, but third-person personal pronouns are gendered. Turkish is a genderless language from the Turkic language family. There are no gendered nouns or pronouns in principle, exceptions are mostly loanwords (e.g. *aktör* – *aktris*). Having no explicit gender markers makes it harder to observe gender bias linguistically, e.g., approaches using pronouns (Rudinger et al., 2018; Zhao

[2] en.wikipedia.org/wiki/Wikipedia:WikiProject_Women_in_Red

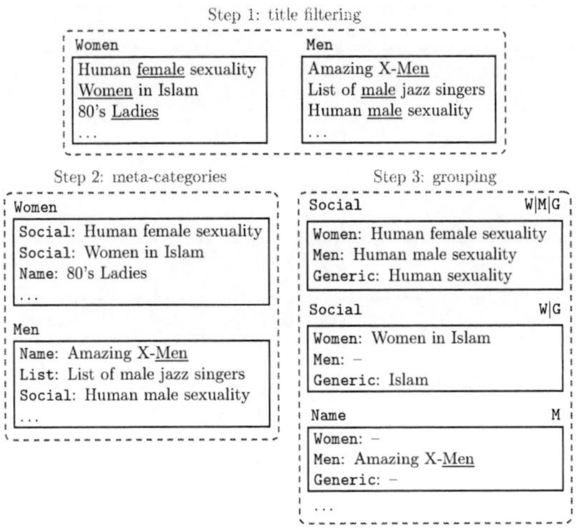

Figure 1: Three-step method used for finding concept-related article tuples.

	Women	Men
English	women, ladies, female, feminine	men, gentlemen male, masculine
German	frauen-, damen-, weiblich, -innen	männer-, herren-männlich
Polish	kobiety, kobiecy, żeński	mężczyźni, męski
Turkish	kadın, kadınlar, bayan, bayanlar	erkek, erkekler

Table 1: Indicators used for filtering gender-related articles. Indicators are mostly words, but also prefixes and suffixes for German.

et al., 2018; Webster et al., 2018) are not applicable to Turkish. Braun (2001) utilizes sociolinguistic tests to demonstrate that Turkish indeed exhibits inherent gender bias that she refers to as *covert gender*.

Step 1: title filtering The first step in Figure 1 consists of filtering all Wikipedia titles that describe a particular topic or concept from a gender-related perspective and dividing them into Men and Women groups. For this, we manually select a list of word indicators, i.e., words such as *men* or *female*, and search for titles that contain at least one of them (underlined words in Figure 1).

Table 1 lists word indicators used for the filtering. We intentionally use plural nouns *women* and *men* and not singular *woman* and *man* for English, German and Polish, since we found that the latter predominantly occur in proper names, such as the movie title *Scent of a Woman* or the island *Isle of Man*.[3] Turkish, on the contrary, has both singular and plural forms, and heavily uses the singular form *kadın* which translates to *women's* and *female* in context, as well as the standard *woman* meaning. Moreover, for German, Polish, and Turkish the list in Table 1 is extended with all inflected forms of the presented words.

It is important to note that by filtering the articles only through Men and Women indicators we leave out non-binary genders (Richards et al., 2016) and do not address the non-binary gender biases in this paper. This decision is based on the current Wikipedia coverage that provides very little content on other genders. For example, we find 125 articles with the word *transgender* in the title, compared to 38385 and 34240 for the words *men* and *women*, respectively. Similarly, according to the *Denelezh tool*[4] only 0.066% biographies in the English Wikipedia are about people of other genders, compared to 18.6% of female biographies.

Step 2: meta-categories In the next step, we assign one meta-category to all the filtered articles. We use five meta-categories that represent the best the majority of gender-related articles: Sports, for articles about sports teams or events, Lists, for listings of particular people or organizations, Social, for articles related to history, awards, gender issues, etc., Names, for proper names, i.e., articles about titles of movies, books, names of universities, etc., and Other, for articles that did not fit into any other meta-category.

The assignment of meta-categories is based on a list of manually selected keywords[5] and takes into consideration the titles of the articles as well as their Wikipedia categories (see Figure 3 and Section 4 for an example Wikipedia page, categories, and redirections).

Step 3: grouping In the final step, we group articles into *concept-related tuples*. Each tuple can be built from three articles: Women, Men, and Generic (notice in Figure 1 that some articles in tuples might be missing).

First, we search for pairs of Men and Women articles that describe the same concept. We determine this by simply removing the gender-related

[3]For example, in the English Wikipedia 81% of titles containing the word *woman* and 71% with the word *man* received the meta-category Names.

[4]denelezh.wmcloud.org/

[5]All the manually-designed filters and source code are available for download on the first author's website and under the address https://github.com/AgnieszkaFalenska/GeBNLP2021.

indicators and pairing articles with the same remaining titles, e.g., *Human ~~female~~ sexuality* and *Human ~~male~~ sexuality*. To limit the number of incorrect tuples, we pair only articles that belong to the same meta-category and completely leave out the ones from the Names group.

Second, we fill the collected tuples with Generic articles using the same approach as in the previous step, i.e., removing gender-related indicators and pairing titles with the same remaining words (e.g., title *Human sexuality* for the example above). However, to increase the coverage at this stage we apply few additional heuristics. Firstly, we search for Generic articles across all Wikipedia titles as well as redirections. Secondly, for languages with inflection, we lemmatize titles to be able to find mappings between such titles as *Kobiety w Islamie (Women in Islam* [case:loc]*)* and *Islam (Islam* [case:nom]*)*.[6] Finally, we apply language-specific and manually designed rules to find mappings between titles with specific noun phrases. For example, in the Polish title above we additionally remove the word *w (in)* to be able to find the pairing with the Generic title *Islam*.

Result The methodology described above provides a list of concept-related tuples of a maximum of three articles. Each of them has assigned one meta-category (Sports, Lists, Social, Names, or Other) and falls into one of six groups: W|M|G (if all three articles are present), W|M (if no Generic article was found), W|G and M|G (if no Men or Women article was found), and W and M (for tuples with only either Women or Men present).

3 Inequalities in Titles

In this section, we apply the described methodology to four Wikipedia editions: English, German, Polish, and Turkish.[7] First, we look at statistics of filtered articles and tuples to provide insights on the coverage of the proposed method (Section 3.1). Then, we detect types of inequalities occurring in titles (Section 3.2) and finally assess which concepts and topics they relate to the most (Section 3.3).

3.1 Statistics

Gender-related articles Table 2 provides the frequency of filtered gender-related articles, i.e.,

	English	German	Polish	Turkish
Women	36241	8679	5568	2400
Men	39069	6356	7994	1585
TOTAL	75310	15035	13562	3985
%WIKIPEDIA	1.23%	0.67%	0.98%	1.04%

Table 2: The frequency of gender-related articles.

	English	German	Polish	Turkish
W|M|G	129	333	128	15
W|M	18033	3480	3712	896
W|G	4438	1895	407	161
M|G	155	52	10	4
W	13641	2971	1321	1328
M	20752	2491	4144	670
TOTAL	57148	11222	9722	3074

Table 3: The frequency of concept-related tuples.

the result of the first step of the method presented in Figure 1. Our simple filtering heuristic finds between 75k and 4k articles, depending on the size of the Wikipedia that it starts from. In three out of four cases this constitutes around 1% of all the articles. German is an outlier here, with only 0.67% of the whole Wikipedia. One of the reasons might be the high frequency of compounds in German. Although we introduce additional heuristics for this language that look at prefixes of words, such as *männer-* in *Männerorchester (Men's orchestra)*, we do not find cases where the gender-related indicator appears in the middle of the word, e.g., *frauen-* in *Deutscher Landfrauenverband (German Rural Women's Association)* or *männer* in *Weltmännertag (Men's World Day)*.

Another reason for German being an outlier might be the fact that it is a gender-marking language. Female-related titles, such as *Liste von Dramatikerinnen (List of female dramatists)* do not contain a separate gender-indicator such as the word *female* in the English translation. Instead, the gender of the subject is indicated by the suffix *-innen*. To cover such cases, we add this suffix to our gender-indicators, however, we accompany it with additional strong filtering rules to not take titles such as *Webspinnen (Spiders)* or *Drei Finnen (Three Finns)* as instances of the Women group.[8]

[6]Lemmatization with spacy v.3.0 (spacy.io/).

[7]Wikipedia IDs: English (2021-03-20, 6144966 non-disambiguation articles), German (2021-03-01, 2241506 articles), Polish (2021-03-01, 1376989 articles), Turkish (2021-03-20, 381908 articles).

[8]Polish is also a gender-marking language. The difference might be that in Polish it is still common to use masculine professions when referring to women, even if feminine equivalents exist (Sosnowski and Satoła-Staśkowiak, 2019).

Article tuples Table 3 provides statistics for the final step of our exploration method, i.e. frequency of concept-related article tuples. The total number of discovered tuples is proportional to the initial Wikipedia sizes, ranging from 3k for Turkish up to 57k instances for English. Interestingly, only around one-third of them belongs to the symmetrical groups `W|M|G` and `W|M`, i.e., tuples that cover both `Women` and `Men` perspectives on the concept or topic in question. Moreover, these tuples cover only around half of all the filtered gender-related articles counted in Table 2 (between 46% for Turkish and 57% for Polish). When it comes to the asymmetrical `W|G` and `M|G` groups the pattern is clear across all the languages – these tuples are much more frequent for `Women`, e.g., 4438 vs. only 155 cases for English. Finally, for the last two groups `M` and `W` no clear pattern can be noticed at this stage; for two out of four languages `M` tuples are more frequent than `W`.

3.2 Types of Title Inequalities

Table 4 presents examples of English articles that fell into each of the six groups and their meta-categories. Interestingly, our filtering method was able to find examples not only belonging to all the groups but also all the meta-categories (at this stage we leave out `Other` articles since they concern a variety of unrelated topics). We now investigate deeper each of the examples to see if we can notice any recurring patterns among them. We mark all discovered inequalities in red in Table 4.

`W|M|G` and `W|M` All articles that belong to these two groups depict how symmetrical gender-related content looks like. In both cases, there are separate Wikipedia articles that describe women and men-related issues regarding the topic under question, such as *human sexuality* or *detective characters*. When necessary, an additional general article exists that describes the topic from a broader perspective. We mark all these examples in green.

`W|G` and `M|G` The next two groups show examples of inequalities among Wikipedia titles. We can notice that the source of the problem across the three meta-categories is different.

In the `Sports` and `Lists` meta-categories, the observed inequalities are a direct result of the decisions of Wikipedia editors. The `Sports` article *Finland national football team* is in fact an article about men's team. Similarly, the article *Town Challenge Cup* refers to a women's event. In both cases, the general titles are missing information about the gender of the participants, and as a result, suggest that the article is about a general concept. In the previous section we found that the male generalization `W|G` is much more frequent, which can be attributed to the *male generic bias*, i.e., the phenomenon in which the prototypical human is commonly assumed to be male (Silveira, 1980).

When it comes to the `Lists` meta-category, a slightly different type of inequality can be noticed. The article *List of Albanian writers* is in fact a proper general article, that covers both female and male writers. However, since the male counterpart does not exist, it makes the concept of *female writer* an exception in the general topic of *writers*. This pattern can be seen as a case of a more implicit gender bias, in which men and women are commonly presented with different levels of *linguistic abstraction* (Menegatti and Rubini, 2017).

Finally, the examples in `Social` group are strongly related to the *societal and biological asymmetries* that apply to people of different genders, such as history or health-related factors.

`W` and `M` Not all tuples belonging to these two groups are examples of title inequalities. `Names` consists of proper names that we treat from the beginning as symmetrical on their own and do not pair with other articles. `Sports` contains articles that similarly to `Names` refer to specific concepts, i.e., names of teams (*Ulster Senior League (men's hockey)*) or events that were held only for men or women (*Danish Ladies Masters*). Therefore, we mark examples that belong to these two meta-categories in green in Table 4.

On the contrary, articles from `Lists` and `Social` meta-categories represent examples of asymmetrical Wikipedia content. Similar to the described above articles from `W|G` and `M|G`, lack of male counterpart for the title *List of Danish women photographers* and female one for *List of male jazz singers* can be attributed to the decisions of the editors. Likewise, the inequalities in `Social` meta-category can be explained by historical and societal aspects.

3.3 Title Inequalities and Meta-Categories

Now that we have established what types of inequalities we can find in Wikipedia titles we investigate how frequent they are. We take only instances of asymmetrical tuples, i.e., only tuples that belong to the groups marked in red in Table 4, and plot their

		Women	Men	Generic
W | M | G	Sports	U Sports women's soccer	U Sports men's soccer	U Sports soccer
	Lists	List of women's magazines	List of men's magazines	List of magazines
	Social	Human female sexuality	Human male sexuality	Human sexuality
W | M	Sports	Argentina women's national softball team	Argentina men's national softball team	–
	Lists	List of female detective characters	List of male detective characters	–
	Social	Bollywood Movie Award – Best Female Debut	Bollywood Movie Award – Best Male Debut	–
W | G	Sports	Finland women's national football team	–	Finland national football team
	Lists	List of Albanian women writers	–	List of Albanian writers
	Social	Women in Islam	–	Islam
M | G	Sports	–	Town Challenge Cup (men)	Town Challenge Cup
	Lists	–	List of Thai representatives at international male beauty pageants	List of Thai representatives at international beauty pageants
	Social	–	Men's health in Australia	Health in Australia
W	Sports	Danish Ladies Masters	–	–
	Lists	List of Danish women photographers	–	–
	Social	Violence against women in Guatemala	–	–
	Names	Four Ladies (TV series)	–	–
M	Sports	–	Ulster Senior League (men's hockey)	–
	Lists	–	List of male jazz singers	–
	Social	–	Male Studies in the Caribbean	–
	Names	–	Anding Men station	–

Table 4: Examples of content-related tuples. We mark in green and red symmetrical and asymmetrical groups, respectively. Names appear only in the last two groups, because proper names are not paired with other articles.

frequency in Figure 2.

Interestingly, the picture is very similar across all the languages (we note that the scales on all four plots are different). Among the asymmetrical cases, the vast majority of tuples include Women articles, i.e., belongs to W | G or W. The largest group across all the languages is W | G and most of the articles that it contains are about sports. These are the titles such as *England women's national football team* and *England national football team* that Criado Perez (2019) pointed out as potential inequalities in how women and men are portrayed in Wikipedia, that inspired our investigation. However, Figure 2 demonstrates that Sports is not the only topic that is asymmetrically covered in Wikipedia. The second most frequent meta-category is Social, especially in the W group, followed by Lists, that although can be noticed for all the groups, are much more frequent for women than for men (cf. W | G vs. M | G and W vs. M). The asymmetrical M titles within the Turkish Wikipedia seem prominent with respect to other languages' distributions (although note that it is only 25 instances). A closer inspection revealed that most cases are award pages that either are worded differently than women's award pages or, although women's awards exist, they are not represented in the Turkish Wikipedia.

4 Beyond Captured Inequalities

Our methodology clearly illustrates that gender bias exists in Wikipedia titles in various patterns. Nevertheless, these patterns do not constitute an exhaustive list; more fine-grained mismatches could be captured if we extend our observations towards asymmetrically named titles and other Wikipedia components.

Before we move on with our observations, we define the structure of a Wikipedia article, exemplified in Figure 3. Aside from the self-explanatory title and content parts, there is a hatnote in some Wikipedia pages that is always placed at the very top of a page and that helps readers distinguish the page they are at, especially after a redirection or visiting a disambiguation page. On the left column

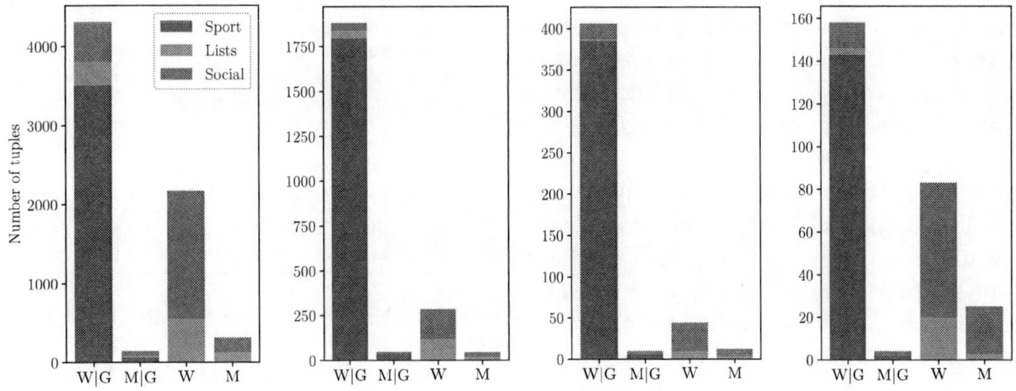

(a) English (b) German (c) Polish (d) Turkish

Figure 2: The frequency of asymmetrical article tuples, i.e., tuples marked in red in Table 4.

of a page, there are interwiki links that connect the page to its versions in other languages. Last but not least, categories are groupings of similar topics. Each page is part of at least one category. To keep category sizes and the number of categories per article manageable, the category structures are hierarchical.

Lexically asymmetric tuples Sometimes it is hard to find concept-related articles because the naming of symmetric concepts hence their Wikipedia titles are not aligned. Articles about the Spanish football league in the English Wikipedia represent such a case. The article about the male league is titled *La Liga*, which is the more commonly known version of the longer name *Campeonato Nacional de Liga de Primera División* (*Division National League Championship*). The women's article, on the other hand, is titled *Primera División (women)*, which is a shorter version of *Primera División de la Liga de Fútbol Femenino*. Our method recognizes the second title as an instance of `Women`, but it is not able to pair it with *La Liga* and the tuple falls into the symmetrical `W (Sports)` group instead of the asymmetrical `W|G` (see Table 4). It is not possible to match these two titles as long as there is a specific hatnote explaining the relationship between these two pages and linking them, neither for human readers nor for automatic systems.

Semantically asymmetric tuples In American collegiate athletics, a common word choice for representing women's teams is adding *lady* to the name of men's teams, e.g. *Statesmen* vs. *Lady Statesmen* of Delta State University (Eitzen and Zinn, 1993; Pelak, 2008). This phenomenon extends to professional sports such as *Professional Golfers' Association* vs. *Ladies Professional Golf Association*. While choosing the word *lady* over *woman* is semantically charged (Lakoff, 1973), both words serve equally for our methodology and capture such article tuples as `W|G` type inequalities.

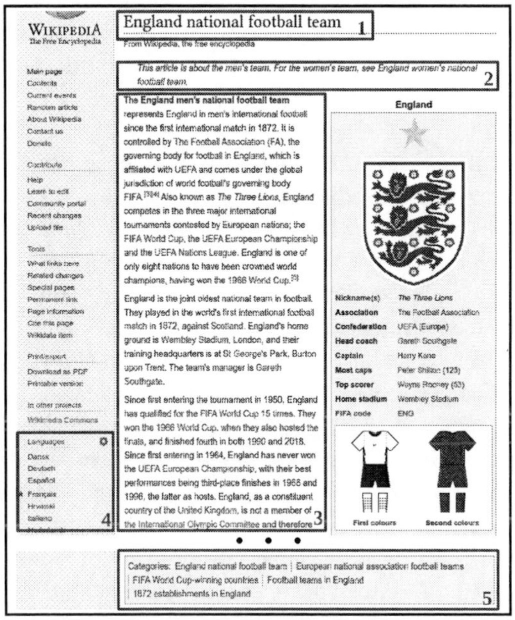

Figure 3: Structure of a Wikipedia article. 1: title, 2: hatnote, 3: content, 4: interwiki links, 5: categories. Example redirections to this article are *England football team* and *English football team*. The page `en.wikipedia.org/wiki/England_national_football_team` was accessed on 2021-04-26.

In Turkish, on the other hand, *lady* is used in the `Sports` category in a different way. The corresponding word *bayan* is used as an euphemism for *kadın* (*woman*), as the latter is considered impolite or has a sexual connotation from a sexist perspective (Arpınar-Avşar et al., 2016). This general use in language is carried over to national federations of Olympic sports. Arpınar-Avşar et al. (2016) report that 27 out of 34 federations use *bayan* to refer to female athletes as of 2016. It is not only in result sections or in regulations, but also in league and team names where male counterparts employ *erkek* (*man*). In terms of automatic processing, the problem is two-way. If we consider, for instance, *Erkekler Ligi* vs *Bayanlar Ligi* (*Men's League* vs. *Ladies' League*) as a concept-related pair, then seemingly there is symmetry; such tuples fall into the symmetric `W | M` group. If we do not pair these two titles, then they belong in `M` and `W` groups respectively, and as `Sports` articles are not treated as inequalities. In both cases, we do not capture the implicit semantic bias behind these two titles, i.e., bias related to historical and societal factors.

Title-content mismatch To remove inequalities in Wikipedia, editors commonly edit `Generic` titles so that they become `Men` titles (e.g. *National Team* $\rightarrow$ *Men's National Team*). An additional approach is to redirect `Generic` titles to `Men` titles to facilitate search. Yet, if this procedure is done uncarefully and the content is not edited accordingly, it can create pages with title-content mismatch. For instance, searching for *Türkiye Millî Voleybol Takımı* (*Turkey National Volleyball Team*) redirects to *Türkiye Erkek Millî Voleybol Takımı* (*Turkey Men's National Volleyball Team*). Since the `Women` article also exists, the tuple belongs to the `W | M` group thanks to editors; the titles are symmetrical. However, the content still uses the `Generic` reference: *"Türkiye Millî Voleybol Takımı ... Türkiye'yi uluslararası erkek voleybol karşılaşmalarında temsil eden takımdır."* (*"Turkey National Volleyball Team ... is the team representing Turkey in the international men's volleyball matches."*). Therefore there is a mismatch between the title and content of the page.

Cross-lingual mismatch Interwiki links are beneficial in NLP tasks such as machine translation (Labaka et al., 2016), bilingual dictionary extraction (Tyers and Pienaar, 2008), or multilingual named entity recognition (Kim et al., 2012). When a title in one language is edited after interwiki links are established between languages, it might cause a cross-lingual mismatch. At the time of writing, the pages for the Turkish national basketball teams are

TR:	Türkiye Millî Basketbol Takımı	G+h
DE:	Türkische Basketballnationalmannschaft	
EN:	Turkey Men's National Basketball Team	
FR:	Équipe de Turquie de basket-ball	
AZ:	Türkiyə milli basketbol komandası	G
DU:	Turks basketbalteam	
ES:	Selección de baloncesto de Turquía	
PL:	Reprezentacja Turcji w koszykówce mężczyzn	M
RU:	Мужская сборная Турции по баскетболу	

Table 5: The titles and content properties of the Turkey men's national basketball team in several languages. G+h: no `Men` in title, a hatnote explaining this is a `Men` page; G: no `Men` in title, no hatnote; M: `Men` in title.

a `W | G` tuple: *Türkiye kadın millî basketbol takımı – Türkiye millî basketbol takımı*. The `Generic` title also has the hatnote explaining that although the title is `Generic`, the page is about `Men`, and there is a separate `Women` article. However, interwiki links connect the page to its English counterpart which is titled *Turkey men's national basketball team*, that is, men indicator is explicit only on the English side. The `Generic` to `Men` mapping in titles depicts a cross-lingual mismatch. NLP tasks that would use this pair would fail to extract an exact translation. Following multiple interwiki links shows that approaches vary across languages, as summarized in Table 5. Moreover, cross-lingual asymmetries in this article can be observed not only in its title but also in its content. The English page reads *The Turkey men's national basketball team (Turkish: Türkiye Millî Basketbol Takımı)* ..., causing a `Generic` vs. `Men` inconsistency between English and Turkish names.

Finally, cross-lingual mismatches come also with semantic asymmetries, such as the use of *bayan* (*lady*) instead of *kadın* (*woman*). Interwiki still links them to non-Turkish titles with the word *woman* or its equivalent, causing a translation mistake.

5 Discussion: Towards Debiasing Titles

The types of inequalities that we presented in this paper call for different debiasing measures. Lexically asymmetric tuples can only be paired via mutual hatnotes. In the specific case of *La Liga*, adding *(men)* to the title in parallel to its female counterpart would at least prevent the male generic bias. Title-content mismatches could be avoided if the content could be updated together with the title. Cross-lingual mismatches are the easiest to catch as there are Wiki bots designed for that purpose.[9]

Among meta-categories, debiasing the `Sports` category is seemingly the simplest one. For instance, the Turkish Basketball Federation[10] symmetrically names national basketball teams by explicitly using *kadın* and *erkek* in their titles. The `W|G` inequality comes from Wikipedia editors. Inserting *erkek* to the `Generic` *Türkiye millî basketbol takımı* (and updating the content consequently) would bring balance to this article tuple. However, sometimes the imbalance is actually in the *real world.* The International Cycling Union (UCI)[11] defines both cups and teams as `W|G` tuples, e.g., *UCI Road World Cup* vs. *UCI Women's Road World Cup*, and Wikipedia titles follow suit. After all, it is not *wrong* to take the actual name of a concrete entity. The next step is subject to a debate: Should Wikipedia editors continue to reflect the real world or should they already convert the title to `Men` and keep the existing `Generic` naming, perhaps with a redirection for search purposes?

The `Lists` category with a `W|G` or `M|G` inequality can be balanced by introducing the missing gender-specific articles or going into the complete opposite direction and keeping only the `Generic` page. If the answer to this question is to create gender-specific pages, the non-binary gender values come into the picture to be represented in separate `Lists` pages. Such lists exist, e.g. *List of transgender political office-holders*, yet, they are few. Wikipedia's metadata system facilitates such a listing by providing non-binary values for annotating biographies; currently, it is a set of seven: male, female, non-binary, intersex, transgender female, transgender male, agender.[12] However, page specification raises more questions: How about the people who do not want to be identified with one of the values, where should they be placed?

A substantial amount of the `W` only tuples in the `Social` category consists of women's rights movements. 10% of the `Social` titles in the English Wikipedia contains the words *suffrage* or *rights.* While `W` seems to be an imbalanced category by definition, the reason behind it is not that women are dominating the scene. On the contrary, it shows the reaction to suppression and that women had to fight over rights that should be the default. Similarly, `W|G` tuples such as *Women in Engineering* vs. *Engineering* seem to be biased towards women by definition, yet the urge to discuss such topics separately comes from the complete opposite reason. Men have been considered the 'norm' such that women are a deviating subset.

It is hard to develop an umbrella strategy for debiasing the `Social` category. For some of these titles, the question is whether they should be *debiased* rather than how they could be debiased. In our opinion, for instance suffrage pages, e.g., *Women's suffrage in Alabama* should remain as is, but the `W|G` tuple *Women's Suffrage* vs. *Suffrage* can be extended to a `W|M|G` tuple. At the time of writing, the title *Men's Suffrage* redirects to *Suffrage.* Instead, a separate `Men` page that very briefly explains the historical developments (i.e., why there has been no need to coin an explicit term for men) would be more informative and more in line with Wikipedia's encyclopedic nature.

6 Conclusion

Inequality in male and female Wikipedia biographies has driven a lot of attention in recent years, both from the research community as well as the press.[13] The editors' community is consequently tackling this problem and fighting the gender gap. As recently shown by Schmahl et al. (2020), these efforts pay off and not only more biographies about women are being added, but also NLP models such as word embeddings trained on Wikipedia articles are exhibiting less stereotypical biases.

In this paper, we aimed at raising awareness that gender inequalities in Wikipedia extend beyond biographies. Women and men are systematically represented in article titles in a different way, especially in such domains as sports and social issues. We showed that such inequalities can be computationally assessed by investigating asymmetrical tuples, i.e., titles that describe a particular topic or concept for only one gender.

The topics we argue here by no means cover all possible inequalities in Wikipedia titles, let alone inequalities in its overall components. Yet, even a simple but competent, systematic approach is strong enough to demonstrate the existing gender bias. With this paper, we hope to draw attention to such bias and open possible solutions to discussion.

[9] meta.wikimedia.org/wiki/Interwiki_bot

[10] www.tbf.org.tr

[11] www.uci.org

[12] P21 'sex or gender' property, www.wikidata.org/wiki/Property:P21

[13] See en.wikipedia.org/wiki/Wikipedia:WikiProject_Women_in_Red/About_us for a list of recent news articles regarding this subject.

Acknowledgements

We thank Pınar Arpınar-Avşar for pointing out real-world sport title inequalities. The second author is funded by DFG via project CE 326/1-1 "Computational Structural Analysis of German-Turkish Code-Switching" (SAGT).

References

Pınar Arpınar-Avşar, Serkan Girgin, and Nefise Bulgu. 2016. Lady or woman? The debate on lexical choice for describing females in sport in the Turkish language. *International Review for the Sociology of Sport*, 51(2):178–200.

Su Lin Blodgett, Solon Barocas, Hal Daumé III, and Hanna Wallach. 2020. Language (Technology) is Power: A Critical Survey of "Bias" in NLP. In *Proceedings of the 58th Annual Meeting of the Association for Computational Linguistics*, pages 5454–5476, Online. Association for Computational Linguistics.

Friederike Braun. 2001. The communication of gender in Turkish. *Gender across languages: The linguistic representation of women and men*, 1:283–310.

Ewa S. Callahan and Susan C. Herring. 2011. Cultural Bias in Wikipedia Content on Famous Persons. *Journal of the American society for information science and technology*, 62(10):1899–1915.

Benjamin Collier and Julia Bear. 2012. Conflict, Confidence, or Criticism: An Empirical Examination of the Gender Gap in Wikipedia Contributions. In *CSCW '12 Computer Supported Cooperative Work, Seattle, WA, USA, February 11-15, 2012*, pages 383–392. ACM.

Caroline Criado Perez. 2019. *Invisible women: Exposing data bias in a world designed for men*. Random House.

Jacob Devlin, Ming-Wei Chang, Kenton Lee, and Kristina Toutanova. 2019. BERT: Pre-training of Deep Bidirectional Transformers for Language Understanding. In *Proceedings of the 2019 Conference of the North American Chapter of the Association for Computational Linguistics: Human Language Technologies, Volume 1 (Long and Short Papers)*, pages 4171–4186, Minneapolis, Minnesota. Association for Computational Linguistics.

D. Stanley Eitzen and Maxine Baca Zinn. 1993. The Sexist Naming of Collegiate Athletic Teams and Resistance to Change. *Journal of Sport and Social Issues*, 17(1):34–41.

Batya Friedman and Helen Nissenbaum. 1996. Bias in Computer Systems. *ACM Trans. Inf. Syst.*, 14(3):330–347.

Andrew Gaut, Tony Sun, Shirlyn Tang, Yuxin Huang, Jing Qian, Mai ElSherief, Jieyu Zhao, Diba Mirza, Elizabeth Belding, Kai-Wei Chang, and William Yang Wang. 2020. Towards Understanding Gender Bias in Relation Extraction. In *Proceedings of the 58th Annual Meeting of the Association for Computational Linguistics*, pages 2943–2953, Online. Association for Computational Linguistics.

M. Hellinger and H. Bussmann. 2001. *Gender Across Languages: The linguistic representation of women and men. Volume 1*. John Benjamins Publishing Co.

M. Hellinger and H. Bussmann. 2003. *Gender Across Languages: The linguistic representation of women and men. Volume 3*. John Benjamins Publishing Co.

Sungchul Kim, Kristina Toutanova, and Hwanjo Yu. 2012. Multilingual Named Entity Recognition using Parallel Data and Metadata from Wikipedia. In *Proceedings of the 50th Annual Meeting of the Association for Computational Linguistics (Volume 1: Long Papers)*, pages 694–702, Jeju Island, Korea. Association for Computational Linguistics.

Daniël de Kok. 2014. TüBa-D/W: a large dependency treebank for German. In *Proceedings of the Thirteenth International Workshop on Treebanks and Linguistic Theories (TLT13)*, page 271.

Piotr Konieczny and Maximilian Klein. 2018. Gender gap through time and space: A journey through Wikipedia biographies via the Wikidata Human Gender Indicator. *New Media Soc.*, 20(12).

Gorka Labaka, Iñaki Alegria, and Kepa Sarasola. 2016. Domain adaptation in MT using titles in Wikipedia as a parallel corpus: Resources and evaluation. In *Proceedings of the Tenth International Conference on Language Resources and Evaluation (LREC'16)*, pages 2209–2213, Portorož, Slovenia. European Language Resources Association (ELRA).

Robin Lakoff. 1973. Language and Woman's Place. *Language in Society*, 2(1):45–79.

Shyong K. Lam, Anuradha Uduwage, Zhenhua Dong, Shilad Sen, David R. Musicant, Loren G. Terveen, and John Riedl. 2011. WP:Clubhouse? An Exploration of Wikipedia's Gender Imbalance. In *Proceedings of the 7th International Symposium on Wikis and Open Collaboration, 2011, Mountain View, CA, USA, October 3-5, 2011*, pages 1–10. ACM.

Michela Menegatti and Monica Rubini. 2017. Gender Bias and Sexism in Language. *Oxford Research Encyclopedia of Communication*.

Cynthia Fabrizio Pelak. 2008. The Relationship Between Sexist Naming Practices and Athletic Opportunities at Colleges and Universities in the Southern United States. *Sociology of Education*, 81(2):189–210.

Joseph Reagle and Lauren Rhue. 2011. Gender bias in Wikipedia and Britannica. *International Journal of Communication*, 5:21.

Christina Richards, Walter Pierre Bouman, Leighton Seal, Meg John Barker, Timo O Nieder, and Guy T'Sjoen. 2016. Non-binary or genderqueer genders. *International Review of Psychiatry*, 28(1):95–102.

Rachel Rudinger, Jason Naradowsky, Brian Leonard, and Benjamin Van Durme. 2018. Gender Bias in Coreference Resolution. In *Proceedings of the 2018 Conference of the North American Chapter of the Association for Computational Linguistics: Human Language Technologies, Volume 2 (Short Papers)*, pages 8–14, New Orleans, Louisiana. Association for Computational Linguistics.

Katja Geertruida Schmahl, Tom Julian Viering, Stavros Makrodimitris, Arman Naseri Jahfari, and Marco Tax, David andj Loog. 2020. Is Wikipedia succeeding in reducing gender bias? assessing changes in gender bias in Wikipedia using word embeddings. In *Proceedings of the Fourth Workshop on Natural Language Processing and Computational Social Science*, pages 94–103, Online. Association for Computational Linguistics.

Deven Santosh Shah, H. Andrew Schwartz, and Dirk Hovy. 2020. Predictive Biases in Natural Language Processing Models: A Conceptual Framework and Overview. In *Proceedings of the 58th Annual Meeting of the Association for Computational Linguistics*, pages 5248–5264, Online. Association for Computational Linguistics.

Jeanette Silveira. 1980. Generic masculine words and thinking. *Women's Studies International Quarterly*, 3(2-3):165–178.

Wojciech Paweł Sosnowski and Joanna Satoła-Staśkowiak. 2019. A contrastive analysis of feminitives in Bulgarian, Polish and Russian. *Cognitive Studies| Études cognitives*, (19).

Dagmar Stahlberg, Friederike Braun, Lisa Irmen, and Sabine Sczesny. 2007. Representation of the sexes in language. *Social communication*, pages 163–187.

Tony Sun, Andrew Gaut, Shirlyn Tang, Yuxin Huang, Mai ElSherief, Jieyu Zhao, Diba Mirza, Elizabeth Belding, Kai-Wei Chang, and William Yang Wang. 2019. Mitigating Gender Bias in Natural Language Processing: Literature Review. In *Proceedings of the 57th Annual Meeting of the Association for Computational Linguistics*, pages 1630–1640, Florence, Italy. Association for Computational Linguistics.

Rachael Tatman. 2017. Gender and Dialect Bias in YouTube's Automatic Captions. In *Proceedings of the First ACL Workshop on Ethics in Natural Language Processing*, pages 53–59, Valencia, Spain. Association for Computational Linguistics.

Francis M Tyers and Jacques A Pienaar. 2008. Extracting bilingual word pairs from Wikipedia. *Collaboration: interoperability between people in the creation of language resources for less-resourced languages*, 19:19–22.

Eduard Fosch Villaronga, Adam Poulsen, Roger Andre Søraa, and B. H. M. Custers. 2021. A little bird told me your gender: Gender inferences in social media. *Inf. Process. Manag.*, 58(3):102541.

Claudia Wagner, David García, Mohsen Jadidi, and Markus Strohmaier. 2015. It's a Man's Wikipedia? Assessing Gender Inequality in an Online Encyclopedia. In *Proceedings of the Ninth International Conference on Web and Social Media, ICWSM 2015, University of Oxford, Oxford, UK, May 26-29, 2015*, pages 454–463. AAAI Press.

Claudia Wagner, Eduardo Graells-Garrido, David García, and Filippo Menczer. 2016. Women through the glass ceiling: gender asymmetries in Wikipedia. *EPJ Data Sci.*, 5(1):5.

Kellie Webster, Marta R. Costa-jussà, Christian Hardmeier, and Will Radford. 2019. Gendered Ambiguous Pronoun (GAP) Shared Task at the Gender Bias in NLP Workshop 2019. In *Proceedings of the First Workshop on Gender Bias in Natural Language Processing*, pages 1–7, Florence, Italy. Association for Computational Linguistics.

Kellie Webster, Marta Recasens, Vera Axelrod, and Jason Baldridge. 2018. Mind the GAP: A Balanced Corpus of Gendered Ambiguous Pronouns. *Transactions of the Association for Computational Linguistics*, 6:605–617.

Amir Zeldes. 2017. The GUM Corpus: Creating Multilayer Resources in the Classroom. *Language Resources and Evaluation*, 51(3):581–612.

Jieyu Zhao, Tianlu Wang, Mark Yatskar, Vicente Ordonez, and Kai-Wei Chang. 2018. Gender Bias in Coreference Resolution: Evaluation and Debiasing Methods. In *Proceedings of the 2018 Conference of the North American Chapter of the Association for Computational Linguistics: Human Language Technologies, Volume 2 (Short Papers)*, pages 15–20, New Orleans, Louisiana. Association for Computational Linguistics.

Investigating the Impact of Gender Representation in ASR Training Data: a Case Study on Librispeech

Mahault Garnerin LIDILEM & LIG
Solange Rossato LIG
Laurent Besacier LIG
Univ. Grenoble Alpes, CNRS, Grenoble INP
FR-38000 Grenoble, France
firstname.lastname@univ-grenoble-alpes.fr

Abstract

In this paper we question the impact of gender representation in training data on the performance of an end-to-end ASR system. We create an experiment based on the Librispeech corpus and build 3 different training corpora varying only the proportion of data produced by each gender category. We observe that if our system is overall robust to the gender balance or imbalance in training data, it is nonetheless dependant of the adequacy between the individuals present in the training and testing sets.

1 Introduction

As pointed out by Hovy and Spruit (2016) in their positional paper on the social impact of NLP, discriminatory performance could be the result of several types of biases. The roots of socio-technical biases in new technology could be situated in its very design, the selection of the data used for training (Garg et al., 2018; Kutuzov et al., 2018), the annotation process (Sap et al., 2019), the intermediary representations such as word embeddings (Bolukbasi et al., 2016; Caliskan et al., 2017) or in the model itself.

Gender bias in ASR systems, defined as a systematically and statistically worse recognition for a gender category is still a working topic (Feng et al., 2021). Pioneer work from (Adda-Decker and Lamel, 2005) found better performance on women's voices, while a preliminary research on YouTube automatic caption system found better recognition rate of male speech (Tatman, 2017) but no gender-difference in a follow-up study (Tatman and Kasten, 2017). Recent work on hybrid ASR systems observed that gender imbalance in data could lead to decreased ASR performance on the gender category least represented (Garnerin et al., 2019). This last study was conducted on French broadcast data in which women account for only 35% of the speakers. If systematic, this performance difference could lead to less indexing of media resources featuring female speech and contribute to the invisibilisation of women and women speech in public debate[1] and history (Adamek and Gann, 2018). Such results would also fall into the category of allocational harms, following the typology proposed by Barocas et al. (2017) and Crawford (2017), because women are more likely to be less represented in corpora (Garnerin et al., 2020), making all technologies relying on speech recognition less accessible for them. It could also result in representational harm such as the maintenance of the stereotype of inadequacy between women and technology.[2] But as other characteristics such as the speaker role, (i.e. his or her ability to produce professional speech) could explain some performance variations, we propose in this paper to address the question of ASR systems' robustness to gender imbalance in training data. As data is now the starting point of every system, we know that the quality of a system depends on the quality of its data (Vucetic and Obradovic, 2001; He and Garcia, 2009). To tackle this question, we work with the Librispeech corpus, widely used in the community and based on audio books recordings. To evaluate the impact of gender imbalance in training data on our system performance, we proceed as follows: we first test the robustness of our model against the randomness introduced at training by the weight initialization stage. We then evaluate

[1] https://www.newyorker.com/culture/cultural-comment/a-century-of-shrill-how-bias-in-technology-has-hurt-womens-voices

[2] see for example, this news report on decreased performance for female speaker in built-in GPS, in which the VP of voice technology stated "many issues with women's voices could be fixed if female drivers were willing to sit through lengthy training... Women could be taught to speak louder, and direct their voices towards the microphone" https://techland.time.com/2011/06/01/its-not-you-its-it-voice-recognition-doesnt-recognize-women/

Proceedings of the 3rd Workshop on Gender Bias in Natural Language Processing, pages 86–92
August 5, 2021.

the impact of speakers selection in training data on model performance. We compare the obtained results to the impact observed when changing overall gender representation in training data. Finally we observe the behavior of our model when trained on mono-gender corpora.

We validate our model robustness against the impact of model seed and observe that overall system is quite robust to gender balance variation. We note that the random factor introduced in the selection process of speakers for the training set seems to have a statistically significant impact on performance. We argue that our model, whereas robust to gender representation variability, is strongly dependent on the individuals present in the training set, which questions the pertinence of gender as a category of analysis in ASR and advocate for a return to a more incorporated conception of language.

2 End-to-end model of Automatic Speech Recognition

For the last decade, the traditional ASR models, based on HMM-GMMs have been coexisting with hybrid models (HMM-DNNs) (Mohamed et al., 2012; Dahl et al., 2012) and for the latest couples of years with end-to-end systems. The former acoustic, pronunciation and language models, made explicit by different modules in the final system, are now collapsed into one big architecture mapping directly the audio signal to its transcription. Since speaker adaptation has been integrated into the entire training process of end-to-end models, we are expecting the gender imbalance within training data to be extrapolated by this kind of systems, resulting in gender-differentiated performance.

2.1 Original data set

We used the Librispeech data set (Panayotov et al., 2015) to perform our experiments. The original training data set contains a total of 5466 books read by 2338 US English speakers. 2671 books are read by female speakers and 2795 by male speakers. As we decide to use the gender terminology over the sex one, we acknowledge that staying within these binary categories is reductive. However, as there is no mention of non-binary speakers in our data sets and believing that the audit of discriminatory performance on non-binary people calls for a thought-through methodology, we stayed within the binary matrix. We are nonetheless aware of the limitations that comes with this choice.

Data set	F	M	Total
train original	2671	2795	5466
wper30	1145	2671	3816
wper50	1908	1908	3816
wper70	2671	1145	3816
test-clean	49	38	87

Table 1: Composition of the different training and evaluation data sets. Numbers reported are numbers of books read by men and women.

The Librispeech corpus comes with two testing sets : test-clean and test-other. The test-clean contains 87 books read by 40 speakers. 49 books are read by women and 38 by men. The test-other set contains 90 books read by 33 speakers, in which 44 books are read by women and 46 by men. The test-clean includes speakers which obtained the best WER according to the results of the WSJ model's transcripts and the speakers left were put in the test-other data set. In this work, analyses are conducted on the test-clean set.

We decide to work at the book granularity. Meaning each point of measure is the WER obtained on a particular book. There is no speaker overlap between train and test sets. For the sake of readability, when we report WER results for male and female speakers, we actually refer to WER results obtained for books read by male or female speakers.

2.2 Controlled data sets

Librispeech being gender balanced by design, we recreated 3 training data sets in which 30%, 50% or 70% of the books were read by women, in order to observe the impact of gender balance on performance. We called the resulting training sets: wper30, wper50 and wper70. To assure comparability, the overall number of books (N=3816) is the same for each training set. The common part between each data set is maximised : the 30% of books read by women in wper30 are also present in the wper50 and wper70 data sets. The same applies to books read by men. We then trained a system with each one of them.

2.3 Model

We trained our systems with the ESPnet toolkit (Watanabe et al., 2018) and used a state of the art model based on an already existing recipe: our model is an attentional encoder-decoder model, with a 5-layer VGG-BLSTM encoder and a 2-layer

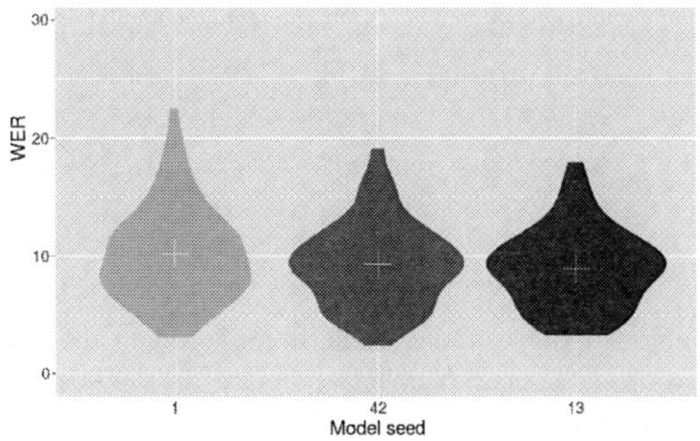

Figure 1: WER distributions on test-clean testing set by model seeds. White crosses represent the mean value of each distribution and color represent each model. Training done on wper50 partition.

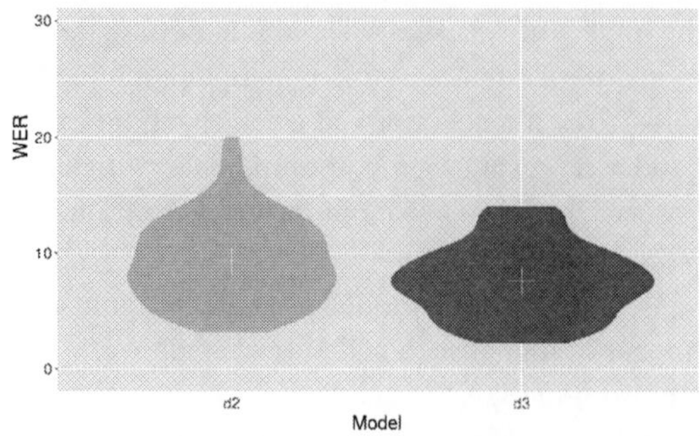

Figure 2: WER distributions on test-clean testing set by data seeds. Both systems have a 50-50% men/women training set. White crosses represent the mean value of each distribution and color represent each model. Training done on wper50 partition.

decoder. The encoder and decoder layers have 1024 hidden units and the output vocabulary is of 5,000 subwords generated through byte pair encoding. We used the PyTorch backend for ASR training and decoding was performed using both an RNN LM trained on the Librispeech text corpus and the joint decoding combining attention-based and CTC scores of the ASR model (CTC weight=0.5, LM weight=0.7).

With this configuration we obtained (with a model learnt on the full train set) a mean WER of 4.2% on the test-clean data set and a mean WER of 14.3% on the test-other set. Reported results on the ESPnet repository were of 4.0% on test-clean and 12.7% on test-other with a similar configuration.

2.4 Statistical testing of WER results

To assess the existence of a statistically significant impact on performance of the different conditions tested, we chose non-parametrical tests, considering our WER distributions do not follow a normal distribution. We used the Wilcoxon Rank Sum test (also known as Mann-Whitney test) and its generalisation to more than 2 samples, the Kruskall-Wallis test (Wilcoxon et al., 1963). Both tests estimate the probability of the WER distributions to be samples of the same population. We set our confidence level to 99% ($\alpha = 0.01$).

3 Impact of the model seed

Our hypothesis that systems might be impacted by a gender imbalance in training data is based on the fact that systems are deeply dependent on the data they are trained on (Vucetic and Obradovic, 2001; He and Garcia, 2009). In order to control that the behaviors we observe are only due to the data variation, we conduct a first experiment where we test the robustness of our model to the seed variability at training. To do so, we train three models with the wper50 (gender-balanced) training set, changing only the model seed. Obtained WER distributions are represented in Figure 1. When performing the Kruskall-Wallis test, no statistical significant difference is observed between the 3 distributions (p-value = 0.17). The same observation is made when comparing the models two by two. We conclude that our model is robust to the randomness introduced at the initialisation stage.

4 Impact of the training data (data seed)

We believe that gender is an attribute of the speaker and that speaker's gender variability goes beyond gender statistics. Following Judith Butler's theory on the performativity of gender (Butler, 1988, 2011), we assume that gender is not expressed in the same way amongst speakers. The intrinsic variability of gender indexing (Ochs, 1992) leads us to consider that two people sharing the same gender "label" will not be interchangeable in a data set.

In order to test this hypothesis, we created two other training sets with a 50-50 men/women balance but with a different random seed for the shuffle and selection process for these training corpora. We refer to this random element as the "data seed". We call the two models d2 and d3 (data seeds values were chosen arbitrarily). We obtained the distributions presented in Figure 2. Wilcoxon rank sum test is statistically significant between the two distributions (W=4771.5; p-value=0.003). Model d2 obtains a mean WER of 9.31% and model d3 a

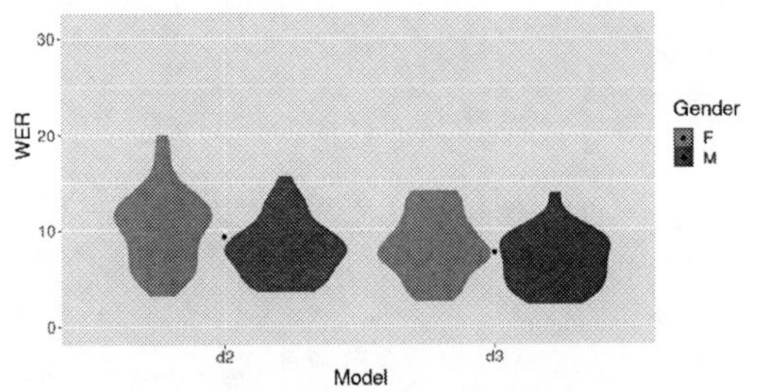

Figure 3: WER distributions on test-clean testing set by data seeds. Black dots represent the mean value of each distribution regardless of gender categories. Training done on wper50 partition.

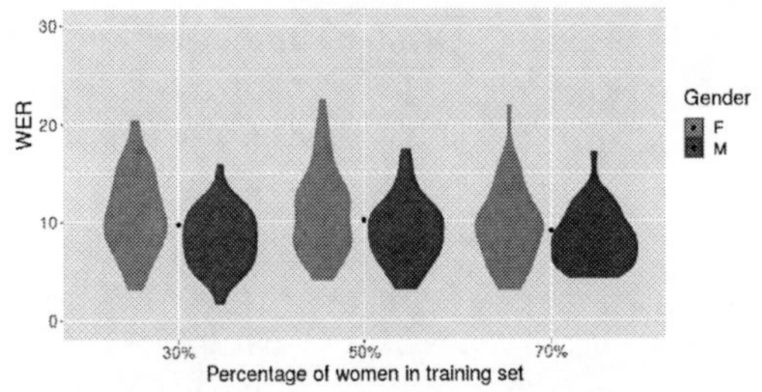

Figure 4: WER distributions on test-clean testing set by gender for the 3 models trained with 30%, 50% or 70% of books read by women in the training set. Black dots represent the mean value of each distribution regardless of gender categories.

mean WER of 7.65%. We argue that the data exhaustiveness is thus a strong factor of performance variation.

When looking at the performance obtained by gender categories (see Figure 3), we also observe distinct behaviors between the two models. WER for books read by male (8.14%) and female (10.2%) speakers are statistically different in our model d2 (W=1240; p-value=0.008). This effect is not found in model d3 (W=1173; p-value=0.038), although a difference of almost 2 points is also observable between the mean WER for men (6.80%) and women (8.31%). There is trend to obtain slightly better WER results for male speakers, with an average difference of 1.7 percentage point. The performance difference between the gender categories is thus of the same order as the difference between our models d2 and d3.

5 Gender balance and performance

In this experiment we try to evaluate the impact of gender representation on the performance. To do so, we trained 3 ASR systems, with our 3 different training sets presented in Section 2.2. Results are reported in Table 2. Overall WERs are of 9.7% respectively 10,2% and 9.0% for our 3 conditions (training set with 30% of books read by women, respectively 50% and 70%). We note a decrease in WER performance for wper50 that could be explained by a different speakers selection for training, as we observed in the previous Section 4. However, no statistical difference is observed between these 3 conditions (p-value = 0.14).

A quick look at our WER distributions by gender category shows that the performance obtained for women are generally worse than the one obtained for men (see Figure 4). This difference is statistically significant (p-value = 0.003) when our training set contains only 30% of books read by women and p-value increases until it exceeds our alpha risk (p-value = 0.04 for wper50 and p-value = 0.10 for wper70). We can argue that an under-representation of a gender category leads to a higher error rate, but the same trend is not observable for male speakers. Surprisingly, when training set contains 70% of books read by women, there is no significant difference between WER obtained for male and female speakers. Even if it is not statistically significant, the trend observed in Section 4 holds because with 70% of female speech in training data, we still observe better WER results for men.

6 What about mono-gender models?

Our overall system performance seems to be robust to the variation in gender representation in training data. In wper30 model we observe a statistically significant gender difference in WER. The better WER results for male speakers are expected as they are more represented in training data. This is not the case for wper70 model, where we expected better results for women. Therefore we trained male-only and female-only models to analyse extreme behaviors. We maximized the size of our training set, reaching a book count in these mono-gender systems of 2671. Hence, it is worth noting that the size of training data in these systems is smaller than the size of training data for our wper models.

Overall WER for the male-only model is of 12.3% and 11.7% for the female-only one without any statistically significant difference. In the male-only model, WER distributions are statistically different by gender category (p-value $< 10^{-6}$), with an average WER of 9.11% on books read by men and of and of 14.7% on books read by

Model	Gender	test-clean
wper30	F	10.9%
	M	8.3%
	all	**9.7%**
wper50	F	11.0%
	M	9.1%
	all	**10.2%**
wper70	F	9.6%
	M	8.3%
	all	**9.0%**

Table 2: Mean WER by gender obtained on the Librispeech test-clean data set for the 3 models trained with 30%, 50% or 70% of books read by women in the training set.

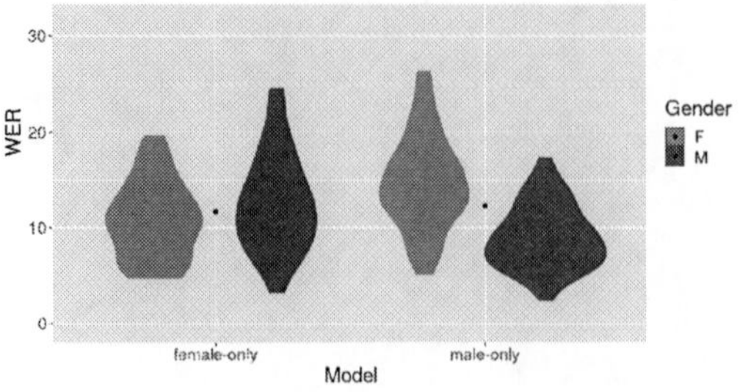

Figure 5: WER distributions on test-clean testing set by gender for our two mono-gender models. Black dots represent the mean value of each distribution regardless of gender categories.

women. But this is not the case for the female-only model (p-value = 0.114 ; WER(F) = 10.9% and WER(M)=12.7%. At last, when we are in a mono-gender configuration with only women-read books at training, we reverse the trend of better WER results for male speakers, but without reaching statistical significance. It seems that an over-representation of women is better suited to the task in our experimental settings.

7 Discussion & Conclusion

It is a common-sense claim to state that all gender categories need to be represented in a training corpus of an ASR system in order to be able to transcribe speech regardless of the user's gender. We expected to find that the performance obtained on each gender category was dependent of their representation in training data. However, if we select individuals while maintaining a balanced gender distribution (see Section 4), we obtain a significant difference in performance of around 1.7 percentage point. It is possible that these differences in performance, between systems and between genders, will not be found for other test corpora, because more than the selection of individuals present at training, it is the "proximity" between voices in the training and test sets that may explain these observed differences. When varying the percentage of female-read books in training sets, we find that the global performance keeps the same range of accuracy, without any statistical significance. As individuals also change when varying the proportion of men and women in training data, we expected our WER distribution to vary accordingly. However, it is worth noting that our three data sets always include the 30% of women of the wper30 set and the 30% of men of the wper70 set. Surprisingly, for the three systems studied, both the gendered proportion and the individuals change without inducing significant differences in overall performance.

We observe that the expected impact is not in terms of overall performance but in terms of performance by gender. There is a higher error rate for female speakers when the system is mostly trained on male speakers but the significance of this difference between men and women decreases slowly as we raise the quantity of female-read books in the training set. However, we do not observe the inverse trend: only with the mono-gender system trained with women voices only, do we achieve better WER results for women than for men, even if this trend is not significant. All in all, we cannot conclude that the gender distributions in the training data have a strong influence on the WER results. While it appears that men's voices are generally better recognised, it seems that increasing the proportion of women's voices in the training corpus helps to reduce gender-differentiated performance, while ensuring the same level of overall performance.

From this study performed on Librispeech, it appears that i) the selection of individuals in the training corpus, ii) the gender distribution with extreme variations and iii) the train/test corpus match have a significant impact on system performance. In this very controlled context of speech production, the gender variation seems to be negligible compared to the individual variation. We believe gender demographics are not enough to ensure the same level of performance on both gender groups. According to our results, it seems that an over-representation of female voices improves recognition of women voices without decreasing overall performance. Further research is needed to disentangle the effects of gender representation in voice and data and the performance of ASR systems. If considering the gender balance in training data is a starting point for fairer systems, trying to quantify the intra-variability of our training sets to estimate a measure of adequacy with our test data appears as a strong lead for future work. We plan on working on acoustic measures such as fundamental frequency and speech rate to assess something that could be named "voice variability cover" and try to finally get out of the binary sex-matrix.

References

Anna Adamek and Emily Gann. 2018. Whose artifacts? whose stories? public history and representation of women at the canada science and technology museum. *Historia Crítica*, 68:47–66.

Martine Adda-Decker and Lori Lamel. 2005. Do speech recognizers prefer female speakers? In *Proceedings of the 9th European Conference on Speech Communication and Technology*, INTERSPEECH 2005, pages 2205–2208, Lisbon, Portugal. ISCA.

Solon Barocas, Kate Crawford, Aaron Shapiro, and Hanna Wallach. 2017. The problem with bias: Allocative versus representational harms in machine learning. In *Proceedings of SIGCIS Conference*, Philadelphia, PA, USA.

Tolga Bolukbasi, Kai-Wei Chang, James Y. Zou, Venkatesh Saligrama, and Adam T. Kalai. 2016. Man is to computer programmer as woman is to homemaker? Debiasing word embeddings. In *Proceedings of the 30th International Conference on Neural Information Processing Systems*, NIPS 2016, pages 4356–4364, Red Hook, NY, USA. Curran Associates Inc.

Judith Butler. 1988. Performative acts and gender constitution: An essay in phenomenology and feminist theory. *Theatre journal*, 40(4):519–531.

Judith Butler. 2011. *Bodies that matter: On the discursive limits of sex*. Routledge, London.

Aylin Caliskan, Joanna J. Bryson, and Arvind Narayanan. 2017. Semantics derived automatically from language corpora contain human-like biases. *Science*, 356(6334):183–186.

Kate Crawford. 2017. The trouble with bias. Keynote at the 31st Annual Conference on Neural Information Processing Systems, NIPS 2017, Long Beach, CA, USA.

George E. Dahl, Dong Yu, Li Deng, and Alex Acero. 2012. Context-dependent pre-trained deep neural networks for large-vocabulary speech recognition. *IEEE Transactions on Audio, Speech, and Language Processing*, 20(1):30–42.

Siyuan Feng, Olya Kudina, Bence Mark Halpern, and Odette Scharenborg. 2021. Quantifying bias in automatic speech recognition. (Submitted to INTERSPEECH 2021).

Nikhil Garg, Londa Schiebinger, Dan Jurafsky, and James Zou. 2018. Word embeddings quantify 100 years of gender and ethnic stereotypes. *Proceedings of the National Academy of Sciences*, 115(16):E3635–E3644.

Mahault Garnerin, Solange Rossato, and Laurent Besacier. 2019. Gender representation in French broadcast corpora and its impact on ASR performance. In *Proceedings of the 1st International Workshop on AI for Smart TV Content Production, Access and Delivery*, AI4TV '19, pages 3–9, Nice, France. ACM.

Mahault Garnerin, Solange Rossato, and Laurent Besacier. 2020. Gender representation in open source speech resources. In *Proceedings of the 12th Language Resources and Evaluation Conference*, pages 6599–6605, Marseille, France. European Language Resources Association.

Haibo He and Edwardo. A. Garcia. 2009. Learning from imbalanced data. *IEEE Transactions on Knowledge and Data Engineering*, 21(9):1263–1284.

Dirk Hovy and Shannon L. Spruit. 2016. The social impact of natural language processing. In *Proceedings of the 54th Annual Meeting of the Association for Computational Linguistics (Volume 2: Short Papers)*, pages 591–598, Berlin, Germany. Association for Computational Linguistics.

Andrey Kutuzov, Lilja Øvrelid, Terrence Szymanski, and Erik Velldal. 2018. Diachronic word embeddings and semantic shifts: a survey. In *Proceedings of the 27th International Conference on Computational Linguistics*, pages 1384–1397, Santa Fe, New Mexico, USA. Association for Computational Linguistics.

Abdel Rahman Mohamed, George. E. Dahl, and Geoffrey E. Hinton. 2012. Acoustic modeling using deep belief networks. *IEEE Transactions on Audio, Speech, and Language Processing*, 20(1):14–22.

Elinor Ochs. 1992. Indexing gender. In Alessandro Duranti and Charles Goodwin, editors, *Rethinking Context: Language as an interactive phenomenon*, pages 335—350. Cambridge University Press.

Vassil Panayotov, Guoguo Chen, Daniel Povey, and Sanjeev Khudanpur. 2015. Librispeech: an ASR corpus based on public domain audio books. In *Proceedings of the 2015 IEEE International Conference on Acoustics, Speech and Signal Processing (ICASSP)*, pages 5206–5210, South Brisbane, QLD, Australia. IEEE.

Maarten Sap, Dallas Card, Saadia Gabriel, Yejin Choi, and Noah A. Smith. 2019. The risk of racial bias in hate speech detection. In *Proceedings of the*

57th Annual Meeting of the Association for Computational Linguistics, pages 1668–1678, Florence, Italy. Association for Computational Linguistics.

Rachael Tatman. 2017. Gender and dialect bias in YouTube's automatic captions. In *Proceedings of the First ACL Workshop on Ethics in Natural Language Processing*, pages 53–59, Valencia, Spain. Association for Computational Linguistics.

Rachael Tatman and Conner Kasten. 2017. Effects of talker dialect, gender & race on accuracy of Bing Speech and YouTube automatic captions. In *Proceedings of the 18th Annual Conference of the International Speech Communication Association*, INTERSPEECH 2017, pages 934–938, Stockholm, Sweden. ISCA.

Slobodan Vucetic and Zoran Obradovic. 2001. Classification on data with biased class distribution. In *Machine Learning: ECML 2001*, pages 527–538. Springer Berlin Heidelberg.

Shinji Watanabe, Takaaki Hori, Shigeki Karita, Tomoki Hayashi, Jiro Nishitoba, Yuya Unno, Nelson Enrique Yalta Soplin, Jahn Heymann, Matthew Wiesner, Nanxin Chen, Adithya Renduchintala, and Tsubasa Ochiai. 2018. ESPnet: End-to-end speech processing toolkit. In *Proceedings of the 19th Annual Conference of the International Speech Communication Association*, INTERSPEECH 2018, pages 2207–2211, Hyderabad, India. ISCA.

Frank Wilcoxon, SK Katti, and Roberta A Wilcox. 1963. *Critical values and probability levels for the Wilcoxon rank sum test and the Wilcoxon signed rank test*. American Cyanamid Company, Pearl River, NY, USA.

Generating Gender Augmented Data for NLP

Nishtha Jain[1], Maja Popovic[2], Declan Groves[2], Eva Vanmassenhove[4]

[1]ADAPT Centre, Trinity College Dublin,
[2]ADAPT Centre, Dublin City University,
[3]Microsoft, Dublin,
[4]Department of CSAI, Tilburg University
[1,2]firstname.lastname@adaptcentre.ie, [3] degroves@microsoft.com,[4]e.o.j.vanmassenhove@tilburguniversity.edu

Abstract

Gender bias is a frequent occurrence in NLP-based applications, especially pronounced in gender-inflected languages. Bias can appear through associations of certain adjectives and animate nouns with the natural gender of referents, but also due to unbalanced grammatical gender frequencies of inflected words. This type of bias becomes more evident in generating conversational utterances where gender is not specified within the sentence, because most current NLP applications still work on a sentence-level context. As a step towards more inclusive NLP, this paper proposes an automatic and generalisable re-writing approach for short conversational sentences. The rewriting method can be applied to sentences that, without extra-sentential context, have multiple equivalent alternatives in terms of gender. The method can be applied both for creating gender balanced outputs as well as for creating gender balanced training data. The proposed approach is based on a neural machine translation (NMT) system trained to 'translate' from one gender alternative to another. Both the automatic and manual analysis of the approach show promising results for automatic generation of gender alternatives for conversational sentences in Spanish.

1 Introduction

Recent studies have exposed challenging systematic issues related to bias that extend to a range of AI applications, including Natural Language Processing (NLP) technology (Costa-jussà, 2019; Blodgett et al., 2020). Observed bias problems range from copying biases already existing in data to claims that the training process can lead to an exacerbation or amplification of observed biases (Zhou and Schiebinger, 2018; Vanmassenhove et al., 2021). The algorithms learn to maximize the overall probability of an occurrence, leading to preferences for more frequently appearing training patterns.

With this work, we propose a method for generating (more) balanced data in terms of one of the main types of bias frequently observed in language: gender bias. Gender bias can occur in language due to the fact that some languages have a way of explicitly marking (natural or grammatical) gender while others do not (Stahlberg et al., 2007). Gender bias in translation is usually manifested when animate entities (e.g. professions) are translated from gender neutral language (e.g. English) into a gendered language (e.g. Spanish) because the instances seen in training data are biased. Also, conversational utterances are prone to bias, both in machine translation as well as in other NLP applications, because systems often do not have the ability to provide multiple gender variants. Therefore, users are simply presented with the most probable option which is prone to bias. In our work, we aim to enable the generation of multiple gender variants by expanding each sentence with the missing gender variants, thus fostering inclusion in online conversations/NLP applications. Generating gender variants can and should also be used to create gender balanced conversational data that can be used to train less biased NLP models such as machine translation models, language models, chat bots, etc.

Unlike previous studies, we did not want to limit ourselves to one specific gender phenomenon, such as gender markings on professions (Zmigrod et al., 2019)) (for which the gender can easily be swapped by using hand-crafted lists) or first person personal pronouns (Habash et al., 2019)). The objective of this research aims to include as many cases as possible of gender alternatives related not only to gender of persons but also to grammatical gender of the objects referred to. In Example 1, (a) illustrates an example of two alternatives for a sentence where

Proceedings of the 3rd Workshop on Gender Bias in Natural Language Processing, pages 93–102
August 5, 2021.

there is agreement with the grammatical gender of an object referred to in the previous sentence, while in (b) there is agreement with the gender of the speaker/writer (i.e. a person).

Example 1.
(a) [MALE] ¿Está complet**o**? – [FEMALE] ¿Está complet**a**? [1]
(b) [MALE] Estoy confundid**o**. – [FEMALE] Estoy confundid**a**.[2]

At this stage, our approach does not discriminate between human referents and objects. It is furthermore limited to the generation of binary gender alternatives. We are aware of the importance and challenge of dealing with non-binary gender(Ackerman, 2019) which we aim to tackle in future work.

The research was carried out in collaboration with an anonymous industry partner with a specific application in mind that deals with conversational sentences. Our approach aims to alleviate gender bias in the said application. We focus on one gender-rich language (Spanish), however, scalability and generalizability were kept in mind while designing the approach. Our approach can be summarized as follows:

1. Identifying (appropriate) sentences/segments that should have the opposite gender variant for some words. POS sequences were used to extract such segments from the OpenSubtitles corpus[3].

2. Creating gendered variants for the words in such segments by applying a rule-based approach.

3. Training a neural rewriter on the compiled gender-parallel Spanish data in order to be able to automatically generate gendered variants on unseen data sets. This additional step makes the approach more scalable as it removes the need for any preprocessing.

The first two steps are necessary since there is a lack of readily available open-source gender-parallel data for training. Although language knowledge and a POS tagger are necessary for these steps, the human effort and necessity for external linguistic tools are minimal (contrary to other approaches which heavily rely on linguistic tools (Zmigrod et al., 2019) or on manually created gender-parallel data (Habash et al., 2019).

2 Related Work

In the literature on gender in NLP, two main approaches for bias mitigation can be identified: (a) approaches that attempt to mitigate bias during model or word representation training, and/or (b) approaches that aim to augment the data by creating more variety in the training set (pre-processing step) or in the output (post-processing step). In the following paragraphs, we focus on the latter as it is most closely related to our approach.

There have been attempts to artificially increase the variety in already existing data sets by creating alternatives to sentences in order to decrease the overall bias (in terms of gender).[4] This approach has been referred to in the literature as 'Counterfactual Data Augmentation'(CDA) (Lu et al., 2018). Their CDA approach consists of a simple bidirectional dictionary of gendered words such as he:she, her:him/his, queen:king, etc. Zhao et al. (2018) does not use the term CDA as this was introduced later, but what they describe can be interpreted as a rudimentary approach to CDA: they augmented the existing data set by adding additional sentences in which personal pronouns 'he' and 'she' had been swapped.

Another CDA approach is described in Zmigrod et al. (2019). Similar to Lu et al. (2018), the approach relies on a bidirectional dictionary of animate nouns. Unlike Lu et al. (2018), pronouns are not handled and the languages worked on are Hebrew and Spanish, languages that have more gender markers than English. Since solely changing the nouns into their male/female counterpart often requires the enforcement of grammatical gender agreement of accompanying articles and adjectives, they introduce Markov Random Fields with optional neural parametrisation that can infer the effect of the swap on the remaining words in the segment. Their approach is limited to mitigating gender stereotypes related to animate nouns and relies on dependency trees, lemmata, POS-tags and morpho-syntactic tags in order to solve issues related to the morpho-syntactic agreement.

In the field of machine translation (MT), due

[1]English: "Is it complete?"
[2]English: "I am confused."
[3]https://opus.nlpl.eu/

[4]Different types of bias exist, however, the current approaches have focused on gender, possibly because many languages have explicit gender markers.

to specific discrepancies between the information encoded in the source and target data, there has been some work on generating the appropriate gender variant for ambiguous source sentences.[5] Vanmassenhove et al. (2019) appends gender tags to the source side of the training data indicating the gender of the speaker. As such, during testing, the desired (or multiple) gender variant(s) can be generated by adding tags. Basta et al. (2020) also experiment with incorporating a gender tag, and investigate adding the previous sentence as additional context information. Both methods result in the improvement of automatic MT scores as well as on gender accuracy for English-to-Spanish translation. Similarly, Bentivogli et al. (2020) developed NMT systems using gender tags and evaluated them specifically on gender phenomena.

The work described in Habash et al. (2019) is the most similar to ours. They proposed an approach for automatic gender reinflection ("re-gendering") for Arabic. They propose a method which consists of two components: a gender classifier and a NMT gender rewriter. In order to build the NMT rewriter, they first manually created a corpus annotated with gender information. Subsequently, each gendered sentence is re-gendered manually in order to obtain the necessary gender-parallel data for training. This way, they are able to provide gender alternatives for sentences with natural gender agreement with the first person singular.

Our research, in contrast, aims to augment existing data with gender alternatives in a broader sense: it is not limited to singular first person phenomena, ambiguity in multilingual settings, or phenomena related solely to gender agreement. It involves the gender of adjectives, past participles, and several types of pronouns for which the referent is not explicitly mentioned within the context of the sentence.

3 Generating gender-parallel data

As mentioned in the introduction, our main objective is to create an automatic gender rewriter using NMT. In order to do so, we need gender-parallel training data that consists of possible gender variants in both directions (masculine-to-feminine and feminine-to-masculine). Such data sets are, unfortunately, not publicly available, which is why we first leveraged linguistic knowledge and rules to generate a sufficient amount of gender-parallel data.

Therefore, we identified the sequences of POS classes that show gender agreement in Spanish and can thus be 're-gendered': adjectives, past participles, and several types of pronouns. A detailed description of how the different word classes are tackled to generate gender alternatives is described below. We would like to point out that our target data consisted of very short sentences, where there is at most agreement with one referent.[6] As such, our approach is limited to tackle sentences alike and cannot handle the generation of alternatives for sentences where more than two gender alternatives could be generated (due to grammatical agreement of the re-genderable word with multiple entities).

3.1 Re-genderable word classes

Past participles In principle, almost all Spanish past participles have an explicit agreement with their referent and can thus be re-gendered. However, in certain contexts they should not be: if they follow or precede a referent noun (*"Película aburrida"*, *"Acceso permitido."*) thus agreeing with the gender of the noun, or if they follow the auxiliary verb *"haber"* thus representing past tense and not a property of a person/object (*"he enviado"*, *"has descansado"*). If they appear in isolation (*"Ocupado/ocupada."*, *"Aburrido/aburrida."*), or merely surrounded by interjections or punctuation (*"Ocupado/ocupada, gracias."*, *"Buenos dias, recibido/recibida, ¡gracias!"*), adverbs (*"muy cansado/cansada"*), or a linking verb (*"Estoy registrado/registrada."*, *"Parece acabado/acabada."*), they can be re-gendered.

We also included pairs of past participles bound by conjunctions, referring to the same person or object, since in these sentences, both instances should be re-gendered (*"aburrido/aburrida y cansado/cansada."*, *"acabado/acabada y pagado/pagada."*).

Adjectives Many Spanish adjectives are gendered and have an explicit gender marker corresponding to the gender of its referent. However, some adjectives are gender neutral. Gendered and

[5]'I am a teacher' or 'I am smart' in English are not marked for gender. However, in many other languages they would be morphologically marked for the male or female gender (e.g. French, Spanish...).

[6]For example, sentences such as "I am happy and they are angry." are not covered by our approach as both 'happy' and 'angry' are in agreement but with different referents, 'I' and 'they' respectively. Such sentences would require the generation of more than two alternatives since both referents are ambiguous.

neutral adjectives can (largely) be identified based on their specific suffixes (for example *"-al"*, *"-nte"*, *"-ble"*, so the adjectives *"genial"*, *"interesante"*, and *"probable"* are neutral), while other suffixes indicate gendered adjectives (for example "o/a", so the adjective *"correcto/correcta"* has variants).

In addition, similarly to past participles, the given context has to be taken into account for gendered adjectives: they should not be re-gendered if they immediately precede or follow a noun (with or without article) which determines the gender (*"Presupuestos adjuntos."*, *"¡Maravillosa idea!"*, *"La información correcta."*). Also, adjectives following neutral demonstrative pronouns *"eso"* or *"esto"* should not be re-gendered (*"Eso es bueno."*). Analogous to past participles, adjectives in isolation (*"Listo/Lista."*, *"perfecto/perfecta."*, *"seguro/segura."*, *"¡fantástico/fantástica!"*), surrounded by punctuation (*"Correcto/correcta, saludos."*), preceding verb (*"¿Estás listo/lista?"*) or adverb (*"Es muy lindo/linda."*) can be re-gendered.

When two adjectives are present, in a conjunction, and refer to the same referent, both should be re-gendered.

Clitic pronouns Some Spanish clitic pronouns, namely *"lo(s)"* and *"la(s)"* should be re-gendered (e.g. *"Lo/la veo."*, *"Lo/la adjunto."*) while *"le(s)"* should not be changed (*"Le veo."*, *"Le digo."*). However, in some cases *"lo"* can represent a general concept not referring to a particular object, such as in *"lo siento"* (I'm sorry), *"lo sé"* (I know). If some of these are re-gendered, the precision will decrease.

Clitic pronouns attached to verbs Clitic pronouns can be attached to a verb infinitive (*"Gracias por acabarlo/acabarla."* (thanks for finishing it), *"Quiero verlo/verla."* (I want to see it)). Similar to the isolated clitic pronouns, there are certain exceptions, such as *"Es bueno saberlo"* (it is good to know). If the gender neutral clitic pronoun *"le"* is attached to a verb (*"Quiero tenerle informado."* (I want to keep you/him/her informed)), it should not be re-gendered. Gendered pronouns attached to an imperative should also be re-gendered (*"Déjalo/Déjala."* (leave it), *"Hazlo/Hazla."* (do it)). On the other hand, clitic pronouns which refer to an indirect object, such as *"mándame"* (send me), are neutral. Finally, if there are two attached clitic pronouns, *"Mándamelo/Mándamela."* (send it to me), only the gendered part (in this case *"lo"/"la"*) should be re-gendered.

Demonstrative pronouns Demonstrative pronouns *"esto"*, *"eso"* and *"aquello"* are neutral, while *"estos/estas"*, *"este/esta"*, *"ese/esa"*, *"aquello/aquella"* are gendered. If the referent is missing in the sentence and the pronoun is gendered, they should be re-gendered.

3.2 Adding gender variants by rules

Whether a gender alternative translation should be generated does not solely depend on the word classes it contains but also on the structure of the sentence. If the referent is missing in a sentence, then an additional variant with the opposite gender should be generated. If the referent is present in a sentence, only one gender variant is grammatically correct, and as such, these sentences are to be left unchanged. The presence or absence of a referent can be determined by the sequence of POS tags in a sentence[7]. For example, if we want to check whether a sentence with an adjective "creo que es correcta" (gloss: "I believe (it) is correct-feminine") needs an additional re-gendered variant or not, its POS sequence "VERB CONJUNCTION VERB ADJECTIVE" indicates that there is no referent noun within the given context. Therefore, another variant of the adjective "correct" should be provided: "creo que es correct**o**". In contrast, the sentence "la solución es correcta" with POS sequence "ARTICLE NOUN VERB ADJECTIVE" contains a referent noun "solución", and therefore it should not be re-gendered.

For each re-genderable sentence, we apply rules for changing the ending of the corresponding word, if necessary. The POS sequences to identify re-genderable sentences and the subsequent rules used to re-gender the corresponding words in such sentences are given in detail in the Appendix. It is worth mentioning we also used POS sequences to identify neutral sentences (those which should be not re-gendered) since we wanted the parallel corpus to contain both.

4 Gender-parallel data

In order to create gender-parallel data, a set of Spanish subtitles was downloaded from the OPUS (Tiedemann, 2012) website.[8] After basic

[7]Assuming that the sentences are short- this approach would not generalize to longer sentences

[8]http://opus.nlpl.eu/

filtering (removing too long and non-alpha numeric segments), a set of short sentences with up to 10 (untokenized) words was extracted. This candidate set consisted of 22 458 968 sentences. This data set was POS tagged using Treetagger[9]. The sentences matching the POS sequences mentioned in the Appendix were extracted from this data set. This set consisted of more than 1M sentences. For each extracted re-genderable sentence, the alternative gender variant is created by applying appropriate rules described in the Appendix. After applying rules on all re-genderable structures, we joined both re-gendering directions (masculine-to-feminine and feminine-to-masculine) in order to create a balanced data set. As already mentioned, the corpus also contains a number of sentences that are not to be regendered. By including these neutral sentences in our training data, we encourage the rewriter to: (a) learn when to generate alternatives and when not to, and (b) how to generate those alternatives, if necessary. In this way, a corpus with about 2.2M gender-parallel sentences was created. This corpus was then separated into train, development (~1k sentences) and test (~3k sentences) sets. The rewritten parts of the development and test sets were revised manually and the errors were corrected for about 6% of sentences and 1.5% of words. The training set, being large, was not verified manually, thus it contained some noise.

In addition to OpenSubtitles, we also obtained data from the industry partner consisting of around 8 000 sentences readily available with all possible alternative versions of the sentences provided. An additional 22 000 sentences had to be revised manually in order to produce the correct gender variant for re-genderable sentences. This set was used as an additional test set for the re-writer. One part of this set can be handled by the described POS sequences and rules ("structured test 1"), while another part contains different POS sequences and cannot be handled by these rules at all ("unstructured test 1"). The latter test set will give a good estimation of the scalability of our approach. An overall split of data sets is described in Table 1. The OpenSubtitles data was split in the standard way for machine translation, namely a few thousands of segments for development and test sets and the rest for the training set.

set	segments
training (OpenSubtitles)	2 193 657
development (OpenSubtitles)	1 018
test (OpenSubtitles)	3 066
structured test1	5 648
unstructured test1	15 892

Table 1: Statistics of data used for building the NMT rewriter.

5 Neural Rewriter

Once we compiled a sufficient amount of gender-paralell data, we were able to train our automatic rewriter. The automatic rewriter is a NMT system trained on the following parallel data: original sentences as the source language, and re-gendered sentence as the target language. For neutral sentences, the source and the target parts are identical.

The NMT rewriter was built using the publicly available Sockeye[10] implementation (Hieber et al., 2018) of the Transformer architecture (Vaswani et al., 2017). The system operates on subword units generated by byte-pair encoding (BPE)(Sennrich et al., 2016). We set the number of BPE merging operations to 32000. We have experimented with the following setups:

- a Standard NMT system without any additional tags
- an NMT system with neutrality/re-genderability tags in the source part

The system with tags was built using the same technique as proposed in (Johnson et al., 2017) for multilingual MT systems and used for many other applications including gender-informed MT (Vanmassenhove et al., 2019). For our experiments, we added a label 'N' (neutral) or 'G' (re-genderable) to each source sentence. These tags are implicitly present in the gender-parallel data – if the source and the target parts differ, it is a re-genderable sentence, if they are identical it is neutral. Therefore, the tags are certainly available for the training and development sets, but they might not be available for the test sets. Therefore, this system was assessed in two ways:

- "NMT-T": neutrality/re-genderability tags are available for the test sets
- "NMT-AT": the tags are not available for the test sets (a realistic scenario) and therefore are

[9]https://www.cis.uni-muenchen.de/ schmid/tools/TreeTagger/

[10]`https://github.com/awslabs/sockeye`

assigned automatically by the gender classifier described in the next section (which is similar to the approach described in (Habash et al., 2019).)

5.1 Gender Classifier

In order to explore potential benefits of automatic pre-classification for automatic rewriting, a classifier to distinguish between 're-genderable' (G)[11] and 'neutral' (N)[12] sentences was also designed. The tags generated by this classifier were used to assess the performance of the "NMT-AT" re-writer by appending them to the sentences.

Data

The classifier was built on the data set of about 8 000 sentences provided by the industry partner. These sentences were balanced in both directions i.e., both masculine-to-feminine as well as feminine-to-masculine counterparts of a given sentence were present and labelled as G. The rest of the sentences were labeled as N.

For the sake of designing a generalised classifier, the development set consisted of sentences from the OpenSubtitles corpus (and was the same as the development set used for the NMT system).

The final classifier was tested on two different test sets - one consisted of the 22 000 conversational sentences sourced from the industry partner and another extracted from the OpenSubtitles corpus.

Features

Following on the work of Habash et al. (2019) for the gender identification step, features using character n-grams, word n-grams and morphological information were created from the training data. To begin with, TF-IDF scores of character n-grams of length 4-7 with maximum features capped at 20 000 and of word n-grams of length 1-3 were generated. These two feature matrices were joined together along with a morphological feature that denoted the presence of a gendered word in the sentence. The resulting training data was a high dimensional data frame with around 40 000 features.

Due to the limited size of the training set, neural network based classifiers were ruled out. Instead, owing to the high dimensional nature of the data, we used a SVM based classifier for training. All the steps described in this section were implemented in Python 3.7 using sklearn[13], pandas[14] and StanzaNLP[15] libraries.

[11] Grammatical gender markings are not related to a referent within the sentence, therefore these markings have to be expanded.

[12] No gender markers that need to be expanded.

	Industry Test Set			OpenSubs		
	Acc.	Rec.	Prec.	Acc.	Rec.	Prec.
Overall	82%	-	-	80%	-	-
G	-	96%	60%	-	97%	76%
N	-	76%	98%	-	56%	93%

Table 2: Gender Classifier Results

Precision and Recall

The SVM based classifier was tested on two sets of data as described in Section 5.1. This was done in order to assess the generalisability of the classifier. Given the small size of the training data, the performance of the classifier looks promising thus far (see Table 2).

It can be observed in Table 2 that the classifier clearly performs better on the test data set consisting of sentences sourced from the industry partner as compared to the data extracted from OpenSubtitles. While the accuracy is comparable on both sets (80%), the precision and recall of neutral sentences is higher on the industry data than the set compiled from OpenSubtitles data. The high recall of sentences labelled as G implies that the classifier is almost always successful at recognising sentences that need to be re-gendered (i.e. sentences that need an alternative variant). However, it incorrectly predicts the labels of a substantial number of N-labelled sentences, which in turn results in a low precision of re-genderable sentences. As we want to avoid generating (incorrect) gender alternatives for neutral sentences, our aim was to first attain a high precision for neutral sentences and then aim towards a high recall for the same. The tags generated by this classifier for the industry sourced data and OpenSubtitles data were used to test the "NMT-AT" rewriter.

6 Results for generating gender variants

Our first experiment consisted of using the implementation of CDA by (Zmigrod et al., 2019) to generate gendered variants. However, this work only tackled animate nouns, which rarely occur in the conversational sentences we investigated in this

[13] https://scikit-learn.org/stable/

[14] https://pandas.pydata.org/

[15] https://stanfordnlp.github.io/stanza/

work. Our re-implementation of their approach generated the correct gender variant for only 1% of the sentences. Because of the very low recall, this implementation was not directly applicable for our research. In addition to this, since our work aims to tackle multiple gender related word classes, we explored extending the implementation by augmenting the list with character adjectives. On doing so, we found that this implementation generated the correct gendered variant in only 9% of the cases. An important point to note is that 3% of the neutral sentences (for which variants should not have been generated) were also converted as opposed to the 1% with only animate nouns, attributed to the presence of more words in the hand-crafted lists. In order to cover more words and improve the performance of this implementation on our data set, we considered augmenting the hand-crafted list with past participles and/or clitic pronouns. However, that increased the size of the list exponentially and made the approach prone to errors, inefficient and not scalable to other languages.

6.1 Automatic evaluation of neural rewriter

The results in the form of error rates are shown in 3. Since we are not performing typical machine translation, namely converting one language into another one, but only converting a few words in the sentence into a sentence in the same language, these error rates are not related to any of the typical automatic evaluation metrics (such as TER, etc.) but to the amount of incorrectly converted words. For each system, numbers in the left column represent the count of incorrectly converted words normalised by the total number of sentences, while numbers in the right column represent the count of incorrectly converted words normalised by the total number of words in the corpus. The numbers in the first row and first two columns can be interpreted as follows: left: 6.4% of all sentences have incorrectly converted words in ; right: 1.50% of all words are incorrectly converted.

First, it can be noted that the error rates are lower for the template-based "in-domain" test sets than for the unstructured "out-of-domain" test sets, which is in line with our expectations. The change in error rate is mainly due to discrepancies in the re-genderable segments. The error rates in the neutral segments are comparable in the out-of-domain and in-domain test sets.

Adding manual tags indicating whether a sentence should get a gender alternative or not (e.g. 'neutral' vs 'regenderable') reduces the error rates on all test sets for both types of segments. A similar performance can not be achieved by adding automatic tags. Automatic tags deteriorate the performance on neutral segments, but reduce the error rates for re-genderable segments, especially for the unstructured "out-of-domain" test set. The manually tagged results indicate the potential of a classifier. These results tie up with the results of the gender classifier (Section 5.1) which is good at classifying the re-genderable sentences as denoted by a high recall of sentences labelled 'G', however it doesn't do very well at labelling neutral sentences as 'N'. It tends to mislabel many of those sentences as 'G', resulting in a low recall and, consequently, incorrect re-gendering.

For the sake of completeness, error rates are reported for the rule-based rewriter, too. The error rates for re-genderable sentences are lower than the NMT rewriter without tags and for neutral sentences the error rate is 0%; it should be noted that the rules are applicable only to data sets which strictly conform to the described template structures.

6.2 Qualitative manual inspection of errors

In order to better understand the nature of errors and remaining challenges, a qualitative manual inspection was carried out on all test sets. First of all, it is observed that in general, the NMT re-writer does not intervene on large portions of a sentence but addresses only specific words, which is exactly what it is expected to do. This is a positive result, as generating gender variants implies changing specific gendered words and does not involve changing entire segments. It also facilitates the evaluation since manual inspection is needed only to identify the nature of incorrect words.

The analysis revealed that the most frequent error for neutral sentences are re-gendered pronouns and adjectives which should not be changed. Also, the most frequent error in re-genderable sentences is leaving them unchanged. These types of errors are predominant in structured sentences, and two examples, one for neutral and one for regenderable sentence, can be seen in Table 4(a). It can also be seen that adding tags can help in some cases.

For unstructured sentences, there are more error types especially for neutral sentences, and examples can be seen in Table 4(b). In the first three

set	type	NMT		NMT-T		NMT-AT		rules	
test (structured)	all	6.4	1.50	4.5	1.03	17.9	4.21	6.1	1.43
	neutral	5.3	1.13	2.5	0.48	33.3	7.07	0.0	0.0
	re-genderable	7.1	1.81	6.0	1.51	6.0	1.72	6.1	1.43
test1 (structured)	all	2.4	0.54	1.3	0.27	4.5	0.99	3.2	0.7
	neutral	4.8	0.95	2.2	0.43	8.7	1.73	0.0	0.0
	re-genderable	0.8	0.19	0.6	0.14	1.6	0.38	3.2	0.7
test2 (unstructured)	all	11.9	2.13	5.2	0.93	10.4	1.87	not applicable	
	neutral	3.3	0.58	0.3	0.04	6.0	1.07		
	re-genderable	57.3	10.7	31.1	5.84	33.4	6.26		

Table 3: Results for NMT rewriter: error rates (%): count of incorrectly converted words normalised by the total number of sentences (left columns) and normalised by the total number of words (right columns).

(a) structured sentences

type	original	correct	NMT	NMT-T
N	esto es perfecto	esto es perfecto	esto es **perfecta**	esto es perfecto
G	está adjunt**o**	está adjunt**a**	está adjunt**o**	está adjunt**o**

(b) unstructured sentences

	type	original	correct	NMT	NMT-T
1)	N	no son lo mismo	no son lo mismo	no son **la misma**	no son lo mismo
2)	N	aquello fue encantador	aquello fue encantador	aquello fue **encantadora**	aquello fue encantador
3)	N	¿a quién aprovecha?	¿a quién aprovecha?	¿a quién **aprovecho**?	¿a quién aprovecha?
4)	N	indíqueme la disponibilidad	indíqueme la disponibilidad	indíqueme la **emperbilidad**	indíqueme la **evelbilidad**
5)	N	indíqueme su disponibilidad	indíqueme su disponibilidad	indíqueme su disponibilidad	indíqueme su **escorpibilidad**
6)	N	unos momentos extraordinarios	unos momentos extraordinarios	unos momentos **extraordinarias arios**	unos momentos extraordinarios
7)	N	indíquenos cuánto	indíquenos cuánto	**indíquenas** cuánto	indíquenos cuánto
8)	G	esta es la adecuada	este es el adecuado	**esta** es ***la* adecuada**	**esta** es ***lo* adecuada**
9)	G	esta la hemos recibido	este lo hemos recibido	**esta la** hemos recibido	**esta** lo hemos recibido

Table 4: Examples of incorrectly generated sentence variants for (a) structured sentences and (b) unstructured sentences.

sentences, the same error type as for structured sentences can be seen, namely some words are changed which should not be changed. Adding tags helped in both cases. However, some other error types can be seen, such as converting some (not gender-related) words into non-existing words in sentences 4) and 5). For sentence 5), generating a non-existing word was triggered by adding tags. Sentence 6) shows an unnecessary re-gendering as well as adding non-existing words. This was also resolved by adding tags. In sentence 7), a word which is not at all related to gender was converted, and this was prevented by adding tags.

As for regenderable sentences, the vast majority of errors are again the unchanged words which had to be changed. If there is more than one word to be regendered, sometimes they all remain unchanged (sentence 8) and sometimes only some of them are regendered (sentence 9). Tags can help to some extent, but only for some words, not all.

Adding tags generated by the classifier also increases the number of correctly re-gendered structures at the cost of a small number of additions of non-existing words.

7 Conclusions and Future Work

In this paper, we describe an initial approach towards enriching short conversational sentences with their gender variants. Unlike other related work, our approach is not limited to tackling the first person singular phenomena, swapping third person pronouns or merely dealing with occupational or generally animate nouns. In addition, with our approach, the reliance on linguistic knowledge and tools is kept to a minimum in order to facilitate real-world deployment.

The main hurdle for this type of research is the absence of large training sets. Although provided with some manually annotated data from the industry partner, the data provided was far from sufficient to train a state-of-the-art automatic gender re-writer.

Therefore, training data was extracted from OpenSubtitles using linguistic knowledge about the targeted language, namely Spanish. Re-genderable types of words (POS classes) were identified and then frequently occurring 're-genderable' as well as 'neutral' POS patterns were extracted. By applying the corresponding rules to the re-genderable sentences, a large gender-parallel Spanish data set was compiled.

Next, an NMT rewriter was trained in order to 'translate' each re-genderable sentence into its gender alternative which showed promising performance both in terms of automatic as well as of manual evaluation.

In addition, it is shown that providing additional information regarding the need for rewriting in the form of tags could be helpful for the NMT system, as similar tags have shown to be useful for other applications such as multilingual translation, controlling politeness and gender in MT, etc. While gold standard labels show better performance than the labels generated by the gender classifier, the classifier shows promising results given the very small training set. Further experiments should investigate a classifier trained on larger amount of data.

In future work, we would like to explore how a similar approach can be applied on more sentence structures in Spanish, as well as for different languages which exhibit distinct gendering rules. Furthermore, different NMT architectures, e.g. character-level NMT or an NMT system with linguistically motivated subword units could be an interesting extension to the conducted experiments, given that gender is usually marked by specific morphemes (usually not more than one or two specific characters). In addition to that, the performance of the gender classifier can be improved to produce more accurate tags by using larger annotated training sets, adding more morphological information in features and using word embeddings instead of TF-IDF scores.

References

Lauren Ackerman. 2019. Syntactic and cognitive issues in investigating gendered coreference. *Glossa: a journal of general linguistics*, 4(1).

Christine Basta, Marta R Costa-jussà, and Noe Casas. 2020. Extensive study on the underlying gender bias in contextualized word embeddings. *Neural Computing and Applications*, pages 1–14.

Luisa Bentivogli, Beatrice Savoldi, Matteo Negri, Mattia Antonino Di Gangi, Roldano Cattoni, and Marco Turchi. 2020. Gender in danger? evaluating speech translation technology on the must-she corpus. *arXiv preprint arXiv:2006.05754*.

Su Lin Blodgett, Solon Barocas, Hal Daumé III, and Hanna Wallach. 2020. Language (technology) is power: A critical survey of "bias" in NLP. In *Proceedings of the 58th Annual Meeting of the Association for Computational Linguistics*, pages 5454–5476, Online. Association for Computational Linguistics.

Marta R Costa-jussà. 2019. An analysis of gender bias studies in natural language processing. *Nature Machine Intelligence*, pages 1–2.

Nizar Habash, Houda Bouamor, and Christine Chung. 2019. Automatic gender identification and reinflection in arabic. In *Proceedings of the First Workshop on Gender Bias in Natural Language Processing*, pages 155–165.

Felix Hieber, Tobias Domhan, Michael Denkowski, David Vilar, Artem Sokolov, Ann Clifton, and Matt Post. 2018. The sockeye neural machine translation toolkit at AMTA 2018. In *Proceedings of the 13th Conference of the Association for Machine Translation in the Americas (Volume 1: Research Track)*, pages 200–207, Boston, MA. Association for Machine Translation in the Americas.

Melvin Johnson, Mike Schuster, Quoc V Le, Maxim Krikun, Yonghui Wu, Zhifeng Chen, Nikhil Thorat, Fernanda Viégas, Martin Wattenberg, Greg Corrado, et al. 2017. Google's Multilingual Neural Machine Translation System: Enabling Zero-Shot Translation. In *Transactions of the Association of Computational Linguistics, Volume 5:1*, pages 339–351, Vancouver, Canada.

Kaiji Lu, Piotr Mardziel, Fangjing Wu, Preetam Amancharla, and Anupam Datta. 2018. Gender Bias in Natural Language Processing. In *arXiv:1807.11714*.

Rico Sennrich, Barry Haddow, and Alexandra Birch. 2016. Neural machine translation of rare words with subword units. In *Proceedings of the 54th Annual Meeting of the Association for Computational Linguistics (ACL 2016)*, pages 1715–1725, Berlin, Germany.

Dagmar Stahlberg, Friederike Braun, Lisa Irmen, and Sabine Sczesny. 2007. Representation of the sexes in language. *Social communication*, pages 163–187.

Jörg Tiedemann. 2012. Parallel Data, Tools and Interfaces in OPUS. In *Proceedings of the Eight International Conference on Language Resources and Evaluation (LREC'12)*, pages 2214–2218, Istanbul, Turkey.

Eva Vanmassenhove, Christian Hardmeier, and Andy Way. 2019. Getting gender right in neural machine translation. *Proceedings of the 2018 Conference on Empirical Methods in Natural Language Processing (EMNLP)*, pages 3003–3008.

Eva Vanmassenhove, Dimitar Shterionov, and Matthew Gwilliam. 2021. Machine translationese: Effects of algorithmic bias on linguistic complexity in machine translation. In *Proceedings of the 16th Conference of the European Chapter of the Association for Computational Linguistics: Main Volume*, pages 2203–2213.

Ashish Vaswani, Noam Shazeer, Niki Parmar, Jakob Uszkoreit, Llion Jones, Aidan N Gomez, Ł ukasz Kaiser, and Illia Polosukhin. 2017. Attention is All you Need. In *Proceedings of The Thirty-first Annual Conference on Neural Information Processing Systems 30 (NIPS)*, pages 5998–6008, Long Beach, CA, USA.

Jieyu Zhao, Yichao Zhou, Zeyu Li, Wei Wang, and Kai-Wei Chang. 2018. Learning Gender-Neutral Word Embeddings. In *Proceedings of the 2018 Conference on Empirical Methods in Natural Language Processing (EMNLP)*, pages 4847–4853, Brussels, Belgium.

J Zhou and L Schiebinger. 2018. AI Can be Sexist and Racist – It's Time to Make it Fair. In *Nature 559*, pages 324–326. https://www.nature.com/articles/d41586-018-05707-8.

Ran Zmigrod, Sabrina J. Mielke, Hanna Wallach, and Ryan Cotterell. 2019. Counterfactual data augmentation for mitigating gender stereotypes in languages with rich morphology. In *Proceedings of the 57th Annual Meeting of the Association for Computational Linguistics (ACL 2019)*, pages 1651–1661, Florence, Italy.

Second Order WinoBias (SoWinoBias) Test Set for Latent Gender Bias Detection in Coreference Resolution

Hillary Dawkins
University of Guelph, Ontario, Canada
Vector Institute, Toronto, Ontario, Canada
hdawkins@uoguelph.ca

Abstract

We observe an instance of gender-induced bias in a downstream application, despite the absence of explicit gender words in the test cases. We provide a test set, SoWinoBias, for the purpose of measuring such latent gender bias in coreference resolution systems. We evaluate the performance of current debiasing methods on the SoWinoBias test set, especially in reference to the method's design and altered embedding space properties. See https://github.com/hillary-dawkins/SoWinoBias.

1 Introduction

Explicit (or first-order) gender bias was observed in coreference resolution systems by Zhao et al. (2018a), by considering contrasting cases:

1. The doctor hired the secretary because he was overwhelmed. [he $\rightarrow$ doctor]
2. The doctor hired the secretary because she was overwhelmed. [she $\rightarrow$ doctor]
3. The doctor hired the secretary because she was highly qualified. [she $\rightarrow$ secretary]
4. The doctor hired the secretary because he was highly qualified. [he $\rightarrow$ secretary]

Sentences 1 and 3 are pro-stereotypical examples because gender words align with a socially-held stereotype regarding the occupations. Sentences 2 and 4 are anti-stereotypical because the correct coreference resolution contradicts a stereotype. It was observed that systems performed better on pro cases than anti cases, and the WinoBias test set was developed to quantify this disparity.

Here we make a new observation of gender-induced (or second-order) bias in coreference resolution systems, and provide the corresponding test set SoWinoBias. Consider cases:

1. The doctor liked the nurse because they were beautiful. [they $\rightarrow$ nurse]
2. The nurse dazzled the doctor because they were beautiful. [they $\rightarrow$ nurse]
3. The nurse admired the doctor because they were beautiful. [they $\rightarrow$ doctor]

The examples do not contain any explicit gender cues at all, and yet we can observe that sentences 1 and 2 align with a gender-induced social stereotype, while sentence 3 opposes the stereotype. The induction occurs because "nurse" is a female-coded occupation (Bolukbasi et al., 2016; Zhao et al., 2018b), and women are also more likely to be described based on physical appearance (Hoyle et al., 2019; Williams and Bennett, 1975). A coreference resolution system is gender-biased if correct predictions on sentences like 1 and 2 are more likely than on sentence 3.

The difference between first-order and second-order gender bias in a downstream application is especially interesting given current trends in debiasing static word embeddings. Early methods (Bolukbasi et al., 2016; Zhao et al., 2018b) focused on eliminating direct bias from the embedding space, quantified as associations between gender-neutral words and an explicit gender vocabulary. In response to an influential critique paper by Gonen and Goldberg (2019), the current trend is to focus on eliminating indirect bias from the embedding space, quantified either by gender-induced proximity among embeddings (Kumar et al., 2020) or by residual gender cues that could be learned by a classifier (Ravfogel et al., 2020; Davis et al., 2020).

Indirect bias in the embedding space was viewed as an undesirable property a priori, but we do not yet have a good understanding of the effect on downstream applications. Here we test debiasing methods from both camps on SoWinoBias, and

Proceedings of the 3rd Workshop on Gender Bias in Natural Language Processing, pages 103–111
August 5, 2021.

make a series of observations on sufficient and necessary conditions for mitigating the latent gender-biased coreference resolution.

Additionally, we consider the case that our coreference resolution model employs both static and contextual word embeddings, but debiasing methods are applied to the static word embeddings only. Post-processing debiasing techniques applied to static word embeddings are computationally inexpensive, easy to concatenate, and have a longer development history. However contemporary models for downstream applications are likely to use some form of contextual embeddings as well. Therefore we might wonder whether previous work in debiasing static word embeddings remains relevant in this setting. The WinoBias test set for instance was developed and tested using the "end-to-end" coreference resolution model (Lee et al., 2017), a state-of-the-art model at that time using only static word embeddings. Subsequent debiasing schemes reported results on WinoBias using the same model, just plugging in different debiased embeddings, for the sake of fair comparison. However this is becoming increasingly outdated given the progress in coreference resolution systems. A contribution of this work is to report WinoBias results for previous debiasing techniques using a more updated model, one that makes use of unaltered contextual embeddings in addition to the debiased static embeddings.

The remainder of the paper is organized as follows: In section 2, we further define the type of bias being measured by the SoWinoBias test set and discuss some limitations. In section 3, we review the 4 word embedding debiasing methods that we will analyze, in the context of how each method aims to alter the word embedding space. In section 4, we provide details of the experimental setup and report results on both coreference resolution test sets, the original WinoBias and the newly constructed SoWinoBias. In section 5, we discuss the results with respect to the geometric properties of the altered embedding spaces. In particular, we review whether mitigation of intrinsic measures of bias on the embedding space, quantified as direct bias and indirect bias by various definitions, are related to mitigation of the latent bias in a downstream application.

2 Bias Statement

Within the scope of this paper, bias is defined and quantified as the difference in performance of a coreference resolution system on test cases aligning with a socially-held stereotype vs. test cases opposing a socially-held stereotype. We observe that gender-biased systems perform significantly better in pro-stereotypical situations. Such difference in performance creates representational harm by implying (for example) that occupations typically associated with one gender cannot have attributes typically associated with another.

Throughout this paper, the term "second-order" is used interchangeably with "latent". Characterizing the observed bias as "second-order" follows from the observation of a gender-induced bias in the absence of gender-definitional vocabulary, resting on the definition of "they" as a gender-neutral pronoun.

Therefore, a limitation in the test set construction is the possible semantic overloading of "they". As discussed, the intention throughout this paper is to use the singular "they" as a pronoun that does not carry any gender information (and could refer to someone of any gender). However, different contexts may choose to treat "they" exclusively as a non-binary gender pronoun.

The gender stereotypes used throughout this paper are sourced from peer-reviewed academic journals written in English, which draw from the US Labor Force Statistics, as well as US-based crowd workers. Therefore a limitation may be that stereotypes used here are not common to all languages or cultures.

3 Debiasing methods

3.1 Neutralization of static word embeddings

3.1.1 Methods addressing direct bias

The first attempts to debias word embeddings focused on the mitigation of direct bias (Bolukbasi et al., 2016). The definition of direct bias assumes the presence of a "gender direction" $\vec{g}$; a subspace that mostly encodes the difference between the binary genders. A non-zero projection of word $\vec{w}$ onto $\vec{g}$ implies that $\vec{w}$ is more similar to one gender over another. In the case of ideally gender-neutral words, this is an undesirable property. Direct bias quantifies the extent of this uneven similarity[1]:

$$DB(N) = \frac{1}{|N|} \sum_{\vec{w} \in N} |\cos(\vec{w}, \vec{g})| \quad (1)$$

[1]The original definition included a strictness exponent c, here set to 1 as has commonly been done in subsequent works.

The Hard Debias method (Bolukbasi et al., 2016) is a post-processing technique that projects all gender-neutral words into the nullspace of $\vec{g}$. Therefore, the direct bias is made to be zero by definition. We measure the performance of **Hard-GloVe**[2] on the coreference resolution tasks.

A related retraining method used a modified version of GloVe's original objective function with additional incentives to reduce the direct bias for gender-neutral words, resulting in the GN-GloVe embeddings (Zhao et al., 2018b). Rather than allowing for gender information to be distributed across the entire embedding space, the method explicitly sequesters the protected gender attribute to the final component. Therefore the first $d - 1$ components are taken as the gender-neutral embeddings, denoted **GN-GloVe**(w_a)[3].

3.1.2 Methods addressing indirect bias

The indirect bias is less well defined, and loosely refers to the gender-induced similarity measure between gender-neutral words. For instance, semantically unrelated words such as "sweetheart" and "nurse" may appear quantitatively similar due to a shared gender association.

One definition (first given in (Bolukbasi et al., 2016)) measures the relative change in similarity after removing direct gender associations as

$$\beta(\vec{w}, \vec{v}) = \frac{1}{\vec{w} \cdot \vec{v}} \left(\vec{w} \cdot \vec{v} - \frac{\vec{w}_\perp \cdot \vec{v}_\perp}{\|\vec{w}_\perp\| \|\vec{v}_\perp\|} \right), \quad (2)$$

where $\vec{w}_\perp = \vec{w} - (\vec{w} \cdot \vec{g})\vec{g}$, however this relies on a limited definition of the original gender association.

The Repulse-Attract-Neutralize (RAN) debiasing method attempts to repel undue gender proximities among gender-neutral words, while keeping word embeddings close to their original learned representations (Kumar et al., 2020). This method quantifies indirect bias by incorporating β into a graph-weighted holistic view of the embedding space (more on this later). In this paper, we will measure the performance of **RAN-GloVe**[4] on the coreference resolution tasks.

A related notion of indirect bias is to measure whether gender associations can be predicted from the word representation. The Iterative Nullspace Linear Projection method (INLP) achieves linear guarding of the gender attribute by iteratively learning the most informative gender subspace for a classification task, and projecting all words to the orthogonal nullspace (Ravfogel et al., 2020). After sufficient iteration, gender information cannot be recovered by a linear classifier. We will measure the performance of **INLP-GloVe**[5].

3.2 Data augmentation

In addition to debiasing methods applied to word embeddings, we measure the effect of simple data augmentation applied to the training data for our coreference resolution system. The goal is to determine whether data augmentation can complement the debiased word embeddings on this particular test set. The training data is augmented using a simple gender-swapping protocol, such that binary gender words are replaced by their equivalent form of the opposite gender (e.g. "he" $\leftrightarrow$ "she", etc.).

4 Detection of gender bias in coreference resolution: Experimental setup

All systems were built using the "Higher-order coreference resolution with coarse-to-fine inference" model (Lee et al., 2018)[6]. It is important to keep in mind that this model uses both static word embeddings and contextual word embeddings (specifically ELMo embeddings (Peters et al., 2018)). Our experimental debiasing methods were applied to static word embeddings only, and contextual embeddings are left unaltered in all cases.

All systems were trained using the OntoNotes 5.0[7] train and development sets, using the default hyperparameters[8], for approximately 350,000 steps until convergence. Baseline performance was tested using the OntoNotes 5.0 test set (results shown in Table 1). Baseline performance is largely consistent across all models, indicating that neither debiased word embeddings nor gender-swapped training data significantly degrades the performance of the system overall.

4.1 WinoBias

The WinoBias test set was created by Zhao et al. (2018a), and measures the performance of coreference systems on test cases containing explicit bi-

[2]Hard debias: https://github.com/tolga-b/debiaswe. All base (undebiased) embeddings are GloVe trained on the 2017 January Wikipedia dump (vocab contains 322,636 tokens). Available at https://github.com/uclanlp/gnglove, based on the work of Pennington et al. (2014).

[3]https://github.com/uclanlp/gnglove

[4]https://github.com/TimeTraveller-San/RAN-Debias

[5]https://github.com/shauli-ravfogel/nullspaceprojection

[6]https://github.com/kentonl/e2e-coref

[7]https://catalog.ldc.upenn.edu/LDC2013T19

[8]"best" configuration at https://github.com/kentonl/e2e-coref/blob/master/experiments.conf

Table 1: Results on coreference resolution test sets. OntoNotes (F_1) performance provides a baseline for "vanilla" coreference resolution ($n = 348$). WinoBias (F_1) measures explicit gender bias, observable as the diff. between pro ($n = 396$) and anti ($n = 396$) test sets. SoWinoBias (% accuracy) measures second-order gender bias, likewise observable as the diff. between pro ($n = 4096$) and anti ($n = 4096$) test sets. Note: accuracy is the relevant metric to report on the SoWinoBias test set, rather than F_1, due to our assertion that "they" is not a new entity mention.

Embedding	Data Aug.	OntoNotes	WinoBias				SoWinoBias			
			pro	anti	avg.	diff.	pro	anti	avg.	diff.
GloVe		72.3	77.8	48.8	63.8	29.0	64.2	46.8	55.5	17.4
GloVe	✓	72.0	67.0	59.0	63.0	8.0	62.8	56.5	59.7	6.4
Hard-GloVe		72.2	66.5	59.1	62.8	7.4	63.6	49.2	56.4	14.3
Hard-GloVe	✓	71.8	64.0	61.9	63.0	**2.1**	77.1	50.1	63.6	27.0
GN-GloVe(w_a)		72.2	63.4	61.1	62.3	2.3	68.0	49.7	58.9	18.3
GN-GloVe(w_a)	✓	71.4	59.0	66.0	62.5	7.0	72.1	69.7	70.9	**2.4**
RAN-GloVe		72.4	72.8	53.2	63.0	19.6	70.2	60.0	65.1	10.2
RAN-GloVe	✓	71.1	60.1	63.8	62.0	3.7	69.5	59.4	64.5	10.0
INLP-GloVe		71.6	67.5	57.5	62.5	10.0	68.4	46.1	57.3	22.4
INLP-GloVe	✓	72.1	66.2	59.1	62.7	7.1	73.4	65.1	69.3	8.3

nary gender words. In particular, pro-stereotypical sentences contain coreferents where an explicit gender word (e.g. he, she) is paired with an occupation matching a socially held gender stereotype. Anti-stereotypical sentences use the same formulation but gender swap the explicit gender words such that coreferents now oppose a socially held gender stereotype. Gender bias is measured as the difference in performance on the pro. versus anti. test sets, each containing $n = 396$ sentences.

Recall that here we are reporting WinoBias results using a system incorporating unaltered contextual embeddings, in addition to the debiased static embeddings. Previously reported results on the "end-to-end" coreference model (Lee et al., 2017), using only debiased static word embeddings, are compiled in the Appendix for reference.

In this setting, we observe that debiasing methods addressing direct bias are more successful than those addressing indirect bias. In particular, without the additional resource of data augmentation, RAN-GloVe struggles to reduce the difference between pro and anti test sets (in contrast to RAN-GloVe's great success in the end-to-end model setting, as reported by Kumar et al. (2020)). Data augmentation is found to be a complementary resource, providing further gains in most cases. Overall, Hard-GloVe with simple data augmentation successfully reduces the difference in F_1 from 29% to 2.1%, while not significantly degrading the average performance on WinoBias or baseline performance on OntoNotes. This suggests that debiasing the contextual word embeddings is not needed to mitigate the explicit gender bias in coreference resolution, as measured by this particular test set.

4.2 SoWinoBias

The SoWinoBias test set measures second-order, or latent, gender associations in the absence of explicit gender words. At present, we measure associations between male and female stereotyped occupations with female stereotyped adjectives, although this could easily be extended in the future. Adjectives with positive and negative polarities are represented evenly in the test set. We will denote the vocabularies of interest as

$$\begin{aligned} M_{occ} &= \{\text{doctor, boss, developer, ...}\} \\ F_{occ} &= \{\text{nurse, nanny, maid, ...}\} \\ F^{+}_{adj} &= \{\text{lovely, beautiful, virtuous, ...}\} \\ F^{-}_{adj} &= \{\text{hysterical, unmarried, prudish, ...}\}, \end{aligned} \quad (3)$$

where $|M_{occ}| = |F_{occ}| = |F^{+}_{adj}| = |F^{-}_{adj}| = 16$, and the full sets can be found in the appendix. Stereotypical occupations were sourced from the original WinoBias vocabulary (drawing from the US labor occupational statistics), as well as the SemBias (Zhao et al., 2018b) and Hard Debias analogy test sets (drawing from human-annotated judgements). Stereotypical adjectives with polarity were sourced from the latent gendered-language model of Hoyle et al. (2019), which was found to be consistent with the human-annotated corpus of Williams and Bennett (1975).

SoWinoBias test sentences are constructed as "The [**occ1**] (dis)liked the [**occ2**] because **they** were [adj]", where "(dis)liked" is matched appropriately to the adjective polarity, such that "they" always refers to "occ2". Each sentence selects one occupation from M_{occ}, and the other from F_{occ}. In pro-stereotypical sentences, occ2 $\in F_{occ}$, such that the adjective describing the (they, occ2) entity matches a social stereotype. In anti-stereotypical sentences, occ2 $\in M_{occ}$, such that the adjective describing the (they, occ2) entity contradicts a social stereotype. Example sentences in the test set include:

1. The doctor liked the nurse because they were beautiful. (pro)
2. The nurse liked the doctor because they were beautiful. (anti)
3. The ceo disliked the maid because they were unmarried. (pro)
4. The maid disliked the lawyer because they were unmarried. (anti)

In total, there are $n = 4096$ sentences in each of the pro and anti test sets. Due to the simplicity of our constructed sentences, plus our desire to measure gendered associations, we further assert that "they" should refer to one of the two potential occupations (i.e. "they" cannot be predicted as a new entity mention). As with WinoBias, gender bias is observed as the difference in performance between the anti and pro test sets.

Firstly, we observe that the second-order gender bias is more difficult to the correct than the explicit bias, given access to the debiased embeddings alone. Methods that made good progress in reducing the WinoBias diff. make little to no progress on the SoWinoBias diff. However, even simple data augmentation was found to be a valuable resource. When combined with GN-GloVe(w_a), the difference is reduced to 2.4% while increasing average performance significantly. Again, we observe that good bias reduction can be achieved, even before incorporating methods to debias the contextual word embeddings. It is interesting that debiasing methods explicitly designed to address indirect bias in the embedding space do not do better at mitigating second-order bias in a downstream task. Further discussion in relation to the embedding space properties is provided in the following section.

5 Relationship to embedding space properties

5.1 Single-attribute WEAT

The Word Embedding Association Test (WEAT) measures the association strength between two concepts of interest (e.g. arts vs. science) relative to two defined attribute groups (e.g. female vs. male) (Caliskan et al., 2017). It was popularized as a means for detecting gender bias in word embeddings by showing that (arts, science), (arts, math), and (family, careers) produced significantly different association strengths relative to gender.

Here we adapt the original WEAT to measure relative association across genders given a single concept of interest. This provides a means to measure whether the set of female-stereotyped adjectives F_{adj} are quantitatively gender-marked in the embedding space.

The relative association of a single word t across attribute sets A_1, A_2 is given by

$$s(t, A_1, A2) = \frac{1}{|A_1|} \sum_{a_1 \in A_1} \cos(t, a1) - \frac{1}{|A_2|} \sum_{a_2 \in A_2} \cos(t, a2) \quad (4)$$

where $s(t, A_1, A2) > 0$ indicates that t is more closely related to attribute A_1 than A_2. The average relative association of concept T is then

$$S(T, A_1, A_2) = \frac{1}{|T|} \sum_{t \in T} s(t, A_1, A2). \quad (5)$$

The significance of a non-zero association strength can be assessed by a partition test. We randomly sample alternate attribute sets of equal size A_1^* and A_2^* from the union of the original attribute sets. The significance p is defined as the proportion of samples to produce $S(T, A_1^*, A_2^*) > S(T, A_1, A_2)$. Small p values indicate that the defined grouping of the attributes sets (here defined by gender) are meaningful compared to random groupings.

Table 2 shows the results of the single-attribute WEAT. We measure association strength of the female adjectives relative to gender in two ways: i) gender is defined using a "definitional" vocabulary ($A_1 = F_{def} = \{she, her, woman, ...\}$, $A_2 = M_{def} = \{he, him, man, ...\}$), and ii) gender is defined using a latent vocabulary – the stereotypical occupations ($A_1 = F_{occs}$, $A_2 = M_{occs}$).

As shown, the F_{adj} embeddings are strongly associated with the explicit gender vocabulary in

Table 2: Single-Attribute WEAT association strength between gender and female-stereotyped adjectives with significance values. Lower association strength (S) values are better. Smaller significance values indicate that the observed association strength is meaningful with respect to gender.

Embedding	$S(F_{adj}, F_{occ}, M_{occ})$	Significance	$S(F_{adj}, F_{def}, M_{def})$	Significance
GloVe	0.0636	0.0001**	0.0694	0.001**
Hard-GloVe	0.0465	0.0001**	**-8.6889e-10**	0.512
GN-GloVe(w_a)	0.0664	0.0003**	**-0.0015**	0.436
RAN-GloVe	0.0402	0.0003**	**0.0153**	0.177
INLP-GloVe	**0.0171**	0.0251*	**0.0054**	0.382

the original GloVe space. However each of the four debiasing methods are successful in removing the explicit gender association, as expected. The Hard Debias method in particular asserts $S(F_{adj}, F_{def}, M_{def}) = 0$ by definition.

In contrast, the F_{adj} embeddings are just as strongly associated with the latent gender vocabulary in the original GloVe space, but this is not undone by any of the debiasing methods. This is somewhat of an unexpected result in the case of the RAN and INLP debiasing methods, as they promised to go beyond direct bias mitigation.

The INLP method makes the most progress in reducing the implicit association strength, however a significant non-zero association remains. Combined with the SoWinoBias test results, we can observe that the WEAT reduction achieved by INLP is not a sufficient condition for mitigating latent gender-biased coreference resolution. Inversely, we observe that reduction of the WEAT measure is not a necessary condition for mitigation when debiased embeddings are combined with data augmentation (demonstrated by GN-GloVe(w_a)).

5.2 Clustering and Recoverability

Clustering and recoverability (C&R) (Gonen and Goldberg, 2019) refer to a specific observation on the embedding space post debiasing; namely, that gender labels of words (assigned according to direct bias in the original embedding space) can be classified with a high degree of accuracy given only the debiased representations. Here we follow the same experimental setup, and report results on an expanded set of embeddings (see Table 3).

In agreement with Gonen and Goldberg (2019), we find that the Hard-GloVe and GN-GloVe embeddings retain nearly perfect recoverability of the original gender labels, indicating high levels of residual bias by this definition.

The INLP method was designed to guard against linear recoverability, and indeed we find that both C&R by a linear SVM are reduced to near-random performance. Recoverability by an SVM with a non-linear kernel (rbf) achieves 75% accuracy; much reduced compared to other debiasing methods, but still above the baseline of 50%. This result is consistent with Ravfogel et al. (2020).

Of interest are the results obtained for the RAN-GloVe embeddings, which have not previously been reported. RAN was designed to mitigate undue proximity bias, conceptually similar to clustering. Despite this, C&R are still possible with high accuracy given RAN-debiased embeddings. Given RAN's success on various gender bias assessment tasks (SemBias, and WinoBias using the end-to-end coreference model), this suggests that complete suppression of C&R is unnecessary for many practical applications. Conversely, it may indicate that we have not yet developed any assessment tasks that probe the effect of indirect bias.

In reference to the SoWinoBias results, we can observe that linear attribute guarding (achieved by INLP) is not a sufficient condition for mitigating latent gender-biased coreference resolution. However, even linear guarding is not a necessary condition for mitigating SoWinoBias when retraining with data augmentation is available.

5.3 Gender-based Illicit Proximity Bias

The gender-based illicit proximity bias (GIPE) was proposed by Kumar et al. (2020) as a means to capture indirect bias on the embedding space as a well-defined metric, as opposed to the loosely defined idea of clustering and recoverabilty. Firstly, the gender-based proximity bias of a single word w, denoted $\eta(w)$, is defined as the proportion of N-nearest neighbours $\{n_i\}$ with indirect bias $\beta(n_i, w)$ above some threshold θ. Intuitively, this is the proportion of words that are close by solely due to a shared gender association. The GIPE extends this

Table 3: Clustering: (reported as accuracy and v-measure (Rosenberg and Hirschberg, 2007)) is performed by taking the $n = 1500$ most biased words in the original embedding space (excluding definitional gender words), and performing k-means clustering ($k = 2$) on the same words in the debiased space. Recoverability: (reported as accuracy) is performed by taking the $n = 5000$ most biased words in the original embedding space, and training a classifier (linear SVM or rbf kernel SVM) on the same words in the debiased space. Smaller values are better (indicating less residual cues that can be used classify gender-neutral words). GIPE: Smaller values are better (indicating less undue proximity bias in the embedding space).

Embedding	Acc.	v-measure	linSVM	rbfSVM	GIPE(V_d)	GIPE(V_{So})	Avg. $\eta(w_{So})$
GloVe	99.8	98.4	100	100	0.1153	0.1844	0.1373
Hard-GloVe	79.0	30.2	92.5	94.6	0.0701	0.1020	0.0894
GN-GloVe(w_a)	85.3	49.7	99.1	99.4	0.1173	0.1650	0.1167
RAN-GloVe	80.4	41.9	95.3	96.0	**0.0399**	**0.0827**	**0.0617**
INLP-GloVe	**57.1**	**1.52**	**52.9**	**74.8**	0.0798	0.1265	0.0967

word-level measure to a vocabulary-level measure using a weighted average over $\eta(w)$.

Table 3 shows the GIPE measure on the entire gender-neutral vocabulary V_d, the gender-neutral vocabulary used to construct SoWinoBias $V_{So} = F_{occ} \cup M_{occ} \cup F_{adj}$, and the simple (unweighted) average $\eta(w_{So})$ on the SoWinoBias vocabulary.

The RAN method mitigates indirect bias as measured by GIPE by design, and therefore achieves the lowest GIPE values as expected (followed by Hard-GloVe, somewhat unexpectedly). However, non-zero proximity bias persists, more so on the stereotyped sub-vocabulary than the total vocabulary. Without extra help from data augmentation, RAN-GloVe achieves the best performance on the SoWinoBias (followed by Hard-GloVe). Therefore further reduction of GIPE may enable further mitigation of the latent gender-biased coreference resolution (cannot be ruled out as a sufficient condition at this time). However, RAN-GloVe does not benefit from the addition of data augmentation, unlike the majority of debiasing methods. Further investigation is needed to determine what conditions of the embedding properties allow for complementary data augmentation.

6 Conclusion

In this paper, we demonstrate the existence of observable latent gender bias in a downstream application, coreference resolution. We provide the first gender bias assessment test set not containing any explicit gender-definitional vocabulary. Although the present study is limited to binary gender, this construction should allow us to assess gender bias (or other demographic biases) in cases where explicit defining vocabulary is limited or unavailable. However, the construction does depend on knowledge of expected relationships or stereotypes (here occupations and adjectives). Therefore interdisciplinary work drawing from social sciences is encouraged as a future direction.

Our observations indicate that mitigation of indirect bias in the embedding space, according to our current understanding of such a notion, does not reduce the latent associations in the embedding space (as measured by WEAT), nor does it mitigate the downstream latent bias (as measured by SoWinoBias). Future work could seek bias assessment tasks in downstream applications that do depend on the reduction of gender-based proximity bias or non-linear recoverability. Currently the motivation for such reduction is unknown, despite being an active direction of debiasing research.

Finally, we do observe that an early debiasing method, GN-GloVe, combined with simple data augmentation, can mitigate the latent gender biased coreference resolution, even when contextual embeddings in the system remain unaltered. Future work could extend the idea of the SoWinoBias test set to more complicated sentences representative of real "in the wild" cases, in order to determine if this result holds.

The SoWinoBias test set, all trained models presented in this paper, and code for reproducing the results are available at https://github.com/hillary-dawkins/SoWinoBias.

Acknowledgements

We thank Daniel Gillis, Judi McCuaig, Stefan Kremer, Graham Taylor, and anonymous reviewers for their time and thoughtful discussion. This work is financially supported by the Government of Canada through the NSERC CGS-D program (CGSD3-518897-2018).

References

Tolga Bolukbasi, Kai-Wei Chang, James Y Zou, Venkatesh Saligrama, and Adam T Kalai. 2016. Man is to computer programmer as woman is to homemaker? debiasing word embeddings. In *Advances in Neural Information Processing Systems*, volume 29, pages 4349–4357. Curran Associates, Inc.

Aylin Caliskan, Joanna J. Bryson, and Arvind Narayanan. 2017. Semantics derived automatically from language corpora contain human-like biases. *Science*, 356(6334):183–186.

Brent D. Davis, Ethan Jackson, and Daniel J. Lizotte. 2020. Decision-directed data decomposition.

Hila Gonen and Yoav Goldberg. 2019. Lipstick on a pig: Debiasing methods cover up systematic gender biases in word embeddings but do not remove them. In *Proceedings of NAACL-HLT*.

Alexander Miserlis Hoyle, Lawrence Wolf-Sonkin, Hanna Wallach, Isabelle Augenstein, and Ryan Cotterell. 2019. Unsupervised discovery of gendered language through latent-variable modeling. In *Proceedings of the 57th Annual Meeting of the Association for Computational Linguistics*, pages 1706–1716, Florence, Italy. Association for Computational Linguistics.

Vaibhav Kumar, Tenzin Singhay Bhotia, Vaibhav Kumar, and Tanmoy Chakraborty. 2020. Nurse is closer to woman than surgeon? mitigating gender-biased proximities in word embeddings. *Transactions of the Association for Computational Linguistics*, 8:486–503.

Kenton Lee, Luheng He, Mike Lewis, and Luke Zettlemoyer. 2017. End-to-end neural coreference resolution. In *Proceedings of the 2017 Conference on Empirical Methods in Natural Language Processing*, pages 188–197, Copenhagen, Denmark. Association for Computational Linguistics.

Kenton Lee, Luheng He, and Luke Zettlemoyer. 2018. Higher-order coreference resolution with coarse-to-fine inference. In *Proceedings of the 2018 Conference of the North American Chapter of the Association for Computational Linguistics: Human Language Technologies, Volume 2 (Short Papers)*, pages 687–692, New Orleans, Louisiana. Association for Computational Linguistics.

Jeffrey Pennington, Richard Socher, and Christopher D. Manning. 2014. Glove: Global vectors for word representation. In *Empirical Methods in Natural Language Processing (EMNLP)*, pages 1532–1543.

Matthew E. Peters, Mark Neumann, Mohit Iyyer, Matt Gardner, Christopher Clark, Kenton Lee, and Luke Zettlemoyer. 2018. Deep contextualized word representations. In *Proceedings of the 2018 Conference of the North American Chapter of the Association for Computational Linguistics: Human Language Technologies, Volume 1 (Long Papers)*, pages 2227–2237, New Orleans, Louisiana. Association for Computational Linguistics.

Shauli Ravfogel, Yanai Elazar, Hila Gonen, Michael Twiton, and Yoav Goldberg. 2020. Null it out: Guarding protected attributes by iterative nullspace projection. In *Proceedings of the 58th Annual Meeting of the Association for Computational Linguistics, ACL 2020, Online, July 5-10, 2020*, pages 7237–7256. Association for Computational Linguistics.

Andrew Rosenberg and Julia Hirschberg. 2007. V-measure: A conditional entropy-based external cluster evaluation measure. In *Proceedings of the 2007 Joint Conference on Empirical Methods in Natural Language Processing and Computational Natural Language Learning (EMNLP-CoNLL)*, pages 410–420, Prague, Czech Republic. Association for Computational Linguistics.

John E. Williams and Susan M. Bennett. 1975. The definition of sex stereotypes via the adjective check list. *Sex Roles*, 1:327–337.

Jieyu Zhao, Tianlu Wang, Mark Yatskar, Vicente Ordonez, and Kai-Wei Chang. 2018a. Gender bias in coreference resolution: Evaluation and debiasing methods. In *Proceedings of the 2018 Conference of the North American Chapter of the Association for Computational Linguistics: Human Language Technologies, Volume 2 (Short Papers)*, pages 15–20, New Orleans, Louisiana. Association for Computational Linguistics.

Jieyu Zhao, Yichao Zhou, Zeyu Li, Wei Wang, and Kai-Wei Chang. 2018b. Learning gender-neutral word embeddings. In *Proceedings of the 2018 Conference on Empirical Methods in Natural Language Processing*, pages 4847–4853, Brussels, Belgium. Association for Computational Linguistics.

A Full test set vocabulary

F_{occ} = { writer, teacher, cleaner, tailor, attendant, librarian, auditor, nurse, nanny, cashier, editor, hairdresser, stylist, maid, baker, counselor }

M_{occ} = { guard, architect, chef, leader, president, developer, lawyer, salesperson, doctor, judge, boss, chief, mover, cook, researcher, physician }

F^{+}_{adj} = { sprightly, gentle, affectionate, charming, kindly, beloved, enchanted, virtuous, beauteous, chaste, fair, delightful, lovely, romantic, elegant, fertile }

F^{-}_{adj} = { fussy, nagging, rattlebrained, haughty, whiny, dependent, sullen, unmarried, prudish, fickle, hysterical, infected, widowed, awful, damned, frivolous }

M_{def} = { man, he, father, brother, his, son, uncle, himself }

F_{def} = { woman, she, mother, sister, her, daughter, aunt, herself }

Table 4: Results on SoWinoBias test set by adjective polarity.

Embedding	Data Aug.	Postive Adj.			Negative Adj.			Total		
		pro	anti	diff.	pro	anti	diff.	pro	anti	diff.
GloVe		69.4	49.2	20.1	58.9	44.3	14.6	64.2	46.8	17.4
GloVe	✓	64.2	60.4	3.9	61.4	52.6	8.8	62.8	56.5	6.4
Hard-GloVe		64.6	49.8	14.7	62.6	48.7	13.9	63.6	49.2	14.3
Hard-GloVe	✓	77.2	51.5	25.8	76.9	48.7	28.2	77.1	50.1	27.0
GN-GloVe(w_a)		71.6	52.9	18.6	64.4	46.5	17.9	68.0	49.7	18.3
GN-GloVe(w_a)	✓	71.5	70.5	1.0	72.7	69.0	3.7	72.1	69.7	2.4
RAN-GloVe		70.9	61.5	9.4	69.4	58.5	11.0	70.2	60.0	10.2
RAN-GloVe	✓	73.6	67.0	6.7	65.3	51.9	13.4	69.5	59.4	10.0
INLP-GloVe		74.2	54.0	20.2	62.7	38.2	24.5	68.4	46.1	22.4
INLP-GloVe	✓	76.4	67.9	8.5	70.4	62.3	8.2	73.4	65.1	8.3

Table 5: Previously reported results on the OntoNotes (baseline) and WinoBias test sets by various debiasing methods when the coreference system was built using the "end-to-end" model (Lee et al., 2017). RAN-GloVe drastically outperforms all methods.

Embedding	OntoNotes	WinoBias			
		pro	anti	avg.	diff.
GloVe	66.5	76.2	46.0	61.1	30.2
Hard-GloVe	66.2	70.6	54.9	62.8	15.7
GN-GloVe	66.2	72.4	51.9	62.2	20.5
GN-GloVe(w_a)	65.9	70.0	53.9	62.0	16.1
RAN-GloVe	66.2	61.4	61.8	61.6	0.4

Author Index

Association for Computational Linguistics
209 N. Eighth Street
Stroudsburg, Pennsylvania 18360

ISBN 978-1-7138-3374-1

CURRAN ASSOCIATES INC.
proceedings.com

9 781713 833741